THE MORAL

THE MORAL MARKETPLACE

How mission-driven millennials and social entrepreneurs are changing our world

Asheem Singh

First published in Great Britain in 2018 by

Policy Press
University of Bristol
1-9 Old Park Hill
Bristol
BS2 8BB
UK
t: +44 (0)117 954 5940
pp-info@bristol.ac.uk
www.policypress.co.uk

North America office:
Policy Press
c/o The University of Chicago Press
1427 East 60th Street
Chicago, IL 60637, USA
t: +1 773 702 7700
f: +1 773 702 9756
sales@press.uchicago.edu
www.press.uchicago.edu

British Library Cataloguing in Publication Data
A catalogue record for this book is available from the British Library.

Library of Congress Cataloging-in-Publication Data
A catalog record for this book has been requested.

ISBN 978-1-4473-3774-4 paperback
ISBN 978-1-4473-3776-8 ePub
ISBN 978-1-4473-3777-5 Mobi
ISBN 978-1-4473-3775-1 ePdf

Cover design by Andrew Corbett
Front cover: image kindly supplied by Jessica Miles
Printed and bound in Great Britain by TJ International,
Padstow
Policy Press uses environmentally responsible print
partners

MIX
Paper from
responsible sources
FSC   FSC® C013056

For Mum and Dad

Asheem Singh is an internationally renowned campaigner, speaker, broadcaster and author. He was the first Director of Policy and Strategy at the UK's leading venture philanthropy fund, Impetus-PEF and was CEO of the UK's leading network for charity and social enterprise leaders, Acevo. He has written widely on social entrepreneurship, leadership, technology, poverty and creativity for a range of international think tanks and publications including *The Guardian*, *The New Statesman*, *The Scotsman*, and *The Spectator*.

Contents

Acknowledgements

The below is just a snapshot of all the thanks I owe but it is the best I can do with the space I have. Thank you to my researchers, especially Simon Dixon who retrieved all manner of statistics for me. Also Emily Wymer, Rosalie Warnock, Kate Brittain and James Wilderspin.

My thanks also to the publishing team at Policy Press. It is a real privilege to release this book through a publishing house that is itself a social enterprise. I couldn't have asked for more. Thanks to Alison Shaw, who encouraged me to stick with it, Isobel Bainton, Laura Vickers, Jess Miles, Jo Morton, Phylicia Ulibarri-Eglite and Rebecca Tomlinson.

Thanks to Sally Holloway, of Felicity Bryan Associates, who believed in this project from the start.

My interviewees and contributors from all over the world – thank you for giving your time and sharing your stories with such candour and grace. Special thanks to Vipin Malhotra, CEO of Keggfarms, and all the people there who treated me so well on my visit. Vinod Kapur, of course. Stephen Burks' team at ReadyMade studios. Cliff Prior of Big Society Capital, Nick Temple of Social Enterprise UK, Tom Fox of UnLtd, Dan Corry of New Philanthropy Capital, Daniela Barone-Soares, Jenny North and Lizzie Pring of Impetus Trust, Rob Owen of St Giles Trust, Catherine Howarth of SharedAction and others too modest to be named here.

My eternal thanks to various advisers and mentors throughout this journey: Baron Glasman of Stoke Newington and Stamford Hill, Lord Low of Dalston, Will Hutton, Nick Hurd MP, Sir

Stephen Bubb and others too numerous to mention. We learn and learn again.

A big shout out to my script readers. You do so much to help dictate the flow and pace of a piece. Thanks especially to Jonathan Lindsell of Charity Futures whose comments were truly insightful.

To the staff and fellow writers and readers at CLR James Library, Dalston Square, a great community facility where the final drafts of this book were written; the Candid Arts Café, a wonderful social enterprise in Angel where 'i's were dotted and 't's were crossed. To Adam Glass, my friend and business partner, and to the rest of you, especially you, you and you. You know who you are.

INTRODUCTION

Behold, the social entrepreneur

Consider, if you will, the following vignettes:

The chicken is huge, with black streaks and an air of menace. It is the size of an adolescent Labrador. It was *invented* only recently in India after years of painstaking research. One man believes it holds the key to ending extreme poverty all over the world. And after much head-scratching, some very important people are beginning to say, 'you know, he might be right'.

This classroom is in a school in Zimbabwe, where millions of young girls are ignored, abused, and face a life of servitude. After the end-of-class bell has rung, some of them stay behind and talk about their lives, and something inside each of them is lit. 'I can do this,' they think.

Buses emerge in formation from a depot in Hackney, East London. The service was created out of protest at government cuts that affected elderly and vulnerable people three decades ago. Today, what began with one community minibus has transformed into a national industrial juggernaut. It takes on major corporations and it wins, and it helps those in need more than ever before ...

There are more. A young mayor in Fukuoka, Japan, has a vision for his city that involves harnessing the many talents of his citizens. A TV chef's flagship restaurant serves food cooked by apprentices from some of the UK's poorest estates. Great Italian design houses showcase the beauty of artisan-made objects from far flung corners of the globe in an elegant, eclectic display, at the centre of which is a many-hued basket covered in designer offcuts ...

At first glance these may seem like quite disparate references; I beg to differ. In the pages ahead I will contend that projects like these, taken together, represent a unique global force, comprising millions of activists from myriad walks of life: restless, unquelled spirits eager to change the world around them.

As we come to understand the ties that bind these folks, something very powerful happens. Their work becomes part of a broader narrative, a global story, if you like. It tells of people on the ground somehow driving mass political and social change; remaking the fabric of state and market from the ground up; transforming millions of lives in the process.

The story of the rise of this movement, the good it does and the transformations it achieves holds a nicely polished looking-glass to our world. It is no exaggeration to suggest that in the movement's collective genius lies the key to our future. That is where this book comes in. We here to learn this movement's ways; to get under its skin and into its heart; to understand the present and future by listening to the stories of those who lead the fight-back against some of the biggest social challenges of our time. By which I mean the stories of *social entrepreneurs*.

A movement on the march

For some time, I have been fascinated by the idea that social entrepreneur are finding a special impetus in our time, in our world of globalised markets, social technology – and seemingly perpetual social, political and economic crises.

Despite the best efforts of academics, practitioners and journalists, social entrepreneurship has been popularly regarded by the older generations as something of a counter-culture; a renegade clan of saints operating in the enclaves of the other, far removed from the world of you and I.

In 2008, 50% of respondents to a comprehensive national survey in the UK had never heard of social enterprise. Fewer than 50% were aware that a social enterprise could be structured as either a non-profit or a profit-making enterprise.[1] Likewise in France in 2014, a poll suggested that fewer than a third of those surveyed had heard of social entrepreneurs. Similar statistics can be rattled off from other countries. There is no doubt that these activists have operated at the margins of the culture, and those who have sought to introduce them to the world have made less progress than they would like.

The archetypal social entrepreneur is a community activist with a deep love of building things. They will use any means at their disposal to platform the people about whom they care. They are campaigners, creatives, technologists … there are many flavours and scents.

Much of our lives are spent buying and selling things, and so, more often than not, social entrepreneurs do the same; they try to influence our buys and rewire our deepest intuitions about how we should splash our cash. Their mantra is that our purchases are democratic choices: when we buy something we cast a vote for the world we want to see.

They study the levers of power and influence; work out how to create ructions in the establishment's fabric on behalf of the communities they represent.

They platform the poor. They superate inequalities of wealth or gender or disability or race, or all of these. They strive for progress on healthcare, on stewardship of the environment, improve the way we eat and more besides. Increasingly, they work together to achieve these aims, graft and scrape and use scant resources in new and innovative ways and use the technologies and opportunities of our time to create record levels of social impact.

The idea that this movement is o the march has been an interest of mine for some time now. I spent large chunks of my working life travelling, learning from and spending time with cadres of social entrepreneurs from all over the world. I ploughed through research and conducted studies. I met tech gurus, politicians and even bankers who came together to work out how they could pull focus onto this fast-expanding dimension of the human experience. I met community members served by social entrepreneurs in some of the poorest parts of nations rich and poor. They urged change in the status quo and support for something better.

Very soon I came to realise that this sense of rapidly rising momentum was no hallucination: each person I met confirmed the hypothesis. Not only was this a wonderful movement full of larger-than-life characters; something radical was afoot.

All over the world, social entrepreneurs have been mobilising, sharing, connecting, forming infrastructure, securing champions, finding new opportunities to do what they do best. Over the past few years, these efforts have shifted into overdrive. You'll see in the chapters ahead there is a leitmotif: the words 'in the past decade,' and 'in the past few years' (or even months).

You might recognise the vestiges of this growth from moments in your own life; symbols and ideas that ebb away at the edges of your consciousness. There are social entrepreneurs driving campaigns like #everydaysexism or #blacklivesmatter that smash taboos around gender and race and improve the lives of so many each and every day.

There are the social entrepreneurs who take aim at what we buy, who bring the political into our lives, almost by stealth. There are supermarkets stocking health foods, run by local communities and constituted as co-operatives; they are social enterprises. There are bottles of Belu water in restaurants, a social enterprise which ensures its profits go towards tackling water shortages in the developing world. Divine Chocolate's brightly wrapped bars are at the treat counter at the local convenience store; created by a company part-owned by the farmers that produce their cocoa – another social enterprise.

There are community-owned gyms: social enterprises. There are arts cafes with no stake in the mainstream that run classes for under privileged kids: social enterprises. There are community land trusts which offer affordable housing in places where the housing market shuts out all but the super-rich: social enterprises. There are empty shops turned into permaculture centres and pop-up venues rather than allowed to be abandoned to the rats by apathetic bureaucracies: social – you get the idea.

These changes are part of the movement's enduring, developing iconography. You need not *know* that these things are the products of social enterprises or indeed that they are the product of trenchant political analysis in order to enjoy what they have to offer and know that they represent a wrong being righted. Think again, though, and the radicalism of it all begins to dawn.

The *modus* of these social entrepreneurs is to take big political questions and bring them into the arena of the everyday. Their work grows like the warmth from a fire. It feels pleasant and nice at first. It slowly fills the room and heats you up. And at some point it makes you a little uncomfortable; makes you sit up; and then you reach out and touch the flame – and it stings you into action.

Of course, this new wave of community radicals – for that is what these social entrepreneurs are – are not just about selling or buying. They are also about spreading good ideas, sharing practices, using the tools we have to support good works and ethical products and ideas. Sometimes they are not about buying *things* at all but about buying *less*, redesigning what we have so that it functions more effectively, doing something great with what we have together.

Today's social entrepreneur is a visionary who augurs a global populace of peak radical potential.

Power and money

Reality check: it may be tempting for the uninitiated to think that social entrepreneurship, admirable as it sounds, is one of those niche metropolitan preoccupations; the pilates or chemical cleanses of the serious business of helping others.

The facts actually suggest that the opposite is true. Social entrepreneurship is making its way into the lives of more of us than ever before. US citizens from all backgrounds are buying social enterprise products at a greater pace than ever before – and the rate at which they buy these things is increasing faster than the rate at which they give to charity. That is interesting, but how about this? Across the world, two thirds of you are more likely to buy a product from a social enterprise than if not. *And citizens from every other continent outside North America and Europe are more likely to buy from social enterprises than people from those two places.* Speaking as a citizen of the latter, *we* are the ones who have to catch up.

This is but one example of one of the bigger narratives that underpin this book – and it is, I suspect, worth keeping it at the forefront of your thinking as the stories of the next few chapters unfold. Social entrepreneurs provide services, fight poverty, help the dispossessed lead more fulfilled lives and improve society. But they are also a radical *economic* movement: the torch-bearers of a generational mission to rewire our system of capitalism in favour of the many.

This mission is fraught with difficulty, yet history yields moments of breakthrough and cause for optimism. Six centuries ago, there emerged in Perugia, Italy, the *Monte di pieta*, or mounts of piety. These were church-backed financial institutions. They used a kind of pawnbroking to create a source of capital for the poor.

In the 19th century the 'Rochdale pioneers' took up the baton and sought to create assets for the many through community ownership of goods such as housing, food production and distribution. They promulgated virtuous principles that connected owner, worker and capital in a democratic business structure. The *co-operative*, they called it, and it remains one of the most important and well-known social enterprise forms we have today.

Move the dial forward to our time, and the lessons of this past are being relearned in our era of globalisation and democracy and given new impetus in the age of the social entrepreneur.

Microfinance, the spiritual successor of the *Monte di pieta*, which involves giving small loans to some of the world's poorest people, has been embraced by social innovators. By 2015 microfinance lending stood at $100 billion worldwide with billions of potential beneficiaries still unserved.[2]

This growth is reflected in the broader movement. Social enterprises in the US alone are estimated to be worth some US$500 billion, or 3.5% of GDP.

Hundreds of billions of dollars are invested globally in so-called impact investment funds, which build these social enterprises up, and craft infrastructure to help them on their way. Their value is hypothesised to reach $US1 trillion by 2020.

Today's co-operative movement, which includes organisations like Spain's Mondragon corporation and British lifestyle retailer John Lewis, has been enjoying renaissance in our time; a steady rise in global turnover. Today the biggest 300 alone turn over some US$1.6 trillion. By my reckoning, that is the gross domestic product (GDP) of the *entire nation* of Spain.

There are trillions of dollars in so-called ethical investments worldwide – many of which are in pension funds and a growing number are invested in so-called solidarity funds across Europe that directly benefit social entrepreneurs through the savings of millions.

All of these investments form part of a group invested per the terms of the UN's 'Principles of Responsible Investment'. Worldwide as of 2015 they totalled US$59 trillion invested. *That is a substantial chunk – much more than half – of all the money in managed funds anywhere in the world and around a quarter of all the wealth in the entire world.*[3]

Focussing, not only on solving problems but on creating a genuine economic movement means that the our aspirations as change-makers can be raised. We set our sights higher, look to deliver on ending poverty or resolving inequalities in ever-more ambitious time-frames. What did you ever hope a community of people working together could achieve? A small change? Improving lives? Saving a neighbourhood? Getting a politician elected? Going global? Remaking capitalism itself?

Even if some of these figures are just echoes from the outer limits (the responsible investment market in particular is mired in jargon, which we will unpick in Chapter Seven), they demonstrate a truth that bears repeating. Unknown to most of us, behind all the suppositions we might once have had about this space, the social enterprise movement has grown from little to a heck of a lot very quickly. It has a long way to grow yet and, as it grows, what big shifts can we expect to see next?

Today they come piling in, looking for their piece of this movement. They come from the trading floor now, these sweaty-shirted loudmouths who hold up slips of paper, who offer pieces of global funds that keep the farms and businesses of the very poorest in order.

They pile in from the parquet floors of national senate houses where notaries rubber-stamp new public bonds that promise to help prisoners reclaim their lives and bring new money to fight childhood obesity.

The super-nerds with their billions whizz along the highways of the internet, mine a piece of Bitcoin from the rig and add to the blockchain. Their story is part of this too.

And this begs another question. How does a growing community movement treat with these huge forces and maintain its integrity, its uniqueness, the care and love that make it wonderful? How does it ensure that its ambition does not lessen or minimise its empathy? With power comes money and with money comes power; when all the services are delivered and all the money is counted, who has been helped? The story of the social entrepreneur's rise is also an inquiry into the struggle for its soul. The reality is that this inquiry is in everybody's interests and is everybody's business.

The moral marketplace

In the chapters and pages ahead you will meet a cavalcade of activists, supporters, businesses, capital, infrastructure, ideas, specialist technologies and philosophies, and ordinary people like you and me on whose shoulders the future rests. Together they form what I refer to as the *moral marketplace*.

Many who walk these paths are quirky and brilliant. Many do work that seems at first glance quite mundane. Their social enterprises create organic waste disposal concerns in rural communities, or consolidated milk distribution facilities, or housing co-operatives. They offer inventory-mapping software to stallholders, sell powdered milk and razorblades in cut-off parts of the country. They build baby-changing facilities and other rudiments.

In some places there is so little infrastructure that even selling basic groceries is revolutionary; a great story of guts and determination in and of itself. In others, quite the opposite. Wal-Mart and Tesco are about as far away from gutsy social enterprises as business can be.

There will be many points of contention, as you'd expect when the subjects at hand are as big as *society*, *money*, *capitalism*, *our future,* and *the future of our most vulnerable citizens*. One little-considered question is the future of the traditional charitable sector. Consider, in the US, around US$370 billion is donated to charity annually. Compared to the money flowing through capital markets, the tax takes of governments, the size of the social problems with which we wrestle, this is a 'tiny, tiny amount,' to borrow a quote from the world's richest man, Bill Gates. One piece of the problem alone, child poverty, costs the US some US$500 billion a year.[4]

In the UK, *per capita* charitable donations are only £165 a year.[5] Citizens of the UK would have to give three times as much to deal with child poverty in their country through charitable donations alone.

And that is before we get to the other, equally great challenges of our era. Such as, say, the 750 million people worldwide who live in extreme poverty on less than US$2 per day, as all the while we grow more unequal.

The point is that traditional philanthropy is far from adequate to deal with these problems; governments too continue to fall short. New combinations and new ideas are the social entrepreneur's stock-in-trade. Who will provide cover for failing public services? Who will deliver in the event that activists secure more money for the poor from the public purse? Who will ensure that our communities receive the care they deserve? These are the problems in the social entrepreneur's crosshairs.

Over the chapters and pages ahead, I will introduce you to the people, the cultures, the philosophies, the innovations that make this movement what it is. I will indulge in those moments at which I believe the enthusiasts that drive this movement get it right. I will also highlight where I suspect they get it wrong, succumb to the hype, misjudge and thereby threaten the progress of the whole. I will not get every framing or assessment right; I may be too quick to criticise an experiment that is ongoing or too slow to call time on a dead end that has had its day.

I will speak from my own experience. I will reflect on my own travels to the farthest shores and my own work with social entrepreneurs all over the world. Indeed this book is not so much an A–Z of this spectacularly diverse movement, but an honest recollection and analysis of those experiences, which I share with you, here and now, in this primer to one of the most important social movements of our age.

The text is written so that you may read it in any order, depending on what interests you most. Here are some personal highlights. The man I met on a trip to an Indian farm who invented a 'super-hen' that has become a key weapon in the fight against poverty is in Chapter One. What connects soccer teams Real Madrid CF, FC Barcelona and Stenhousemuir is considered in Chapter Seven. The cryptocurrencies Bitcoin and Ethereum are unchained in Chapter Eight and considered for their socially enterprising qualities. Hip-hop artist Akon, he of the lights in Africa, shows up for Chapter One. There is some technical debate on measuring how social a social enterprise is in Chapter Four. The future of the traditional charity is discussed in Chapter Five. The issues at stake throughout: poverty, climate change, recycling, where to get a decent vegan lunch … I'll leave you to unpick these as you go.

For those of you who crave more structure, here is how the ideas of the book are laid out.

The first chapter will introduce you to social entrepreneurship, social enterprise and their evolution into radical change movements. It offers a number of alternative approaches to getting to grips with the field and a guide to help you argue with your friends about what 'counts' as a social enterprise.

The second chapter considers where social entrepreneurs come from. It will introduce you to pyramids and incubators, and other kinds of community support that seek to empower and develop our most socially minded citizens..

Next up, in the third chapter, is a consideration of the great global co-operative and mutual movement, one of the cornerstones of modern social enterprise. Here we also take on the rising phenomenon of ethical consumption.

The fourth chapter looks at how you measure the good this sort of activity actually does. It discusses the theories and philosophies that attempt to discern, amid all this growth, what 'good' looks like.

The fifth chapter examines the space where corporate bruisers meet social enterprise and social enterprise meets more traditional charitable forms: venture philanthropy. It presents a code for non-profit survival and flourishing in the era of the moral marketplace.

The sixth chapter will introduce you to social enterprise cities and communities. Here we take on mass-local transformation, and consider the social entrepreneur's most powerful community-building techniques, such as leveraging community assets and social design. This is what 'taking back control' – an important mantra in the social entrepreneur lexicon – looks like on the ground.

The seventh chapter will introduce you to social impact investment and the nascent-though-rapidly-expanding place where social enterprise meets the financial markets. This is where the social or solidarity economy becomes real and makes trillions of dollars.

The eighth chapter brings social technology into the mix, considers the galvanising effect of online movements, and brings despatches from a whole bunch of fascinating developments, from citizen journalism to social 'P2P' lending to blockchains.

The final chapter examines how government must refind its heart if it is to regain its legitimacy in the era of the social entrepreneur radical. There are some 30 ideas in total, split into six major groups, which outline the case for a political dispensation that harnesses the incredible force that is the moral marketplace.

I conclude by thinking about the ultimate impact of all this on the economic, social and political settlement we have. I consider the role of social entrepreneurship in the search for an improved capitalism. And I offer four keys to realising the best possible future for the moral marketplace and for those around us.

If you are not an enthusiast of the social entrepreneur by the end of this book, you will at least be a connoisseur though it may not surprise you even at this early stage to know that my preference would ever so slightly be for the former.

R.A.S., London, 2017

The man who invented a chicken:

introducing a global generation of entrepreneurial social activists

> Begin with an individual, and before you know it you find that you have created a type: begin with a type, and you find you have created – nothing. (F. Scott Fitzgerald, *The Rich Boy*)

> Social entrepreneurs are not content just to give a fish or to teach people how to fish; they will not rest until they've revolutionised the whole fishing industry. (Bill Drayton, founder, Ashoka Foundation for Social Entrepreneurs)

A journey into the Indian village

Vinod Kapur was working at a Swedish company based in India that specialised in the making and selling of matches when he decided to leave it all behind and dedicate his life to rearing chickens.

He had considered this for a while, for he had a brother and he thought that chicken farming might be a way of helping him into some kind of trade. But one day in 1963 Kapur was told he had a shadow on his lung, and with a second child on the way he wondered if it might be the case that chickens were for him too.

He heard about new chicken varieties imported from Canada that could survive and withstand tough Indian conditions. He could start small, grow incrementally. When I met him in India in 2017, he was sporting a comfortable cardigan and a tidy mop of white hair. He was 82 by then, seated behind a large desk. He leaned forward as he reminisced on this and said to me: "This, young man, is how destiny works."

The plan at first was to import chickens for rearing in India. However, the government of the day didn't much like the idea of creating an Indian industry that was dependent on foreign imports. So Kapur and his associates had a second idea. From an American supplier he obtained a quantity of *germplasm*, pure breeding stock that could give rise to new generations of healthy birds.

This made the idea self-sufficient enough for the bureaucrats. Over a few years, supported by loans from his family, from these seeds he would build India's first genetic poultry breeding business.

It did well. In the early 1970s, he moved his head office to some land just off a major highway in the growing city of Gurgaon, to the south west of India's capital, New Delhi. Here things would really take off. The business known as Keggfarms was born.[1] For years it held its own in the poultry trade and things went swimmingly, until the rules of the game changed again.

In 1991, the Indian government made a dramatic intervention and raised the old nationalist–focused market restrictions, and India's economy changed virtually overnight. Kapur found himself in a new reality and in a bind. Keggfarms was successful but it was a relatively small business in the grand scheme of things, no match for the big, multinational juggernaut which now entered the market. Once again Kapur was forced into the position of having to improvise. He could, of course, sell out to one of the major multinationals. "Not for me," he told me. "I don't like the herd." In which case he needed another approach.

He had one, or at least the germ of one, in his back pocket. Kapur was of modest beginnings himself and had always wanted to 'give back' in some way through the work that he did. This, allied to years of experience at the head of the field, culminated in an idea. *This chicken business could work wonders when repurposed to fight poverty.*

To understand what he meant by this, dwell for a moment on the business of rearing chickens. Chicken farming is relatively low-tech. Eggs can provide nutrition and the selling and buying of eggs can create a sort of micro-economy in the rural environment. The assets of this economy are easy to understand: you have mothers, chicks, roosters, pure breeding stock, eggs and meat. The barriers to entering this marketplace are therefore low, and, he reasoned, if the fruits of this business could be harnessed to help some of the poorest of his fellow citizens, good things could happen.

Kapur was into this idea – in his teens he had been something of an activist – and after some more research, he began to clock its true potential.

He had something quite unique here that his multinational competitors did not. The tempo of his voice quickened as he told me:

> "There were nearly 30 million families connected through this raising of poultry, in some way or the other, in rural India. This was low-tech industry with little up-front cost but you could get so much out of it. You could get eggs to eat or to sell. And you could ultimately get meat also. People's attitudes to these matters in India were changing. This was no longer just something that rich people would eat. There was a big opportunity."

Multinationals would not help these people. Part of the reason was that their stock was just too weak. They had controlled production facilities, temperate environments. These produced relatively sensitive chickens that would seldom survive the harsh conditions endured by the poorest of the poor. The big bang of economic liberalisation, the mass production and distribution of these birds across the nation risked unleashing an unintended consequence: harsh and punishing inequality.

When all was said and done, Kapur realised that if he did not concentrate on the poorest of the poor, those who reared chickens in their backyard, against all odds, no one would.

And so he did.

Throughout the early 1990s, Kapur conducted intensive studies and reapplied Keggfarms to this new idea. He realised early on that the challenge here was not only about changing Keggfarms' focus; it would require major innovation. He would not only have to amend aspects of his business, but he would have to reimagine the bird itself if the enterprise and its beneficiaries were to survive and prosper as a poverty-fighting enterprise.

Inventing a new kind of chicken was exactly the kind of challenge a veteran cross-breeder like Kapur relished. He began a wishlist. It would have to be good for meat and eggs. It would have to be hardy enough to survive in the dust and heat of the village as well as in the easier streets of the more affluent farms. It would have to be wily, camouflaged. "The challenge," Kapur summarised, "was to create a dual-purpose bird that could produce meat and eggs, and survive in the Indian villages."

A process of selective breeding began, the summation of decades of experience as a businessman-turned-chicken-breeder. Think development montage in a superhero film, with clucking roosters rather than sparring dukes at its centre. And after all that work and sweat and toil from all of this emerged an entirely new breed of bird, which would come to be known as the Kuroiler.

If you go to Keggfarms today, you drive in off a dusty road through a large gate next to which is the sign pictured below. As you leave the beeping horns of the road and sounds of heavy drilling behind, the gates close behind you and you find yourself in something of an oasis. There are rows of red and pink flowers, smartly suited workmen run water along bushes and trees. There

Photo 1.1: Entrance to Keggfarms

are snaking pathways and the soft sound, quite pleasant in a strange way, of chickens crowing in unison.

The process of building the Kuroiler happened here. And, today, the Kuroiler and the social mission that sparked its creation has taken over the entire identity of the organisation.

Kapur explained to me how breeding the chicken was only part of the task of creating this socially-focused business. He had to do what the multinationals could not and get it to the communities that could benefit from it, at a price that would make it viable for all parties. He also had to understand the households in question so as to ensure the intervention would create real life change for the households involved. Selling a product is one thing, making a difference is quite another. Each of these things was a new and complex conundrum.

Transportation was a huge challenge. There were few nice, flat roads in the farming villages; there were muddy plains or alleyways that would soon finish off an egg. He tried many experiments, for example selling day-old chicks instead of eggs, but he soon found that they were easy prey for cats, dogs and snakes.

The fix they alighted on was rather elegant. Keggfarms would sell chickens to 'mother units'. These were controlled environments in which eggs could be harvested within a 500 km radius of the hatchery, about half way in to the very poorest areas. They were owned by individuals and sometimes there would be small loans – 'microfinance', they call it, and we will speak more of this phenomenon in due course – that would help get the business going. A few weeks later, the by-now-sturdier chicks could be sold to rearers in the villages, typically women in the poorest rural households.

To get them that extra 500 km into the village, Kapur's team made use of a distribution network already in place that reached right into the yards of the poor and dispossessed: vendors on bicycles – known locally as *pheriwalas* – who pedal from village to village selling everything from blankets and chewing gum to medicines, incense and oil lanterns. Now they would carry entire businesses too. "It's not about introducing something new, it's about working with what is there," Kapur told me. "The pheriwalas were able to do this better than anyone. They were part of the community . What better distribution network than that?"

Then there was the question of who purchased the Kuroiler and how it was used. From his earliest research, he knew the focus had to be women. "Some of the women in these households have terrible lives," he told me. "They work all hours of the days, they raise the children. The husbands, well …" – he is not very complimentary.

> "It's no life really. But I'll tell you what. If you give them money or you give them a task and they can see it will help the children, they don't spend it on drink or anything. They apply themselves. They can do it. And some magic happens, some fire is lit, when they can earn for themselves."

Keggfarms workers would spend time assessing how best chickens could be reared in rural environments so as to shape and form their breeding. They noticed that there was considerable nutrition in the leftovers from meals, typically rice water and lentils, in cooking pots and pans. This could be nutritious enough, alongside other food that could be scavenged for chickens of a certain variety. The women to whom the Kuroiler was directed became skilful farmers in their own right as a result of this activity, and their status as breadwinners and co-providers improved as a result of taking part in the programme. "There is a real change you see when huts become replaced by brick, and it happens slowly, in pieces, but it is wonderful."

More of the world would hear about what Vinod Kapur and his team had done in the middle of the 2000s. It began when he spoke on stage before a gathering of the world's great and the good about this entirely new way of connecting with rural farmers based on this new breed of chicken. "I was giving a talk at a global poverty-fighting symposium. I was introduced as a chicken farmer. They saw this guy in a tailored suit. I don't think they expected anything like it."

He told them how the Kuroiler targets the most vulnerable people in the world and gives them a genuine economic destiny. "For the lady of the house, the Kuroiler is like an ATM," he said in a typically direct flourish. "It scavenges like a jackal but will survive even if it only feeds on household waste that one would find in a kitchen or a yard. It is thus a quite unique 'biowaste converter'." It grows far larger than the typical broiler chicken and it lays 150–200 eggs a year – four times more than its peers. "The SUV of the bird world," he dubbed it. Villagers liked them because, with all the care and love that had been put into its creation, it simply tasted better than the mangy leftovers to which they had, on special occasion, been accustomed. Despite its meagre dietary requirements of rice pap, lentils, insects and scraps, it produces eggs and meat in sufficient quantities to be eaten by a large family several times over. It is a survivor: some early studies found that 80% of hatched eggs go on to become chicks, compared to just 47% among its cousins.[2] "They were pretty shocked," he said. "I've never had so many people want to talk to me at once. And I live in India."

In that crowd were a number of influential people who would come to define the next stage of the Kuroiler's development. There was Harvard academic Dan Isenberg, who ventured with Kapur to rural enclaves in Calcutta in order to see for himself what Kapur had created. "Seeing is believing," Kapur told me.

He is right. I was genuinely astonished, having read Isenberg's study, to see a Kuroiler in the flesh. The thing is huge, the size of an adolescent Labrador. It has a large, puffed out breast and a stately air of menace. I had never seen anything like it. "This is what they call the bird of hope," Keggfarms CEO Vipin Malhotra told me as he and his team showed me around.

Connections bred more connections. A world-leading expert in vaccines at the University of Arizona clocked this story too and he asked whether this approach might be used for farmers in other countries, not just India. Kapur needed no convincing. But poultry at the time was not fashionable in development circles as a way to tackle poverty. "They weren't interested in us." The moment of inspiration came when a picture emerged of then new US President Barack Obama's relatives in a farmyard in Kenya surrounded by chickens, and once more the proverbial lightbulb-in-a-cloud appeared above Kapur's head. "We had to try then!" he told me, and he laughed mischievously.

Kapur made the pitch to the Bill and Melinda Gates Foundation, who support some of the most interesting interventions in global poverty today and whose work we will encounter several times over the course of this book. The response? "Stop talking just get the Kuroiler."

In 2010, at the initiative of Arizona State University and the Government of Uganda, Keggfarms supplied start-up capital and parent stocks to Uganda. They struck a deal that was to take the Kuroiler across the Indian ocean, aided by a grant from the Bill and Melinda Gates Foundation. On 12 July 2010, the first Kuroiler chicks were hatched in Entebbe, Uganda. "We lit this fire and it just went mad," he recalled.

The Ugandan government would support the initiative for a time and the project was taken on by a company called Chickmaster. "The private sector lit a bigger fire," said Kapur. The Kuroiler travelled well and plans were drawn up to expand the bird's province into Nairobi, Kenya, Ethiopia, Nigeria and Tanzania. For Keggfarms, selling pure breed stock to these economies opened up a new revenue stream. The micro-economies created at rural level were now being replicated internationally, a sort of mass–micro engagement, both local *and* global. "We are getting calls all the time. There was all this reluctance at first. Now people are looking to India, not the west for ideas. After 50 years of doing this, this business is today going through the roof."

No wonder he has so much energy about him for a man in his ninth decade. He has had added a new set of pro-social companies to his portfolio. There is Indovax and Evitech, both of which produce services to help rural farmers produce healthier animals. Kapur oversees it all, even now. "He's the boss and he gives the best advice of anyone," said Keggfarms CEO Vipin Malhotra, a formidable pro-poor businessman in his own right, with the impressive silver moustache of a major-general. "You think of these images," said Kapur, laughing once more.

> "Bill Gates standing outside a New York skyscraper holding a chicken saying 'this is the future!' And you think, this is it. It is not the only way to beat poverty, but it is changing everything. Building these local economies. And you go back to India, to Bihar [India's poorest state and an avid consumer of Kuroilers] and you see how the villagers are getting on after three to five years and it is not just brick walls but brick houses. And that's why it all changes. They used to call the Kuroiler The Bird of Hope. Now they call it The Bird of Choice. They used to say that livestock wasn't the answer to beating poverty. Now they know: it is chickens."

The language of choice is important here. Keggfarms remains a business and the diversity of its income streams enables the activity in rural India to flourish. They produce a premium egg, or Kegg, alongside the Kuroiler. "Japan, Taiwan, Korea: they are our biggest Keggs customers. And it's a wonderful thing." At this point a Keggfarms worker takes me through a quite bizarre but interesting comparison of the yolk and albumen qualities of various competitor eggs cracked onto a succession of clean white plates.

> "I believe it is the best egg in the world. And it all helps fund the Kuroiler. For each major Keggs customer at the end of the year we write them a letter saying thank you for buying these Keggs and for doing what you do. In this way, we connect the richest of the rich with the poorest of the poor, not through any charity, but in a dignified way, through business."

By 2011, Kapur was selling over 1,500 Kuroiler mother hens a month and 1,500 Keggfarms outreach workers were delivering the chicks to the villages. Around 1 million village households bought them. With the Kuroiler going multinational since then and the world's most influential people lining up behind it, who is to say what the limits might be?

The rudiments of social entrepreneurship

Across the planet, millions of *social entrepreneurs* attempt to make similar manoeuvres, to find ways to demonstrate with a degree of permanence and credibility good, socially conscious outcomes while maintaining, often in the face of incredible odds, business models that last. In this chapter we will sketch in broad terms the breadth and scope of their movement and highlight a few questions that attend their definition and classification.

They are extremely diverse in style, approach, ambition. Some are not-for-profit. Some are owned by members of poor communities.

Some make profits and achieve large-scale social change with clearly identifiable results.

There are one-person-bands and large institutions, sustainable soup kitchens and socially minded multinationals. Groupe SOS in France is one of the biggest. It employs 15,000 people in more than 400 sub-businesses covering 36 countries and areas as diverse as elder care, services for young people, health (it was a pioneer in HIV testing and clinics) and more. Despite being more than three decades old, its turnover has leapt by a quarter year on year in the last few. It is worth $900 million at the time of writing; the social entrepreneur who set it up, Jean-Marc Borello, says he'll retire when it hits a billion.[3]

The variety of causes covered here is almost infinite. Their various approaches are diverse. Some are able to sustain themselves in spite of the difficulties that come with their efforts. Others take a more pragmatic approach to their business model, supplementing their turnover with gifts and grants, or contracts for services with government agencies to keep the wheels oiled.

Others still – Keggfarms is one example – flip the 'problem' of being socially aware on its head. The fact that they reach the hard-to-reach *and no one else can* gives them first position in a whole new market in which to work. For them, this altruism is not a burden that holds them back in the marketplace but an enhancement that makes their business flourish. This is their niche. And they do well, not in spite of doing good, *but because of it*.

There are global hotbeds of this movement. Social entrepreneurship flourishes at pace in some places, takes a little longer in others. Why is this the case? We'll unpick this question over the course of this book but it is worth dwelling on this question here in brief for a moment, for it gives us an insight into the structures that create and support this movement globally.

In broad terms there are four big drivers of local success. The first is **clientele**. Not all social enterprises sell things to customers, but most of them do. Businesses such as Trashy Bags in Ghana, which creates eco-friendly recycled bags and laptop sleeves, rely mostly on the quality of their product to shift units. They are helped also by a rising tide of ethical consumer who want to make a difference – and certainly not wanting to cause harm – when they purchase goods or services.

Worldwide, this trend is on the rise. According to the Nielsen agency (2015) 66% of people worldwide are willing to pay extra if they know a company is committed to positive social or environmental outcomes.[4] Other surveys yield similar statistics and while the field is not yet mature for organisations that help consumers discern what a 'good' product looks like in an easy way, as the technology and information flow develops, this percentage is likely to rise.

Second, a big one: **infrastructure**. Developing, growing, securing funding and support is, of course, crucial to the success of any social enterprise. While many social enterprises seek to be self-sufficient, this goal is rarely achieved instantaneously. Initial injections of capital ensure that barriers to entry are minimised; support and encouragement from mentors, financiers and communities are almost as valuable.

The right business development environment is essential. We will uncover several types of development technique that marry support and funding for social entrepreneurs. There are pyramids and incubators, there is venture philanthropy, social capital markets, crowdfunding and 'solidarity finance'. The last of these includes schemes such as that used in France, where all organisations with over 50 employees are mandated to provide a socially orientated pension scheme. As reported by the OECD in 2013, in the first year of this scheme it provided over €100 million to social enterprise.[5]

A critical mass of funders, investors and supporters who maintain a positive attitude towards social entrepreneurship is essential. Often these accumulate in large collections or communities of social enterprise, some of which we encounter in Chapter Three.

Then there is **government**. Governments set the rules of the game, have it in their gift to make or break new industries, to set them up with incentives or let them fail. The tech industry in

Silicon Valley would never have grown with the vigour and success it did were it not for venture capital task breaks and government funding from defence innovation projects. The social enterprise industry is no different.

It should be said that an absence of government intervention need not hamper the growth of social enterprise. This was the conclusion of a study undertaken by the British Council in 2015 of social enterprise in India.[6] Nevertheless, in territories with sophisticated pro-enterprise and particularly pro-social enterprise policies, things move that much more quickly.

The interests of business and social enterprise tend to overlap on issues such as tax breaks, support for skilled and unskilled workers, liberal attitudes to labour flow, government acting as advocate rather than owner and a bottom-up approach to industrial strategy. As I hope to show you throughout this book, they may diverge on a range of other subjects where social enterprise seeks to show conventional business an alternative way.

Linked to this is the **allocation of international aid funding**. Often it goes like this. In developing countries, there is significant outside funding of many non-governmental organisations (NGOs) – largely drawn from international development budgets. As countries grow more affluent, this reduces. Such a change may prompt NGOs to seek a diversified income stream in order to survive and become more entrepreneurial. While this represents a different route into social enterprise than that followed by the Vinod Kapurs of this world, the end result is the same. And indeed, in Chapter Five we will see many charities in developed economies following the same route.

In 2014 the Overseas Development Institute noted this *aid to trade phenomenon* in countries as disparate as Vietnam and Kenya. Regulation often stimulates this change. Consider a 2013 law that prevents Kenyan NGOs from receiving more than 15% of their funding from international sources. Given the large role now played by such organisations in providing a range of public services, this has prompted a major pull towards social entrepreneurship. The balance between government support and the work of independent organisations is a recurrent debate.

A vexed question: defining social enterprise

Here's an interesting problem: there is currently no single universally accepted definition of a social enterprise.

Sure, we have already specified a couple of lines in order to describe the phenomenon. We can use our common sense and apply it to what we have seen thus far. You get what Vinod Kapur was trying to do, why he had to do it and why he was ultimately successful. Breaking it down goes something like this:

(i) His work was not traditional business and not traditional charity and yet at the same time was rooted in both traditions.
(ii) It was not publicly owned or specified but it had public benefits.
(iii) It was not managed through a pure profit-driven shareholding companies and neither was it a traditional alms-seeking non-profit.
(iv) Its purposes were resolutely ethical or social (though, as with all questions of ethics, the question of degree is up for debate).
(v) Profits, where generated, broadly travelled in the direction of the people that the enterprise was set up to help, the poor and vulnerable, though this money need not necessarily be locked into the organisation so as to preclude all future outside investment.

These are well-respected principles across the movement but the call is often made for something tighter, especially for the purposes of regulation and to aid the ordinary consumer. This is an interesting challenge that reveals much about some of the tricky and nuanced questions that emerge when you get into the detail of the social enterprise movement.

There are many starting points. Research firm Virtue Ventures offers one:

any business venture created for a social purpose –
mitigating/reducing a social problem or a market failure
– and to generate social value while operating with the
financial discipline, innovation and determination of a
private sector business.[7]

Many would-be definitions like this assume much and issue can
be taken with most of them. In the Virtue Ventures definition, for
example, we see the assumption that the private sector is the standard
bearer of financial discipline or innovation or determination. Most
of us can think of examples to the contrary.

The Austrian approach

So how should we define it? Let's go back to first principles.
Writing in the period between the First and Second World Wars,
Austrian economist Joseph Schumpeter wrote of entrepreneurship
as a means to bring about 'new combinations' of the means of
production.[8] Schumpeter's colleague Ludwig von Mises meanwhile
defined an entrepreneur as:

acting man in regard to the changes occurring in the
data of the market ... those who have more initiative,
more venturesomeness, and a quicker eye than the
crowd, the pushing and promoting pioneers of
economic improvement.[9]

By this rubric, the entrepreneur is a hero; a maverick who is by
nature promethean; a person or persons willing and able through
idiosyncratic genius to promote a new idea or invention; who take
the clay of ideas and fashion it into a successful innovation that results
in the replacement in whole or in part of inferior innovations. This
brings a 'gale of creative destruction,' as Schumpeter famously put
it, and this he supposed, was largely responsible for the dynamism
of industries and the long-term growth and health of economies.

Thus conventional entrepreneurs are not made 'to serve'; they are 'unquelled, restless spirits'.[10]

This is a reasonable approximation of Vinod Kapur the man. But it is incomplete. Even the most impressive 'acting man' was trained somewhere and depended on someone. Per Kapur, "I am a man of ideas, but I depend on the excellence of people around me to deliver." We know the importance of formal and informal networks of relationships and associations; of information to businesses of all kinds, shapes and sizes. We recognise the importance of grounding, of education. The entrepreneur is no Randian rugged individual: she stands on the shoulders of many. Austrian conceptions of social entrepreneurship only get us so far towards understanding the reality on the ground.

The role of the market

The role of the market in social entrepreneurship is also a source of contention. Social entrepreneurs are those who change systems and communities for the long term, using any of the means at their disposal, of which the market *may* be (and most often is) one. Consider, entrepreneurship in this context does not solely commend financial returns as its measure of success. It is about leveraging what author David Bornstein referred to as 'the power of new ideas'.[11] In a market economy this will *most often* involve treating with the marketplace – but not always. A great example of the latter is the Girl Child Network, which we encounter in the next chapter and which is as socially entrepreneurial as they come because growth is built into its model; but this growth is social rather than financial with successive generations of young women being encouraged to lead and empowering entire new cadres of young women in turn.

Ethical contortions

There are further levels of oddity. Conceptions of what is 'social', 'ethical' or 'socially acceptable' vary from country to country and generation to generation, beyond a penumbra of minimum moral regard. We have considered Vinod Kapur's ingenuity and diligence, but vegetarians and vegans raise their own heckles about working with animals in this way. Kapur shrugged when I put this to him. He has other things on his mind.

This does not please everyone. Such lines are blurry and yield debate. Furious arguments rage over whether this or that social enterprise 'counts' or whether it is social enough, as questions of regulation are caught up in culture wars around veganism or abortion or fracking.

The approach of the world's lawmakers

How do governments and regulatory authorities all over the world do it? Here we are subject to the nuances of domestic law, business and non-profit regulation.

Some examples. In Australia, a generally accepted definition sees profits substantially reinvested for the purposes of the businesses. In the US this is diluted to businesses that conform to some overarching standard of profit, social purpose and potentially environmental concern but there are differences between the way that 'non-profits' can set up trading arms of their operation and how those regulations work in other jurisdictions (such as the UK, where things are less strict).

In Italy, the organisation has to be not-for-profit and is given the status of a legal category within the umbrella form of co-operatives – a kind of company with a particular cultural significance. In Finland, South Korea and the Czech Republic, such organisations must be appropriately registered, often with a central government agency.

South Korea especially is a fascinating case. In the early part of the 20th century, South Korea was a welfare-lite state, with the smallest portion of social expenditure relative to the overall government budget in the advanced industrial countries. To deal with these issues, the Korean government introduced in 2006 a law promoting social enterprises. Certified social enterprises were created that sold goods, created jobs for disadvantaged folks and improved lives – all at the stroke of a government edict.

Until January 2010, 288 social enterprises had been officially certified, employing 7,228 people. This is social enterprise, but wrought from the clay of government, uniquely Korean, which led some commentators breathlessly to proclaim that they had created a national social enterprise movement on a sort of fast track. Is it sustainable? We shall see.

The British government has veered between attempting to legally define, worrying that this would unduly constrain and instead throwing their weight behind self-certification standards such as the 'social enterprise mark', and steering clear of the question altogether. I counsel the latter course. Government regulation cannot tell a grassroots movement what it is. Fascinating how many people forget that, regulators especially.

The movement defines itself

All of the above has not deterred several respected voices from attempting to create internationally credible approaches to definition, classifications, or typologies. They are often based on survey data, testimony or supposition. If you want to learn about the depth and diversity of this most contemporary of global community movements in more detail, this is a good way to get into it.

The social enterprise typologies game

The academic Kim Alter created a very useful typology of social enterprise, which was based on observations of a number socially minded organisations.[12] It outlined various types of organisation that lie between traditional not-for-profits and traditional profit-making enterprises, categorised according to their motive, accountability and use of income.

Organisations sitting on this spectrum can be divided into two groups, depending on their purpose. Categories 1 and 2 in Figure 1.1 are driven primarily by social impact, whereas categories 3 and 4 are primarily motivated by profit. Social enterprises, by this rubric, are driven by social impact, but use commercial activity in order to ensure their sustainability.

The Alter Typology is clear, concise and lends itself very well to argument and disputation. There is a peculiarly fun kind of game that you can play where you assess a particular business and decide whether it is a social enterprise or not. Take the archetypal vegan café. As a lapsed vegan my instinct is to suggest that these will be social enterprises as a matter of course, unless something really bad is happening under the hood. If a dollop of soy is being presented as a 'super burger' or similar and the owners and shareholders are getting rich from the profits, then it would closer to a scam. But this is quite a high threshold and for me any number of organisational models, from co-operative, to socially responsible business, to business with community responsibilities, to charity would bring such an anti-animal cruelty vegan business into the social enterprise family. Others, who are not so committed to this cause, disagree. They want to see more stringent social purpose tests applied to the business side of such an enterprise because for them veganism, of itself, does not count as a useful social object.

The issues of profit and non-profit, conventional and social business regularly kindle the embers of debate when it is applied to social enterprise. A business that employs people is not necessarily a social enterprise; for that is just what businesses do. Neither

Figure 1.1. The social enterprise spectrum

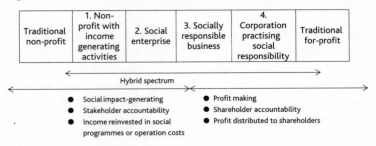

Source: Adapted from Alter (2007).[13]

is a business that employs and trains people a social enterprise necessarily: depending on its practices it is most likely to be a conventional corporation or at a push a socially responsible business. Training, after all, is what smart businesses do. A business that employs and trains long-term unemployed people might be a social enterprise in a particular area though I suspect it would have to be a pretty rigorous programme with proper milestones aimed at a targeted group. A business that trains people who are being systematically underemployed – say the deaf and mute communities employed by Mirakle Courier Company in Mumbai, India, or the refugees employed by Magdas Hotel in Vienna, Austria – is definitely a social enterprise. For me, this holds whether it is for or not for profit; the social purpose is crystal clear so as to make the financial model broadly irrelevant save for when that model is exploitation. I suspect that the long-term unemployed example could well qualify if it were constructed as an asset-locked or not-for-profit institution. I would need further evidence of the parameters of the aid being given, the scope of the problem being solved and the relationship of the intervention to the business: more evidence in other words. The strength of the Alter Typology is that it facilitates discussion and debate like this, and compels evidence-based analysis – or at worst a healthy sort of 'smell test' – that is good for the movement. And it is quite fun to have these arguments too, though perhaps that is just me.

Note that many social enterprises indeed, including Kapur's own, are set up as non-profits. This is a slight problem with the typology; failure to rigorously define the boundary between categories 1 and 2 – precisely because this boundary is porous – tends to pull the schematic apart. An example Alter gives for category 1 is a charity that sells products as a side line, and makes no effort to expand this range, while category 2 might be a charity selling the same product, but as a commercial opportunity which they have expanded considerably and constitutes their main operation. Yet in practice it is hard to see this distinction hold. If a product offered by a charity that trades is attractive, it will be in demand (and most products will be offered with a view to getting to that point, else what is the point?) and this is an example of social entrepreneurship. If not, and the product is only bought by people because it is offered by the charity, and there is no entrepreneurial attitude behind it, then this is akin to soliciting a donation. And so you are back in the realm of the traditional non-profit.

Similarly, the boundary between 2 and 3 (and more rarely 4, though in India, to take one example, such organisations are more likely to be referred to as social enterprises) is porous too. A 'new wave' of new hybrid forms have emerged and gathered steam since Alter first conceived of this typology. New kinds of socially responsible business model, such as B Corps and L3Cs (Chapter Three will explain all) make the barrier between the socially responsible business and the social enterprise communities ever more mutable. Moreover, social entrepreneurs, like the clutch of employees at mobile giant Vodafone who created mobile money juggernaut M-Pesa, a highly effective development tool which provides people all over the world with access to funds, show that even large corporations and governments can encourage and develop social enterprises within the integument of their own systems.

Ultimately, fitting everything in these boxes is not really the point of all this; getting a strong sense of the limits of each and the purposes that we are trying to achieve with these structures matters that much more. The debate, generating discussion and energy around this space is the thing. The typology, as amended above, is just one guide.

It is worth mentioning one more type-based approach here: that championed by Nobel prize winner and development financier Professor Muhammad Yunus. In his view, a 'social enterprise' is any entrepreneurial organisation that has a social purpose; while a 'social business' reinvests most or all of its profits into that purpose or is owned by its beneficiaries, provided they are from poor backgrounds.[14]

I am not alone in finding the distinction between social business and social enterprise pedantic but the notion that a social enterprise either (i) helps the poor through its business or (ii) is owned by the poor in some way, while (iii) ensuring that the poor are not used exploitatively as the worst sort of 'cash cow' is helpful.

The social impact approach

This approach reserves the term 'social enterprises' for those organisations that have a 'social impact', which is calculated in some way, and that seeks to create definable measures of that impact and demonstrate improvement against those measures.

This calculation is a considerable challenge. Businesses of all kinds have social impacts; they offer jobs and livelihoods for example. Social enterprises may make profits, but those profits are (mostly) directed to the end of doing something good for others, something beyond the good things that businesses already do. Understanding, measuring and improving on this impact, understanding its ethical and social dimensions, each present huge challenges, and we devote a chapter to this controversial science: Chapter Four.

A cultural point: note that not all countries see impact in quite the same way. Returning to India, there are a variety of forms of social enterprise. The closest to the understanding we have outlined above is a 'Section 25' company – registered under section 25 of the Indian Companies Act 1956, a form which effectively prevents the assets of such companies from being distributed.[15] Otherwise, definitions are broad and inclusive. Take the criteria applied by projects such as the Tata Social Enterprise Challenge, which takes a definition that simply requires organisations to demonstrate some kind of social impact to count as a social enterprise irrespective of legal form.[16]

In India, the work of academic C.K. Prahalad remains highly influential. His analysis of 'bottom of the pyramid' businesses – those selling to the poorest in society – as a form of social enterprise focuses on the power of profit-making activities to tackle extreme poverty.[17] In a vast country, bringing the fruits of commercial networks, Vinod Kapur-style, to those who have been cut off for generations is in and of itself a social good. Merely selling to the poorest would not qualify as a 'social impact' in most countries; in others it is seen at times as a radical act.

The stakeholder approach

Another approach sees organisations identified as 'social enterprises' by virtue of the different constituencies to which they try to appeal. This speaks to the daily work of the social entrepreneur in their role as a leader; it contends that social entrepreneurs must never be motivated by purely business concerns or purely social concerns but all of the above and more.

Generally, social entrepreneurs appeal to three different sorts: the charitable, the public and business. You need charitable types to keep them on mission. You need the public to support their endeavours (and governments to platform their work). And you need business to assure them that they will last. Political skills are required to negotiate the fields between the private, public and charity sectors. Coalition building, persuasion, negotiation with key parties including volunteer groups, funders, government agencies are top of the social entrepreneur's skillset. This sounds like hard work – and it is – but it has benefits on the other side too. For example, like charities, social entrepreneurs are often starved of funding for their causes. Social enterprise grant funders tend to cover a much smaller proportion of these organisation's overall needs for shorter time periods than in more traditional grant-seeking charities. This can make things difficult, but it can also make these organisations more diverse, more resilient, more future-proof than your alms-dependent organisation.[18]

The animal kingdom of social enterprise

This approach identifies the method by which groups of social enterprises do their thing: how they interact with the marketplace or their target community to do lasting good.

The principal types, a sort of animal kingdom of social enterprise, are below. They are based in part on a similar exercise conducted by Kim Alter, partly on my own investigations and studies from the field. New categories and ideas emerge all the time.

Social activist social enterprises. This sees a would-be entrepreneur enter into a community, understand problems from the bottom and devise useful, innovative solutions that treat with the local, national or indeed global marketplace or find some other way to create considerable ructions in the community's social fabric. From Vinod Kapur's network, to Muhammad Yunus's Grameen Bank, these organisations prospered because they were close to the people that mattered and offered them something new that could make a difference for now and for the long term.

One of the most innovative reform movements of our time is the drive to reform business and finance, and social activist social entrepreneurs are at the heart of this. There are great examples such as the entrepreneurs driving the rise impact investment, aided by enterprises such as GIIN (Global Impact Investing Network).[19]

Market access social enterprises. These enterprises enable the very poorest to gain better access to the market. They may purchase goods from beneficiaries and then sell them on the market or introduce and broker relations with the markets. Stephen Burks of Readymade Studios' work with artisans all over the world to produce design pieces for major fashion houses is but one example, one kind of linkage that can be made. Online microfinance lenders such as Kiva.org enable entrepreneurs in poor countries to seek small loans online. Indian enterprise Drishtee enables local entrepreneurs to manage their inventories better, giving them sophisticated technological tools to move key consumer goods into areas of great need.

Employment social enterprises. Some social enterprises employ beneficiaries to provide services or produce goods which are then sold on the market. Jamie Oliver's Fifteen restaurant hires apprentices from local estates to learn their trade in the kitchens. The Magdas Hotel in Vienna is a beautifully designed space that employs refugees from dozens of backgrounds and peppers quirkily presented information about the iniquities of the asylum system about the place. India's Mirakle courier company employs and empowers people with disabilities.[20]

Cross-subsidy social enterprises. India's Aravind Eye Care is one of the great social enterprises. It offers low cost eye surgery to poor people, and makes use of 'cross-subsidy' to do so. In this case, a subsidy from more commercial healthcare ventures is applied to pro-poor endeavours to create staggering multinational impact. On a similar yet smaller scale, Talia Frenkel's L. condoms works by promising a condom to a woman in a hard-to-reach area of high need for every condom purchased online or in pharmacy stores. Blake Myckosie's Tom's Shoes gives a pair of shoes to someone in the developing world for every pair they sell. Inspired by the sight of bare-footed children on the outskirts of Buenos Aires, the designs are based on *alpargatas* canvas slip-ons, with 12 million pairs donated by 2012. And a particular favourite: WGAC (Who Gives a Crap) was set up by three Australians. They make eco-friendly toilet paper and donate a portion of profits to sanitation programmes that ensure that billions of people on our planet who cannot afford access to a proper toilet are helped. WGAC got going after a crowd-funded online campaign which saw one of the founders sit on a toilet in the WGAC warehouse until enough money was raised to get production under way.

Charitable support social enterprises. Here, a socially beneficial organisation decides to sell socially useful products to its beneficiaries to support its core work. For example, the elder care charity Age UK provides its beneficiaries with all sorts of offers such as travel insurance for the elderly. At the farther end of this scale, commercial activity may be unrelated to social programmes, with income used to fund social programmes. The vast majority of charity shops, such as those run by legendary American philanthropic organisation Goodwill, which turnover billions in the US alone, are the typical examples of this. There are subsets of these organisations, which we discuss in Chapter Five.

Bottom of the pyramid commercial social enterprises. Under certain limited circumstances, it can be an act of social activism to provide key products to the lowest income members of our society in cases where local conditions make those products unaffordable. Aravind Eye Care's work driving down the costs of lenses and surgeries is one example.

Social tech social enterprises. These enterprises are a unique variant of social activism and specifically attempt to give people (or even businesses) innovative tools to reflect on and change the way government and society works. For example MySociety was set up by social entrepreneur Tom Steinberg, and gives citizens the information they need to have an impact on politics in a simple, accessible form. Videre, founded by Israeli Oren Yakobovich, provides equipment to people to document human rights abuses. Dubarah ('I've got your back' in Arabic) is an online network created by Ahmad Edilbi, which provides Syrian refugees with online peer support, information and knowhow on their countries of resettlement so that they can become productive and knowledgeable citizens and help shift the at times shamefully xenophobic narrative that persists around all refugees. The entrepreneurship here lies in the new and sophisticated use of products, innovations and resources to push the boundaries of the good.

Public service social enterprises: These enterprises go with the grain of public service and welfare provision and attempt to improve it, often using new digital media. This can range from providing data banks to improve the quality of field research to creating web services to help rate public services, or working with local government using video and innovative game design in order to improve the quality of services. A key player here is often government, though it can also be trade unions or indeed any other organisation with an interest in the policy matter at hand. One example of this are the plethora of US Living Wage campaign groups incubated by the Tides Foundation (Chapter Two) around the turn of the millennium or British social enterprise In Control (Chapter Nine) which helps differently-abled people manage their care budgets.

New Mutuals. The type of market engagement we see here is redistribution of financial ownership. These social enterprises are often co-operatives or 'solidarity-based' organisations and are about giving property and wealth to those who do not have it. Community land trusts across the developing world and the developed world are but one example, giving people a stake and a say in where they live. There are food co-operatives like Park Slope in Brooklyn in the US or the People's Supermarket. There are textile co-operatives like Becky John's Who Made Your Pants, which until 2015 supported women working in the industry who also took a stake in the organisation. There are many more variations besides, and a variety of new pro-social company forms to consider with them.

Support social enterprises ('hubs'). These organisations are the infrastructure that helps all of the above. They advise, support and keep the movement going. They ensure that new social entrepreneurs are found, often from within disadvantages communities, who personally understand the networks and relationships that people like Vinod Kapur were trying to understand from the outside. The Tides Foundation in the US supports groups of local social enterprises, businesses with ethical ideas or charities that want to improve their impact. Consider also the park dedicated to the subject in Bilbao, Spain, grand organisations such as the Skoll forum, or great social enterprise 'fests' such as SoCap in the US. Individual social entrepreneurs dedicate huge energy to supporting others. Consider, at the investor end of things, continental Venture Philanthropy Networks (as they are called) that span Europe, Africa and Asia, which were set up by philanthropist Doug Miller. Or Michael Young, who created Which? and Language Line as social businesses, Open University and National Extension College as public agencies and the Young Foundation which seeds social ventures. As mentors and role-models, the movement is channelled and enhanced through them; it owes them a great deal as do we.

The global community activism scene

As early as 1980, social entrepreneurship was identified as a nascent, breakout idea; a movement worthy of factoring in to the concatenation of ideas that determine the world's future. Bill Drayton was a key figure. A former head of the US Environmental Protection Agency, he reflected on the work of charitable luminaries like Nobel Laureate Muhammad Yunus, who pioneered tiny loans to rural-dwelling women in Bangladesh that freed them from the grasp of loan sharks. He reflected on the broader, more ancient heritage of activism that seeks to change the system. He reflected on the protagonists of this movement's willingness to treat with the market, with finance and with business in order to deliver more for the people they wanted to help. He referred to the people behind these organisations as social entrepreneurs. He explained with reference to that old phrase 'Give a man a fish, he'll eat for a day; teach him how to fish and he'll eat forever.' As he put it:

> social entrepreneurs are not content just to give a fish
> or to teach people how to fish; they will not rest until
> they've revolutionised the whole fishing industry.

His organisation, the Ashoka Foundation, is an educational and support foundation that supports a range of social entrepreneurs, many of whom we will meet over the course of this book.

But as we can see from the above, it is really in the last few years that social entrepreneurship has begun to fizz, to rapidly reach boiling point. There are several reasons for this: a critical mass of brilliant ventures, a globally hyper-connected economy and society and a generation – I call them mission-driven millennials – who have appropriated social entrepreneurship as their thing. We'll get further into the detail of these arguments over the course of the chapters ahead.

In light of the definitional issues, getting a handle on the *size* of the social entrepreneur movement in various countries and localities is not as straightforward as one might hope. There is no simple definition, no global register that must be ticked (though there are individual forms, such as the UK's Community Interest Company, that offer such a register). Once again, this is about sketching outlines, broad contours, and make inroads based on the often differing assumptions used by different countries.

The first Great Social Enterprise Census took place in the US in 2013 and the results demonstrated the extent to which social enterprise has emerged as a leading social and economic movement of our time. According to analysis of the first wave of submissions, around 60% of US social enterprises were created in 2006 or later, with 29% created since 2011. The results, while not comprehensive, suggested that in the US alone, the movement could be worth some US$500 billion, representing 3.5% of US GDP, and 90% of those enterprises worked on US-based social issues. Around a third were not-for-profit, a third were standard companies with social objectives and a growing set were 'hybrid forms', new mixtures of the two that create new possibilities for mixing growth and good.[21] The UK has developed a particularly effervescent culture of social enterprise. In September 2013, 180,000 people were employed in social enterprise in the UK, contributing approximately US$80 billion to the UK economy. More generally, around a fifth to a third of nascent or early stage entrepreneurship in the UK was in the social domain. Of all funding required by social enterprise, 60% was expansionary – investment for new projects or service development, capital investment such as plant or buildings. Consonant with the relatively large size of its economy, there are more social entrepreneurs in the UK than any other country in Western Europe and, as awareness grows, the number of people who are interested in setting up a social enterprise increases too. In India, economic reform has been accompanied by a boom in social entrepreneurs. According to the 2010 Beyond Profit survey,[22] 68% of social enterprises there had been in business for up to five years; 90% were small, with a turnover of $500,000 or less. And crucially, almost a third grew rapidly – by as much as 50% in the year prior to the survey.

In China, despite the words 'social' and 'entrepreneur' operating in a different cultural context, reformers agitate for loosening regulations to help the growth of social entrepreneurship as we understand it here. Stories of growth and advocacy for this new form of bottom-up business-cum-charity continue to sprout right across our ailing planet.

As they should and as they will continue to do. This is not just about the breadth of the movement and the scale of the problems we face. There is clean energy, childcare services, hospices, cancer treatments, working with differently-abled children. It is also about the people best placed to articulate solutions to our problems, to drive the debate and design the future. I hope that the huge canvas I have presented in this chapter begins to convince you of one thing: they are not found in the old institutions or among the old orders. They are on the ground, supporting, working with, empowered by, or being social entrepreneurs.

Many conventional business brains, government ideologues or charity activists do not quite have the measure of the movement yet and are suspicious of it. I say: good. Let's spend some time opening minds and examining our prejudices, and let's see how we fare by the time we get to the other side.

There is no comprehensive answer to the question of what puts the 'social' in social enterprise. I say: good. The minute we believe such a statement exists, we have ceased to believe in our endless capacity to debate and discern new frontiers of the good.

The debates and typologies , legal classifications and censuses are useful of themselves but also because they allow us to get a feel for the idea of social enterprise and the kind of conversation we are about to have about it.

The road ahead

Knowing what a social enterprise, roughly, is and understanding the incredible changes that Vinod Kapur and his fellow ambitous community activists seek to create in the fabric of our established orders so as to tackle some of the biggest problems we have are two very different things. Our time brings huge challenges; these are the stories of how we face them, with local action and global connection. Regulation and definition, where it exists, must look to empower and free that spirit.

As we move through the chapters ahead, I want you to think about that spirit, about the need for change and the people who will deliver it. And I suggest the following as particularly apt characteristics of the movement with which we are now familiar that render it particularly suitable to come together and slay the giants of inequality, want and hypocrisy that mar our time.

(a) *Challenge and competition.* The old order inevitably becomes complacent. Not-for-profits, governments and businesses get used to doing things their own ways. Social entrepreneurs enter the arena and compel change, adaptation, learning. They open new doors and cause bad practices to be shelved.

(b) *Democratic and community empowerment.* Community action gives the social entrepreneur her power. You saw this in Vinod Kapur, whose work really took flight when tested and tempered in the fire of the Indian village and the lived reality of the woman of the house. Social entrepreneur channels something very powerful: it puts communities, the voiceless, those on the ground, right in the driving seat of change.

(c) *Collaboration and institutional disruption.* Social entrepreneurs hungrily make and test new partnerships; new ideas are implemented. Institutions are disrupted and small movements grow to become capable of mounting challenges to established orders. These partnerships transform our terrain, enter our consciousnesses through expressions like the anti-fat-cat Occupy movement, the #everydaysexism and #blacklivesmatter online movements and, indeed, the political groundswells of our time, orchestrated online, that rewrite the rulebook.

I end this chapter with Mr Kapur's words. "Every day I wake up my work gives me so many reasons to be happy and so many reasons to be hopeful," he told me as I was packing up my things to leave Keggfarms. And as I left the Keggfarms oasis and drove onto the highway and once again saw that sign with its slogans (Photo 1.1), three words from it connected by arrows set in my mind:

ALLEVIATION

SECURITY

EMPOWERMENT

As my car sped off to the airport, I contemplated that the definitions, the health checks, the reports and the rest are crucial to show us how far we have come. But the real joy of this movement, lies in thinking about where this journey might take us next, and simple three word statements like these present the work of the social entrepreneur in elegant summary.

2

Raising the voices of girl-children:

pyramids, incubators, and the fight for equality

I prefer to be a dreamer among the humblest, with visions to be realized, than lord among those without dreams and desires. (Khalil Gibran)

The mentor

For Mzuvare Betty Makoni it sprang from a grave and terrible betrayal. As a child growing up in Zimbabwe in the 1970s she sold tomatoes and candles. Then at the age of only six she was raped by a local man in her neighbourhood. The crime, shamefully, was hushed up. She would later recall:

'I remember my mum using salt and whatever she could use to treat me. The whole abuse left physical and psychological trauma, everything stuck into my sub-conscience ... He thought raping little girl would make him rich ... a belief that raping virgins brings luck. I grew up a very angry girl ... I told myself whatever happens, I will confront every rapist.'[1]

In time she would become a teacher, looking after classrooms of young girls. She knew what many of them were going through all too well; terrible crises of adolescence and outrage and, sadly, many had been through similar things to her. She became their trusted, compassionate confidante. In her classes, beyond the numbers and letters of the curriculum, the seed of something grew. It would, through care and application, become the Girl Child Network (GCN).[2]

As the girls shared their stories and encouraged each other, as they spoke and were listened to, something wonderful happened. Girls who appeared to be at risk of going off the rails found a new strength and purpose in this safe environment. Results improved; aspirations grew. Some girls found that they were particularly effective listeners and facilitators and they brought new girls into the network. Some even came to run their own groups.

To give you a sense of the scale of the problem we are dealing with here, consider GCN's own statistics. Some 60 million girls are said to leave school before they are 15 years old. In Zimbabwe alone thousands are raped annually, with many going unreported. Genital mutilation, child marriage and other 'harmful cultural practices' mean that girls are five times more likely to be exposed to HIV/AIDS than boys. Girls in the classroom may be encouraged to marry or be raped by teachers. Girls are often easy targets to be co-opted into local militias in conflict states. The scale of the response marches out of step and behind the size of the problem.

But networks like GCN offer hope because tied into their method is the means by which they develop and replicate. In those classrooms, quiet girls become leaders and those leaders create new movements of their own, driven by people who have been there who understand. And, when it is at its most powerful, it is driven by people who know just how this feels.

Spurred by Makoni's drive, but moreover by the leadership of bright young women who have passed through the network, GCN has become one of the world's great social enterprises: a movement dedicated to leadership that relies on the wealth of talent in people who have often been overlooked and ignored.

The network today proactively identifies girls who are at risk of not pursuing their education and supports them to open up and continue. It provides a community of people who have been through some of the things they have been through and encourages those girls to speak up and take an active role in that community. Its strength lies in that dynamic of support that offers hope to millions.

GCN does not only relieve the pressure; in the best tradition of the social entrepreneur it seeks to revolutionise the narrative, to turn the story around, to secure and empower. The model is purposefully ambitious; the scale of the problem is so huge that souls cannot be saved one at a time. Instead, there is a sort of production line of social leadership, where girls are helped, empowered and then encouraged to empower others. As they put it:

> We inspire girls to take leadership in gender equality at community level. We believe girls are not victims. They only need their potential unleashed so that they reach their full potential. We are here to inspire and empower so that girls aspire and achieve. We are confident of what we do because we have over 300 000 girls we supported through girls clubs in Zimbabwe and now they are women leaders all over the world.[3]

Social entrepreneurs like Betty Makoni offer a very pure kind of hope and inspiration in a situation that in their absence seems desolate and bleak. Its mode of action is simple and replicable. The possibility that bad things might not be hushed up, or that the further assaults of wars, predators, quack cures, threats, mental and physical harm in these girls lives might be spoken about and avoided is in many places revolutionary. You only need a classroom, or a living room, and a generous ear for it all to work.

Another way of looking at all of this is that Makoni's organisation is developing hundreds of thousands of potential future social entrepreneurs. Each young person takes their place in a pyramid of socially minded activity, spurred on and inspired by those who inspired them to inspire others in turn. This chapter is about manoeuvres like these, organisations that stare down the seemingly insurmountable problems of inequality and injustice and, against all odds, prosper. Social entrepreneurship is their weapon and their elixir.

Finding the lost generation

Consider the case of Malala Yousufzai. She was barred from an education by repressive forces in her home country and suffered horrible physical violence as a result. Now, like Betty Makoni, she is a campaigner, not only for her own education but for the rights of girls and women all over the world. She is a symbol, a story of success, a humanitarian activist of global standing and she has been there.

Much of the power of her message comes from her authenticity and experience. She is not just talking about the problem and the solution, she has faced the problem and lived the solution and when she speaks with erudition and grace the imbecility of a convention that prevents girls from receiving an education is made clear several times over. Giving those who have suffered the chance to articulate and drive the change needed to alleviate suffering is just about the most powerful, radical and moral platform we can create.

Social entrepreneurs like Malala and Makoni are often extremely adept at highlighting the scale of the problem that faces us. We have discussed some of the statistics already, but a paper by Betty Makoni even more adeptly presented the scale of the problem – social, economic, cultural and political – that activists like her take on. Her five 'charges' and additional statistics are worth quoting in full, not least because they have cultural resonance in many parts of the world:

1. In many places, parents believe it is more advantageous to have sons than daughters.
2. A case of five boys indecently assaulted by a teacher took two weeks to be heard in the courts, while another case of 32 girls who were sexually abused at school took more than a year to be heard.
3. During the domestic violence debate in Parliament, Zimbabwean parliamentarians said that in the eyes of God, men and women are not equal.
4. There is a Ministry of Women's Affairs, but it is very poorly funded compared to other government ministries.
5. Women occupy only around one-fifth of key decision-making positions in Zimbabwe.

In addition, the incidence of HIV and AIDS in Zimbabwe is 60% amongst girls aged 13 to 25 years, compared to 10% amongst boys of the same age. Ninety-three per cent of girls are sexually abused in Zimbabwe compared to 7% of boys. One in four girls out of 6,000 believed to have been raped is infected by HIV and AIDS. Due to early forced marriages, the widowed, orphaned girl child has become a common sight in most poor communities. The youngest rape survivor in Zimbabwe is a day-old baby. There was a big outcry in Zimbabwe when one 16 year old boy married a 45 year old woman, compared to hundreds of girls under 16 years of age who are married in some apostolic sects to men of 70 years and older.[4]

This level of knowledge, expertise, experience and eloquence is a key weapon in the social entrepreneur's armoury.

Social entrepreneurs are often characterised by as the archetypal 'Harvard MBA types'; people who have chosen to take the high road and apply their *educations* to the cause of fighting poverty. Some of the most effective social entrepreneurs use their own *experiences* to craft transformative organisations. We are not just talking about helping or empowering vulnerable people: we are asking people who were once considered to be victims to step forward as leaders and CEOs, precisely because they are the best people for the job. And so we are talking about driving an armoured tank through privilege and class.

It is not enough to have a great idea, it must be a great idea done well. Social entrepreneurs cannot rely only on the strength of their feeling, on emotion, on the heart. They use their heads too and must be seek business success with hunger so that they build something that not only helps but lasts.

Education, experience, emotion, advocacy, insight, business smarts: together they form a uniquely heady balance of skills, competences and visions that must be balanced if a social enterprise is to gain momentum. Conventional entrepreneurs have a tough enough time getting their enterprises off the ground; social entrepreneurs like Betty Makoni have it all to do. Studies of social enterprises operating in the health and care sector have suggested that, given that social enterprises do not always look like standard businesses – and social entrepreneurs do not always look like standard business people – there is a danger that investors might be wary of helping them develop.[5]

Practitioner surveys further suggest that in some environments, the founders of social enterprises may lack the requisite knowledge of the local investment landscape, being from outside the local business 'bubble' and discriminated against for precisely that reason.[6] In one of my own studies on this subject, conducted in 2010,[7] I noted the tendency of new social entrepreneurs to undervalue their enterprises and not shoot for the proper goals that might keep their business afloat. This all results in a vicious *cycle of ignorance* wherein relatively few social enterprises access the capital they need in the form in which they need it so that they might make their visions real.

This is very costly indeed. My research on the UK scene showed that around a third to a fifth of all new business ventures are created by social entrepreneurs and that around a third of these ventures are capable of producing sustainable social enterprises. If the cycle of ignorance could be broken to the extent that appropriate support were to reach just 10% of them – a credible target to be sure – we could witness the creation of approximately 8,500 viable expanding social enterprises or equivalent vehicles immediately. On current figures that would represent growth in the UK market of some 12%.

This cohort, absent from our lives, our communities, our society and economy, I referred to as *the lost generation* of social entrepreneurs.

Remember, that these figures reflect the situation in one country, from research conducted in 2010. As demand for such services increases, as the old orders and offices of the good continue to teeter and crumble, how much greater are the losses now? Just how huge is this lost sea of potential globally, in our time today?

Incubators and pyramids

One of the most exciting moments in my work with social entrepreneurs is when I meet a new one. That mix of inspiration and ideas, of meeting someone who wants to change the world and has a way of doing it that reveals their ingenuity or dedication is one of the best feelings. It has led to many lost hours, rapt in conversation, analysis and thought. Little wonder then that, all over the world, a great deal of energy is expended in finding new ways to develop and support social entrepreneurs; to help make their visions become real.

Bill Drayton, who coined the term 'social entrepreneur' (as we noted earlier), recognised from an early stage that to build the social entrepreneur movement, we would need to create a unique form of business support that helped it to find its way. Today, that sub-movement is rich and diverse.

In this section, we'll take a look at its ways. Principally, it divides into two major families, with several sub-forms and related approaches. Those families are: *incubators* and *pyramids*.

The incubator

Incubators are perhaps the better known of the two families. Putting it simply. *incubators harness the capacity of good people to create fabulous social enterprises that make a big difference.*

Incubators like Echoing Green in New York City search for 'world class leaders' to join their fellowship and have invested tens of millions of dollars in them. They give them funding, advice, support to mature their business idea into a working model and might pair them with investors in order to achieve large scale social initiatives.

One of Echoing Green's investees was Wendy Kopp, founder of the Teach for America programme. Kopp's pathway is a sort of archetype for the action of the pathway of action of an incubator graduate. She was a Princeton alumna who argued in her undergraduate thesis that postgraduate teaching might help harness the civic energy of her peers. Teach for America sprang from that idea, offering teaching placements to graduates in classrooms in some of the most difficult areas. Working in partnership with government, business people and philanthropists, success would follow and Kopp would come to expand Teach for America into a global network, Teach for All. The trajectory of her impressive organisation has been consistently growth focused; it now reaches graduates and children all over the world.

The incubator model tends to work best with those with high-achieving folks who have a hinterland of such good ideas: our archetypal Harvard MBA grad. It tends to focus on those who are less difficult to reach than many of the girls dealt with by, for example, GCN. Echoing Green claims a local mayor and former US First Lady Michelle Obama among its investees. It helps these bright sparks achieve great things in the social sphere. When it works they create marquee social enterprises based on a need identified through rigorous research, study or field-experience.

Sandbox incubators in India, supported by businessman and philanthropist Gururaj Deshpande, give similarly stellar social entrepreneurs the space to pilot and validate their ideas, with 'periodic' mentoring and peer-to-peer workplace learning. This yields mission-driven businesses and innovative ventures.

The alumni list is impressive, spanning water purification, irrigation and even a company called Nanopix, an image-based food sorting technology that automates the process and lowers the costs for producers. The Sandbox approach, which reaches across India in several hubs, is very much geared towards the educated social entrepreneur, with prior business experience or an academic track record – and of course a great idea.

Teach for All bequeathed the Teach First programme in the UK. The latter's founders took the idea and grew it into a viable, long-term, successful concern using native and acquired business knowledge. One of them, Nat Wei, went on to co-found an incubator himself, the Shaftesbury Partnership.

The partnership is a classic incubator; it insists on a careful selection process that systematically weeds out the non-scalable social entrepreneur from the viable and stellar.[8] Those that are chosen to continue are prepped and tailored through an impressive network of support. They offer their Fellows 'crowds' sourced from their network, who help during various phases of their projects.

In their words, they create 'techniques to model and develop the relational capital among stakeholders that power effective reforms'.[9] They take smart people and place them within a community in order to develop their work, give them influence within their industry or sub-sector and give their work the best possible chance of making the difference.

Franchising is one favoured tool that many incubators directly promote. The term is more often associated with companies like McDonald's or Starbucks, but organisations may be incubated in order to have groups of people with the right qualifications create branches or arms, outposts or chapters. Strong brand presence and corporate-wide marketing campaigns are cited as the reasons for their success.

The Shaftesbury Partnership has been particularly keen to leverage this idea in the past. It says it is a way to 'overcome systemic risks that often paralyse stakeholders'.[10] Incubators make this sort of tool hitherto reserved for the coffers of big business accessible to the social space by working with people who know that anything and everything is possible.

Throughout this book, as things develop and get more complex, you will see complex commercial ideas translated into the world of the social entrepreneur, promising aid and transformation to billions. It is the spirit of the incubator that helps seed this ambition from the start among a great many of the social entrepreneur movement's members.

Incubators come in all shapes and sizes; they are not only restricted to graduates of much maligned western universities. The Centre for Social Initiatives Promotion is a Vietnamese body aimed at the incubation of social enterprise within Vietnam. As well as investing directly in the work of social enterprises, it aims to create a more amenable economic and cultural environment, in which social enterprises have the opportunity to thrive. By introducing new financial players to the idea of investing in social enterprise, it is able to significantly increase the ability of social entrepreneurs to access the seed capital which they need.[11]

One close to my heart having spent some time in the country of Lebanon while writing this book is AltCity. AltCity supports and encourages entrepreneurship in Lebanon and across the Middle East and North Africa region. One of its focus areas is around what it describes as 'for-profit social impact ventures'. It provides a physical hub, in which entrepreneurs can work together, as well as access support from AltCity advisors. This represents a far more granular, practice-focused incubator than many others. Lebanon has been wracked by conflict on all sides; its people keep admirable focus on creating a better world. This too is AltCity's mission.[12]

Incubators are a vital part of the movement. They have enabled social entrepreneurs like Andrew Youn, whose One Acre Fund helps farmers in East Africa buy in bulk, access a range of financial and educational products and thereby improve their livings. Their graduates are often, though not invariably, amenable to being invested in, being replicated and grown. They are the embodiment of the *mission-driven millennial* whose support has taken the social entrepreneur movement this far already.

The pyramid

The undoubtedly more radical – and risky – approach is taken by the *pyramid* family of support hub.

Think of it this way: fewer than 1% of people who want to start a social enterprise are actually reached by funding agencies of any kind. The rest rely on personal or family money, the less fortunate do not have this luxury.

And yet, as we saw earlier, it is precisely those who are less fortunate – those who are directly affected by a social problem – whose ideas can help solve it, not only for them but for others in their community. They may not be educational or business stars; they may not even be graduates. How is their potential to be tapped?

British support hub UnLtd has described itself as part of the pyramid group. The difference between what they do and that which an incubator does is to be found in the screening process for those who come through the door. "The point," former CEO Cliff Prior told me, "was to find people from a diverse array of backgrounds who have direct experience of the problem they are trying to solve."

It is a one-stop development shop. It provides mentorship and a shoulder to lean on. It provides technical support such as financial modelling. It deploys quite sophisticated measures to assess not only the quality of the idea presented, and also the extent to which a person's life – and even their community's life – might be turned around if things were to come off and their enterprise was to make it.

Cliff Prior was the driving force behind all of this. He is an interesting character; we'll spend some more time with him a little later. I remember quite vividly how he explained all this to a sceptical young author one grey day in 2010, liberally peppering his discourse with a bewildering array of examples from the UnLtd stable, adjusting his fashionable rimless glasses as he went along.

The UnLtd indicators attempt to catch the breadth of the various types of people who could qualify for their support and so quantify the extent to which supporting them benefits wider society.

A traffic light system (red, amber, green) would be correlated with a measure of individual impact (greatest learning impact so needing most support, potentially less social impact) and social impact (needing least support, potentially more social impact). They looked for a diagnostic trait (there is something wrong here) and an activist trait (intention to do something about it). Success, here, Prior told me, "is measured quite differently to the success measured by incubator models or indeed success as defined by conventional business."

Prior's successor at UnLtd, Mark Norbury, has added to this a further layer of impact assessment: the extent to which the social entrepreneur meets key societal challenges. As he put it, "the priority is for social entrepreneurship to not only develop leadership skills to deliver successful ventures with individual impact, but also delivering collective impact sufficient to move the dial on particular social issues." So it's not only 'how much do you support your community?' but also 'to what extent do you support the health/employment/truancy problems in your community?'

This trend, of making the impact of such ventures that much more transparent can be witnessed across the piste and is part of what Norbury refers to as "taking social entrepreneurship mainstream". That is a key concept for us and we will come to it again in Chapter Four.

To take further examples of the kind of thing such organisations might be looking to achieve, over and above creating successful social enterprises and social entrepreneurs, I had a look at UnLtd's research and evaluation archives.

In a study by UnLtd of its social entrepreneur cohort, it was revealed 86% of those moving through the programme felt able to make a difference their community as a result of running their project.[13] This is an important finding; we'll return to it in the next chapter.

Similarly interesting was the evidence it gave for social entrepreneurship acting as a sort of democratiser that encouraged more people to find their voice. Giving belief to one person tends to transmit it to those around them.

Those who are time-rich – such as the newly retired for example – see something good and get involved. Those with the requisite skills can perform vital advice services or volunteer.

Indeed, in various evaluations, while 70% of UnLtd investees reported that they gained confidence as a result of inaugurating their social enterprise, 62% also believed that they gained leadership skills.[14] These gains are precious.

Both pyramids and incubators contribute to the greater movement. The incubator is a sort of fast-track to global public leadership. The pyramid may be this too, but I think of it as more of an everyday, homespun thing. It is about grassroots, on the ground activism; ventures that may not be quite so sexy as super-chickens or prestige restaurants with a social twist. They may not be terribly innovative but in the communities where they make their entrance, they make an incredible difference.

They are not limited to the developing world. They are the community owned café that does those cupcakes. The local gym that is run by residents. The urban allotment-cum-permaculture centre or indie-girl music venue that provides classes to oft-ignored kids.

In some places, there is so little that even beginning to sell things like basic groceries is an act of social entrepreneurship. Elsewhere,

where such things are often provided by the Wal–Marts or Tescos of this world, they represent an incursion on our lives that is as far away from social enterprise as one can be. This is what you get when you build a global movement in a world of such contrasts.

If the incubator's graduates must check their privilege and soul search about the ethics of building a career on selling to the poor, the operation of the pyramid is to take on that privilege at source.

The social enterprise movement somehow manages to bring these two ideas coherently together. The idea of growth and the idea of groundswell are two forces in one package, connected by the spirit of empathy: global and local.

This messiness, this diversity, this resistance to simple definition or convenient classification: this is what makes the movement so interesting and so alive.

The boundaries between pyramid and incubator are porous. Some support hubs may use either approach according to who comes through the door. The Tides Foundation is a US fund that incubates a number of discrete initiatives, but it displays the behaviours of a pyramid organisation when the project demands it. Its aim is to 'accelerate the pace of social change'. It does not only work with social enterprises – it also engages with everyone from foundations to individual donors and government institutions. Its interventions cover a broad spectrum, including facilitating grant making, providing shared workspaces for non-profit organisations and advocacy to shift public policy such as around delivering a 'living wage'.[15] It is eclectic, democratic, a genuine force for progress.

All that is good, in short.

Global ambitions

Let's return to Bill Drayton, one of the godfathers of social entrepreneurship, for a moment. His Ashoka Foundation is a social support hub for thousands of social entrepreneurs – whom it refers to as Ashoka Fellows. It names Betty Makoni and indeed many of the other social entrepreneurs in this book among its number.

Support hubs like these tend to be local, focused on entrepreneurs in a particular area, a little like a local chambers of commerce, networking club or business link for small conventional businesses. As social entrepreneurship is a local *and* global movement, however, in the past few years there have been moves made to join up this infrastructure in some rather interesting ways.

UnLtd has been at the forefront of realising these ambitions. Its goal is to enable its model to be used by everyone who needs it. And so since its foundation in 2000, UnLtd has been sharing its experience and learning of supporting social entrepreneurs with numerous other countries.

Since 2013, this has been carried out under the auspices of the Global Social Entrepreneurship Network (GSEN), which aims to support communities around the world to develop social entrepreneurship in their own countries in the way that works best for them.[14]

GSEN estimates that its members have supported over 2,600 social entrepreneurs since its foundation in 2013. In this way, the networks of ideas, talent and enterprise that spring from support organisations form their own, ever expanding variant on the conceit of the global community movement.

The idea of a genuinely globalised support infrastructure for social entrepreneurs is no pipe dream: it is our present.

People like Doug Miller have been building such transnational networks for years. After a career in the US army and then in business, Miller's retirement consisted of spending thousands of hours on a plane each year, travelling to China, Singapore, India and across Africa in a bid to set up new international support networks for venture philanthropists who support groups of social entrepreneurs using a variety of models. He creates, in short, continental support networks for the support organisations of this world.

His endeavours helped to create the American Gathering of Leaders of US venture philanthropy funds (we will consider the venture philanthropy movement in Chapter Five), the Asia Venture Philanthropy Network and the Africa Venture Philanthropy Association.

When I met him in 2012 it was clear that he saw his role as if he were still in combats. "I'm like a soldier taking a hill," he told me. He was not the one who took the hill, he said, but he was "marking the territory with flags, explaining the plan, bringing the troops together." Ending poverty, hunger, poor education, and so on were the goals here. We've met quite a few soldiers already.

Infrastructure is being built on infrastructure; growth multiplies. Networks like the Global Impact Investing Network (GIIN) share information, conferences like 'SoCap' in the US hold funding meetings for social start-ups and those that seek to invest in them and are the training grounds for the next generation – at SoCap 2010 25 pioneer funds were announced that support social entrepreneurs, representing some US$1.2 billion in 200 countries. By the end of 2012, this had grown to 53 funds, managing a total of US$1.9 billion.[16]

From its beginnings in Drayton's pioneering Ashoka Foundation, the market in social support hubs has grown too. There is the Schwab Foundation for Social Entrepreneurship, created in Switzerland in 1998 by Klaus Schwab, the founder and president of the World Economic Forum, Geneva, Switzerland. There is the Skoll Foundation, based in Palo Alto, California, and founded in 1999 by Jeff Skoll, the first president of eBay.

There are approaches that are entirely discursive in character. For example, the School for Social Entrepreneurs (SSE) is an international support agency. Its method focuses on group events where active social entrepreneurs speak and work through their problems. It is a bottom-up approach, where criticism is peer-driven and there is a Chinese wall between the funder and the support so that neither is compromised. This is outside the incubator/pyramid dichotomy and all the more interesting for SSE's global success.

Globalisation creates the opportunities here; globalisation makes it tick. Globalisation has turned into something of a political swear word of late, but this is globalisation tailored to developing local societies and economies; globalisation done right. Just as social entrepreneurship breathes life into localism, could social entrepreneurship also give moral meaning to globalism?

Turn that thought into action: a global response is needed if we are to further ramp up social entrepreneur support. Of the 1.6 million non-profits currently in operation in the US; the millions more across the world; the panoply of one man bands, large social businesses, digital entrepreneurs that came with the internet boom: the world is full of potential successful social enterprises. The call to break the cycle of ignorance that prevents social entrepreneurs from reaching their potential – and to avoid future lost generations – is ours to make.

There will be failures along the way. However well we support the movement, a large number of its members will not make it. Around two in three do not have the idea to get there. Of those that do, other things may get in the way. It is the way of things and certainly no reason to abandon hope or give up on them.

A very sad story was told recently of a social entrepreneur who emerged from prison, experienced a lack of support and decided to set up a social enterprise to provide such. She was helped by a pyramid incubator which developed her confidence, skills and her idea and the enterprise became hugely successful, was both sustainable and contributed to lower reoffending rates among users of the service. Unfortunately, some years later, with the enterprise still on an upward curve, she was involved in an incident that saw her go back to prison. We lost that one.

But we will win many more. The numbers are in our favour and right is on our side. We have here the potential to enable people create wealth not through their privilege, but through lack of it. We have in a very practical form the pith and substance of how we create equality of opportunity across the world in our time.

Among UK social enterprises, 91% have at least one female director.[18] Over 40% of Ashoka Fellows are women. Across the globe, women are using this movement to get active. UnLtd's survey figures from 2010 suggest that at the time in the UK, 57% of the entrepreneurs involved with them in new social start-ups were women. Additionally 13% are from refugee backgrounds and 44% started out on welfare themselves.[19]

War, famine, sanitation, exploitation: today's giants that stoke unrest and unhappiness demand radical responses. The social entrepreneur contends that the solutions to the problems of our time are already with us, we need only open our ears, reach out; look deep into communities that have been cast aside or written off. We will find them.

The social entrepreneur will help us. Incubating excellence and building pyramids that make our societies more equal are but two tools at their disposal. All they ask for in return is that we support them. A radical scaling up of our offer to them should be the least our gratitude delivers. For ultimately social entrepreneurship is about possibility and opportunity; realising the right of children all over the world at least to be given the chance of making the best of their lives. The statistics look terrible, the odds seem insurmountable. But somehow we are proving that we can overcome them. People like Makoni are creating lasting legacies for good, the most compelling of which is a confident, empowered global generation of girl-leaders.

3

The incredible rise of co-operatives:

conscious consumption ... slow fashion ... ethical exploration ... and more ...

Money makers are tiresome company, for they have no standard but cash. (Plato, *The Republic*)

The community of makers

Stephen Burks is an icon of industrial design. He leads Readymade Projects, a studio with offices in Brooklyn and Barcelona. He is in the business of creating beautiful things and winning awards for his endeavours. His partners and commissioners read like a who's who of design: Missoni, B&B Italia, Cappellini. You get the idea.

But Burks has another string to his bow. As he says in his mission statement, available online:

> "I make no distinction between [Readymade Projects'] product design for the Cappellinis or Missonis of the luxury design world and my collaborations with socially conscious non-profit organisations like Aid to Artisans and the Nature Conservancy in places like South Africa, Peru and India. In fact, I consider community,

generosity and authenticity to be the new watchwords of the future."

There is a lot to consider in that small statement, so let's take it step by step.

The Aid to Artisans of which he speaks is a social movement that has been around for decades.[1] In that time it has helped manufacturers and designers build relationships with workers from Africa to Asia, helped to reframe the marketplace for their wares and elevate their livelihoods thereby.[2]

Burks has been one of their best-known supporters. He had been serving a long apprenticeship in design, in the US and in Europe, when he and Aid to Artisans crossed paths. At the time he was well on his way to becoming one of the premiere US industrial designers at the time, and then a piece came out about him and his art titled 'Puff Dada'.[3]

"They were referring to me, *I* was Puff Dada," he said, suppressing a grimace during a talk in 2016, which he shared with me. Burks is of African-American descent. When he gave that talk he cut a languid, lean figure with a buzz cut, a Dries Van Noten suit and a soft, sophisticated patois. He was every inch the trope of the worldly design guru and nothing like the stereotype of the bling-king implied by the headline, and one can't help but think that it was a vulgar nod to Burks' heritage. "It made me think how little diversity there was in design."

Nevertheless that headline became something of a lightbulb moment. Burks ramped up a process of self-questioning, of feverishly and deliberately deconstructing identity and authenticity in his work, of trying to understand our often contradictory and fractious relationship to artisanal products and 'the other' in more detail.

Burks' work with Aid to Artisans was part of this journey. In South Africa, he challenged a local souvenir producer who worked with hand-wrought wire to try to make something larger than they had ever before made. After much craftsmanship, the result would come to be known as TaTu, a 'weather resilient modular collection of side and coffee tables' (as it was described in the press kit); a very beautiful piece of furniture.

There were other projects like these, and Burks came to see for himself the artisanal and economic potential locked in these communities. There was a story here that he felt he could tell his own industry. "As a designer, you can sit down with a CEO at a Missoni and talk about things like this, about the future," he said. Many of the great fashion houses emerged out of such craft traditions, and were initially family-owned artisanal business in Italy. There was an opportunity for the social entrepreneur to "build a bridge from [developing world] craft traditions into the future".

Burks is not the only designer with such ambitions. Dutch-born designer Tord Boontje is known among the general public for his collaborations at the retail end of the marketplace, for example with British homeware store, Habitat. In 2004 he worked with a women's collective in Brazil, a collaboration that resulted in a lampshade design that Boontje asked Italian homeware brand Artecnica, with whom he was working at the time, to produce commercially.

Earlier, similar attempts to work with such artisans had failed. The products yielded, when all of the liaison and research had been completed, were too expensive for the general Artecnica customer. By 2004, with Boontje's impetus behind the project, the company learned from its mistakes.[4] The lamps were a hit – and so emerged Artecnica's *Design with Conscience* range, which now includes pieces by Fratelli Campana, who also designs for Italian design giants Alessi, among others. They were all developed with and made by artisans from Asia, Africa, Central and South America.

The model is not perfect. Creating luxury goods, while interesting, does not necessarily represent where Burks wants this work to be. He expresses his frustration that, for all of his work bringing these worlds together, his products remain the preserve of the rich. "There is all this value," he says, "And I want to find a way of bringing it back down to people."

There are real, aesthetic questions too. What, after all, is 'authentic' about creating luxury items for the elite from the work of the very poor? What is particularly 'socially conscious' about encouraging this sort of conspicuous consumption? Isn't it aesthetically nullifying to take the work of the artisan and decontextualise it by placing it within this over-priced consumer frame?

Burks admits to wrestling with these problems constantly in his search to create a platform for these artisans that is useful and sustainable; that brings their stories to the world beyond.

Such projects, emerging as they do from the world of high fashion and design, are apt to be lampooned. Swedish flat-pack furniture juggernaut Ikea's collaboration with so-called artisanal makers received the treatment in the Hollywood movie *Fight Club*, which was based on the Chuck Palahniuk novel. The insomniac protagonist addicted to the consumer lifestyle is impelled to purchase the furniture for his flat with 'little imperfections' to show that they have been produced by artisans. This is nothing more than a sop to his degraded conscience, a further excuse for the all-consuming addict to keep buying things he doesn't need. He orders most of it while sitting on the toilet.

Burks' work is on a different plane; he is not culturally appropriating but empowering. As a 'market access social entrepreneur' he has evolved from those roots with Aid to Artisans to cover yet more artisan communities in some of the farthest reaches of the world. He is not usurping their voice but facilitating it.

Every day he brokers crucial connections between producers and consumers, the marketplace and artisans, between ideas and consciousnesses. He brings these communities' wares to the marketplace, into plain view, exposes them to more of the awe-struck public in some of the biggest couture brands in history. "For the first time in history with committed investment, we can all help foster the growth of influential brands out of Africa, Peru or India," he says. He is talking about what he calls "economic transformation by design".

Burks is committed to the hypothesis that corporations can form a platform for these communities to show their best selves. This chapter is about the organisations that test that hypothesis; the businesses set up to work in solidarity and co-operation with communities all over the world in order to shift realities. It is about the past and the future of perhaps the greatest social enterprise movement we have ever seen. It is about the co-operative and the culture that gives it meaning.

The greatest social enterprise

Co-operatives are the Koh-I-Noor diamond in the social enterprise crown; a hugely successful company form that represents one of the major foundations on which the moral marketplace rests.

Their heritage is considerable. They have existed in some guise since the 1400s, but it was with the establishment of the 'Rochdale Society of Equitable Pioneers' in 1844 that the movement was truly established.[5] The seven principles set out by this 28-strong band of weavers can still be found in the International Co-operative Alliance as the moral ballast for the movement (see Figure 3.1). In many parts of the world, Italy (where it is a protected company form), Denmark, Germany, in various guises, the co-op has always been strong. Indeed, the tradition of structuring an organisation as a co-operative, a 'mutual', a worker-owned enterprise or similar has been the foundation of European business for centuries. This was a model where the concerns of the community of members and wider society were placed alongside the contentions of capital. Often such organisations are referred to as being part of a 'social economy', an idea that has nice resonances with the wider 'moral marketplace'.

If you think that the above principles might somehow impair the conducting of business or hamper its ability to diversify or evolve: think again. Let us take in this movement, in all its myriad forms, for a moment.

Figure 3.1 The seven principles of the international co-operative movement

Principle #1: Voluntary and Open Membership
Co-operatives are open to all people able to use their services, without gender, social, racial, political or religious discrimination.
Principle #2: Democratic Member Control
Co-operatives are controlled by their members—those who buy the goods or use the services of the co-operative—who actively participate in setting policies and making decisions.
Principle #3: Member Economic Participation
Members contribute equally to, and democratically control, the capital of the co-operative. This benefits members in proportion to the business they conduct with the co-operative rather than on the capital invested.
Principle #4: Autonomy and Independence
Co-operatives are autonomous, self-help organisations controlled by their members. If the co-op enters into agreements with other organisations or raises capital from external sources, it does so based on terms that ensure democratic control by the members.
Principle #5: Education, Training and Information
Co-operatives provide education and training for members, elected representatives, managers and employees so they can contribute effectively to the development of their co-operative.
Principle #6: Co-operation among Co-operatives
Working together through local, national, regional and international structures.
Principle #7: Concern for Community
While focusing on member needs, co-operatives work for the sustainable development of communities.

Source: International Co-operative Alliance[6]

Spain is where we begin. Its Mondragon co-operative is one of the oldest around. It represents the top end of the European co-operative scene – one of the largest of around 250,000 organisations. Some 9% of the Spanish economy is 'social'.

Many of them are not only big but durable: of particular note has been Mondragon's ability to weather the financial crisis in Spain, which began during the great recession of 2008, and which saw many others fall by the wayside.

The global financial markets are our next stop; here we see the presence of co-operative principles in at least some of these organisations. Of the 15 largest co-operatives globally, eight are banks or insurance brokers. These include Credit Agricole and the Rabobank Group – companies of an impressive size, regardless of their form.

Heading east, India has seized on the opportunities offered by this form of organisation, especially within the agricultural sector. One of these is the dairy co-operative Amul. Amul was set up in 1946 by dairy farmers around the city of Anand, in Gujarat. Over 70 years, Amul has expanded to cover an estimated 3.6 million milk producers, giving them a turnover of around US$3.4 billion.[7] Not bad for what started off as a small group of dairy farmers disgruntled with the low market prices they were getting for their wares.

Co-operative housing pops up in places of poverty and affluence alike. Affordable housing is a constant need. Housing associations have a secure asset base. And so they pioneered forms of private, public and social impact investment to deliver new homes in a way that foreshadowed many of the investments we encountered earlier, offering rents and even ownership to underprivileged citizens in the 1980s, 1990s and 2000s. Even as affordable housing becomes unaffordable, co-operative housing is mooted as a solution. Community land trusts involve members subscribing to organisations that jointly own land and housing stock independently of associations. Such land trusts are being used in rural India among other places to empower people and provide homes.

To Germany now and a fascinating fusion of co-operative principles and social impact investment, a form of social enterprise finance that we will meet in Chapter Seven. The Vauban building project in Germany is our stop. An 'eco-neighbourhood located in Freiburg, it comprises energy efficient homes with solar panel roofs and countless other ideas. It emerged as locals felt that rising house-prices had left the neighbourhood lacking in diversity.

A group called the Oekegno co-operative decided to challenge this by setting up a housing co-op, 'La Vaubanaise', which has constructed a building in the middle of the neighbourhood that respects the community's ethics but encourages the young and the poor to move in with smartly priced rental and purchase offers.

Partly this project was paid for by social impact investment – a simple loan in this case. Partly it was paid for by the co-op ('solidarity-based') savings schemes of the members, similar to the solidarity funds we encountered at the end of the previous chapter. It issues bonds to sister co-ops across Europe and offered a 3–4% return.

With all of this growth and innovation, with people all over the world brought together by this most venerable and easily understood of iterations of the social enterprise movement, current predictions posit co-operatives as the fastest-growing organisational form globally by 2020.[8]

Even today, the movement is huge, buoyed by the surging interest in social entrepreneurship and the support for their model. UN Secretary-General Ban Ki Moon recently expressed the view that co-operatives are one of the keys to delivering on our globally agreed goals to eliminate poverty and improve lives. He praised co-operatives' 'underlying values of self-help, equality and solidarity offer a compass in challenging economic times'. He concluded, 'By contributing to human dignity and global solidarity co-operatives truly do build a better world'.[9]

The field touches an increasing number of the industries that impact on our everyday lives. Our food buying is largely colonised by major chain supermarkets like Wal-Mart or Tesco, or health food juggernauts like Whole Foods. Meanwhile, a number of co-operative providers offer an alternative.

There are the pioneers like Park Slope Food Co in Brooklyn, NY. Founded in 1973, it has 16,000 members.[10] Each adult member gives two hours and 45 minutes of voluntary service each week, which enables them to reduce the mark-up on their items, relative to those offered by the supermarket giants. As such, they have played major roles in offering cheap produce from local farmers, environmentally conscious items and in boycotting goods, such as those of apartheid-era South Africa.

There are other major players like the UK's Co-Op food store and newer players like the People's Supermarket in London, whose members pay a fee to be connected with food from 'local producers at a reasonable price'.

Another really interesting example of co-operative growth: football (or soccer). Football clubs in the UK are often run as traditional businesses; indeed the UK's Premier League, the world's richest, which benefits from enormous global television deals, has stolen a march on rivals as result.

Yet even in the UK, a yearning for an alternative is compelling owners and fans to think again. The rationale, well understood by European sport administrators, is that football fans do not change teams if their club is badly run, so the shareholders tend to be in a position to hold fans to ransom.

As such, a few pioneering football clubs at the lower levels of English football are adopting a new structure, which was invented but a decade ago: the *community interest company*. This allows social purposes to be inserted into the articles of a profit-making company's association and locks assets, so that unscrupulous owners are not in a position to cut and run.

In Spain, the biggest clubs are entirely fan owned. Barcelona FC and Real Madrid FC are icons, football and financial powerhouses. They are political symbols: Barcelona of the insurgent Catalans; Real Madrid of the unified Spain. They have full-time members, or *Socios*, who own the club. They elect the president, who often comes promising marquee transfers; the corporate and the political are intertwined, not always for the better.

There is, it must be said, only one other club in Spain's top division structured like Barcelona and Madrid; the rest are more conventionally structured as trading companies. German clubs operate under somewhat different conditions, mostly half fan-wned with only half of the club operating as a trading company.

This has not reduced the on-pitch success of these clubs; Bayern Munich, or 'FC Hollywood' as some call the club, is a colossus. Yet English teams, and Scotland's teams, whose league shares common cultural roots with those of the English, have rarely considered that such structures might be appropriate to run professional football clubs – until recently.

Ultimately, football is more than a trading business. Some owners do make a great deal of money from the business of football, but they are few and far between.

There are objective measures of a successful club: to win matches or trophies, to buy players, to stay alive rather than pay out dividends and get relegated from their divisions. Clubs' supporters are not customers who buy a ticket in order to receive a service (indeed the reverse was argued by the under-fire CEO of English club Charlton FC in 2015 to considerable opprobrium).

There is a real feeling of ownership among the fans of a club and this ownership is central to the club's fortunes, to the match day atmosphere, to revenues and to moral support, often across generations. There is little choice or competition; most supporters would not defect or go to another club in the event of poor service from the owner or the board. A co-operative structure and the principles that undergird it reflects the reality of the supporter experience; the bond between the club-as-company and its supporters. It can give them comfort that their goals and the goals of the club are aligned. Football supporters of all stripes, take note: corporations structured the co-operative way, with supporters at their centre, could and should be your club's future.

The co-operative evolves: B Corps and more

This is a golden era for co-operatives, a time of growth and rapid expansion. The rise of the co-operative in our time is a direct rejoinder to the culture of business – actual and perceived – that we have. The financial crash of 2007/08 has been but one stimulus. Research firm Ipsos Mori's recent survey data based on 18,000 interviews in 23 countries suggests considerable mistrust of conventional business. Less than a third of Britons (31 per cent) trust business. Only people in South Korea (28 per cent) and France (27 per cent) were more suspicious at the time of asking.[11]

In that same poll, less than a quarter of Britons (24 per cent) felt they could trust business leaders to tell the truth. Less than a third (32 per cent) felt they could trust businesses to improve the economic and social conditions of their communities and around the same number said they didn't trust business to produce domestic economic growth. In other polls, similar results have been recorded, with Gallup's annual indicator suggesting that only a fifth (21%) of Americans trusted 'big business' 'quite a lot' or 'a lot'. Compare that to nearly a third who trusted the Presidency.[12]

Stories of tax avoidance, sharp practices, trampling on workers' rights and environmental degradation continue to be shared and continue to plague the sector. Little wonder that the search for community-focused, co-operative alternatives gathers pace.

And the movement is not resting on its laurels. In April 2010 a new law in the state of Maryland was introduced that inaugurated the 'benefit corporation', usually referred to as a B Corp. This was a new addition to the moral marketplace; a form of 'socially responsible business' that sits alongside and at times overlaps with the social enterprise movement.

To qualify as a B Corp, a firm must have an explicit social or environmental mission, which is assessed on a points basis by a rigorous set of metrics. Having passed the test, it takes on a legally binding fiduciary responsibility to take into account the interests of workers, the community and the environment as well as its shareholders. It must publish independently verified reports on its social and environmental impact alongside its financial results. Other than that, it can go about business as usual, making profits and delivering on its social purposes.

The form proved popular. California became the sixth state to allow B Corps in January 2012. Twelve Californian firms registered in the first month. Across the USA, there is a thriving community of B Corps.

Spurred by demand, smart legislators everywhere are inaugurating similarly innovative company forms that allow philanthropic and private money to be mixed. There is also the 'flexible purpose corporation' (FlexC), which allows a firm to adopt a specific social or environmental goal, rather than the broader obligations of a B Corp. Or the low-profit limited-liability (L3C) company, which can raise money for socially beneficial purposes while making little or no profit, thus allowing it to veer between not-for-profit and for-profit status depending on its funding mix.

The UK has its own version of a L3C-style company form for socially responsible business: the Community Interest Company (CIC). This form is about a decade old, and has its own regulatory framework and the added imperative that the company is asset-locked: money cannot be taken out by shareholders. It has been adopted by a number of forward-thinking organisations that privilege its revenue-raising, entrepreneurial flexibility over the tax breaks afforded to new charities.

A subset of global research and advocacy bodies have emerged in the last few years to support and interrogate the B Corp concept, the efficacy of B Corps and their cousins. GIIRS (the Global Impact Investment Reporting System) considers social purposes and performance of social investments and counts these new forms among its objects of analysis. They are all part of a drive towards understanding the true social impact of these developments.[13]

This space develops quickly. One of the best known social enterprises, Divine Chocolate, relies in part on a hybrid-ownership model of this kind. This multinational business whose wares can be found in their pretty wrapping on confectionary shelves in supermarkets in the USA, in Europe, in Canada, Australia, South Korea and Japan is actually 45% owned by the Kuapa Kokoo farmers' co-operative of Ghana, with price protections, voting rights and a democratic voice in the working of the industry available to their representatives. It is an attractive package in every sense of the word.

The shared value idea

Amidst all of these new social enterprise forms, while the co-operative movement marches on, conventional business continues to seek a way back into the public's affections. The term 'corporate social responsibility' (CSR) emerged in the latter part of the 20th century to describe socially purposeful endeavours involving corporations, many of them multinationals, above and beyond their ordinary business. So well supported is this activity that we saw it on our typology in Chapter One, as one of the many heads of the intersection between society and business – and one of the many facets of the moral marketplace.

Not everyone believes it deserves to be there. In the book *Good Business*, Steve Hilton, former adviser to the UK's Prime Minister, and his co-author Giles Gibbon, CSR consultants themselves, noted in 2002 that

> most people ... would be amazed if they lifted the stone
> of contemporary business activity and saw the armies
> of consultants, experts, charlatans and do-gooders
> scurrying around inside and outside companies trying
> to help them become more socially responsible.[14]

The industry continually gives itself a poor reputation. Breathless calls for businesses to 'save the world' using their CSR budgets are hollow, for these budgets are tiny compared to the size and impact of the whole.

It is often delivered like this. Companies graft actions onto their core work in order to demonstrate their regard for the society or environment in which they operate. They have an event, do a press release, give some money to a charitable cause. And that, more or less, is it.

When so executed, it is a curious idea, lacking in substance. In the most typical incarnation it appears to be something of a confidence trick constructed by the public relations people for a quick headline and a spike in sales.

What's more, this work does not always sit well with those who preach the gospel of the free market. Milton Friedman, the academic hero of the libertarian right, argued that such flirtations are a 'fraud on the shareholder',[15] diverting resources from the purpose of the business.

He is in one sense absolutely right; after all, if the only reason a company is working in these spaces is to achieve some notional idea of the good, disconnected from its main purposes, spurious and set adrift, an obvious PR stunt and nothing more, then it will not deliver shareholder value. The public will see through it. Customers will be turned off by it. Social entrepreneurs will not stand for it. And neither should we.

Academics are doing their bit to cajole the corporates along and give community activists the framework with which somehow find a common social purpose with the business elite.

Professor Michael Porter at Harvard, writing alongside Professor Mark Kramer, whose work we encountered in Chapter Five, argues that the truly socially responsible company, whatever form it takes, subscribes to the notion of *shared value*: a socially responsible concordat between investor, corporation and community.[16]

The good corporate citizen begins by using the tools of CSR, the special projects, events, articles and internal awareness sessions that demonstrate that they care about the community in which they are based. This activity can be interesting but, per the shared value thesis, is not sufficient. There is a more radical road to travel:

to form a sort of shared set of goals and ideas with important organisations within their communities of operation.

They are no longer separate from those communities, attempting to demonstrate their worth, but an active and engaged part of the fabric of society. They form common objectives.

Co-operatives are set up to do this as a matter of course. B Corps and CICs are well placed to do so also. But the shared value thesis extends to traditional companies as well. Porter and Kramer argue that such activity falls well within the remit of their duties to their shareholders.

An example of how this works in practice is found in the case of MA's Tropical Food, Sri Lanka. The traditional supply chain of spices in Sri Lanka consists mainly of small-scale producers. Over 200,000 small-scale growers are involved in spice cultivation where 70% of production comes from smallholder farm units of less than 1 hectare of land. Many of them are part-time farmers with other sources of income.

As a response to this, MA's Tropical Food Company assisted smallholders in different ways, by helping them organise themselves in farmers' organisations; training extension officers to support farmers; setting standards and paying premium prices to farmers who achieve them; improving logistics and inspection.

This model mutually benefited the parties involved in the supply chain. For the company, it improved corporate income, volume of trade and turnover. For smallholders, it improved farm income, created more jobs and enabled other social benefits such as better information sharing.

It is not perfect. Transport costs were somewhat high. Labour was expensive and their money from their wilier suppliers did not always come through on time. The company is only so big and can take on only so many farmers.

Yet when MA's set its own standards and sent extension officers to assist smallholders, the quality of products increased. Quality engagement minimised risk. Those in the supply chain also began to better organise themselves spontaneously, sharing labour, introducing democratic systems among themselves, keeping records and improving their bargaining power.

This is an example of a business acting as a sort of pyramid for support: showing the regard usually reserved for social entrepreneurs by engaging with communities, listening to them and offering solutions

Some companies do this better than most. Take Yara, a major global player in the chemical industry. It attracts investors who care about improving the quality of global agriculture, about feeding the hungry and fighting famine.

Yara tries to improve local food output, reduce emissions from fertilisers and make local areas more self-sufficient alongside meeting its corporate objectives. It is, interestingly, controlled by the oil-rich Norwegian state, which informs its ethics and in turn the necessity of its adoption of a shared value approach.

Porter and Kramer are bullish. They invite all businesses to think about what they are doing and what they could do more for the many stakeholders affected by their operations, in part as a service to society, in part as a service to the broader capitalist idea that provides the basis for their sustenance.

Self-serving it may be, but 'shared value' is not just part of the strategy, it is the strategy. Shared value gives us a framework to hold companies to account, to get them to do more for their wider community, and to require such companies to explain their processes for meeting their obligations or lose our custom.

I should 'CoCo': from conscious consumption to ethical exploration

Ultimately, our biggest weapon in the drive to reform capitalism is – you've guessed it – our wallets. And this leads us to what is potentially the great corporate reform movement of our time, initiated and evolved by social entrepreneurs: conscious (or ethical) consumption.

More of us do it than ever before. In the US, it increased more quickly from 2013 to 2014 than charitable giving.[17] Per Nielsen, two thirds of us buy things because they are not only good for us but are good for the planet. And most of those, believe it or not, are people who come from outside Europe and the US.

Conscious consumption (CoCo, for short) is a considerable lever in the hands of a willing community of activated citizens. Agitating for more of us to say 'I should CoCo' – and participating in this activity can make the difference between corporations testing their products on animals or not; corporations using unsustainable food sourcing practices or not; and so on.

The barrier here is not willingness but information: giving you the facts in an accessible form so that you can make good choices for yourself and your family. Social entrepreneurs are on this case too. They create tools, websites such as ethicalconsumer.com, that list ethical considerations that attend common products in detail.

Social entrepreneurs lead campaigns to support such endeavours and raise awareness. Social Enterprise UK, a national support body for social enterprises, inaugurated the 'Buy Social' campaign that encourages companies to shift their behaviour and provides a directory of social enterprise suppliers. It also encourages consumers to 'buy social'.

More and better consumer tools will help, not only to give us the low-down on how we buy better but also to remind us about the volume of what we buy. After all, many activists will argue that the best thing that we can do is purchase less, not more, and that is fair enough.

Here is an excuse to talk about a whole range of interesting social enterprises, like Tom Szaky's Terracycle. Terracycle's first business line is organic fertiliser sold in Target and Wal-Mart that is made from 'worm poop'. Terracycle also collects trash and turns it into colourful products, for example, messenger bags made out of used Capri Sun drink packages and 'urban art trash cans', which have been described as 'trippy'. The company donates two cents to charity for each waste item it recycles, raising millions so far.

Another really interesting example: the Plastic Bank, headquartered in Vancouver, Canada, which incentivises recycling of plastic destined for the ocean, repurposes that plastic as items and even turns some of it into a form of currency, and whose projects in Haiti and elsewhere have made waves.

To bring all of this along, we will need an array of retail offers, apps and guides and augmented reality maps and the like for the world's individuals to help make these choices and bring these alternatives to life. A number of these are beginning their process of occupying the mainstream consciousness, including the ethical exploration social enterprise movement I co-founded to source socially positive experiences and events.

There will be limits to the consuming public's willingness to ditch the buzz of buying or replace it with an ethical alternative. Some people will buy the latest gadget ten times over in every colour and want their own no matter who has to suffer in its production.

But there are alternatives now. The choice for the ethical consumer, corporate or individual is widening every day. You may be the sort of person who just *has* to have the latest Xphone, but the ascent of social enterprises, like Fairphone, that eschew unethical production processes makes this sort of decision much more difficult – and might just cause you to think again.[18]

All business is social

This chapter began with a foray into the world of co-operative couture; 'slow fashion' (as opposed to the buy-it-one-season, junk-it-the-next attitude of so-called 'fast' fashion) and design. Here, at the intersection of business, beauty and community activism, a new generation of mission-driven millennials create wonderful things. Stephen Burks' work and that of his peers shows how amenable industry can be to helping create these social enterprise enclaves, especially when there is reputation to be garnered.

Some industries need this association more than others. Fashion, particularly, has a keen interest in this area of activity. The business has been wracked by accusations of sexism, child labour, animal cruelty. Contrast this with inspiring stories of social enterprises, like that of soleRebels, a 'slow fashion' shoewear brand set up in Ethiopia by social entrepreneur Bethlehem Tilahun Alemu,[19] who uses eco-friendly materials and local community workers to produce fashion lines that have made the organisation Africa's fastest growing footwear brand and that have seen her dubbed by *Forbes* magazine as 'Africa's most successful woman'.[20] Little wonder then that co-operative couture is ablaze, not just in one area but everywhere.

Similarly the shared value thesis enables companies to overcome Milton Friedman's objection that social actions by shareholder companies are a 'fraud'. In this eventuality, social purposes become a part of what the shareholder buys. Ensuring that social benefits are realised through the work of the company not only becomes a 'product marketing' exercise, but a 'market-shaping' exercise that means your future product lines have a chance in a field of competitors all of whom have a social story to tell.

It protects future product lines from rejection by socially savvy consumers or regulators. Consider taxes on sugar that may be the result of food or drinks companies not paying sufficient heed to matters around healthy living and the role their products play therein. Companies avoid such constraints by becoming better citizens before they are hit. Social value is an example of social entrepreneurship *par excellence*, because it changes behaviour for the better, now and forever.

There are many who will continue to recoil at this, but I suspect we are only at the beginning of this journey. Stephen Burks is positive about the power of corporations, not only to show interest, but to learn from communities of artisans. 'I'll weave a basket with a business person,' he said during that talk at Bloomberg in 2016, 'as long as they are willing to travel down that dirt road with me.'

Many business have begun the journey of travelling that dirt road. In a number of key industries, people expect more social regard from their businesses than ever before. In others, such as hedge fund management, we have barely begun. Perhaps this too will change. Perhaps social entrepreneurs will drag these business people too, yank those who are apathetic into the world of you and me. The boundaries between businesses with a strong sense of shared value, socially responsible businesses that use specialised structures and social enterprises could become increasingly porous. And the project to reform the perpetually crisis-stricken institution that is capitalism might yet be completed to satisfaction by the anger and ingenuity of this generation of social entrepreneur.

How do you know you are making a difference?

The metrics and measurements that keep the social entrepreneur on-mission

Distortions. Interference. Real data is messy. (Tom Stoppard, *Arcadia*)

The science of charity

At the end of the 19th century a new idea began to capture the imagination in the poorer parts of New York City. Institutions were set up to help the poor and disadvantaged, inspired by the work of English vicar Samuel Barnett and his wife Henrietta, whose East London project Toynbee Hall encouraged the nation's future leaders to volunteer with the needy and destitute.

The New York versions were called Charity Organization Societies (COSes). They were staffed by a number of well-wishers, redoubtable types many of them, perhaps the best known of whom were Josephine Lowell and S. Humphrey Gurteen.

Lowell believed that 'idleness' was a major cause of poverty. She advocated giving those who requested relief a 'labor test', such as breaking stones or chopping wood, before they received assistance. During her life, she developed several principles to guide her work.

'Charity must tend to develop the moral nature of those it helps' was one such rule of thumb.[1]

Gurteen had a kindred vision and developed Charity Organization Societies to bring together various groups already providing to the poor to work to that end. There was a central office where 'friendly visitors' or 'agents' would meet to compare notes to determine who was worthy of relief. This would result in a sort of 'doomsday book' of those receiving assistance.

Gurteen honestly believed that COSes would end outdoor relief, stop pauperism and reduce poverty for good. Flash forward several decades and views on this vision veer between it being eccentric, morally repugnant and vaguely ridiculous. Its protagonists conjure up comical visions of the Victorian schoolteacher with scale and callipers, checking the circumference of a potential applicants' thigh in order to see if they are sufficiently emaciated to warrant the poorhouse's money.

The deserving and undeserving poor idea has gone the same way, relegated to the ranks of eccentricity in social science circles; to the ranks of cant most often used to justify policy decisions based on prejudice.

Nevertheless, the ideas of Lowell and Gurteen came to be known as the *scientific charity* movement. Its advocates articulated their goals with admirable clarity. They would improve society by subjecting the poor to discipline and religious education. They would to cut the cost of providing services to the poor. They would to use what funds were available for such services wisely and thriftily.

For all the comical imagery, it is not difficult to see that scientific charity had, at its heart, a comprehensible intention. Funds for social good were scarce and there was a duty incumbent on all to do what they could do get by. It was intended as good practice, the kind of good practice that those involved thought would make the relief of poverty that much more rigorous.

Indeed, we may go so far as to say that the exponents of scientific charity planted a seed that would nag at the heart of those who are interested in helping others for more than a century.

There is a certain attraction to the idea that there really ought to be a scientific – or at least a quasi-scientific – way of holding to account the billions or indeed trillions of dollars of donations and investments in the offices of good that we make each year. Social interventions are not experiments; people are not test subjects – generally.

But if we can find acceptable ways of measuring the things that matter and holding organisation and institutions more effectively to account, the idea is that we could do better with what we have; make our money work that much harder for the many people it needs to help.

Such approaches exist but, as with most things in the social space, they come with health warnings, assumptions of practice and philosophy, and huge caveats. They beg the simple the question: how can you honestly measure something as apparently intangible as 'doing good'?

Other questions flow naturally therefrom. Do such measurements offer us a chance to talk in simple, comprehensible terms about the good that social entrepreneurs and their supporters actually do? Does their use offer our best hope of delivering what we might think of as a maximal happiness with the money at our disposal? Or is this all a whole load of old trout, a distraction from the real business of getting things done? This chapter is about a group of people who believe that when someone tells you their movement is changing the world, you shouldn't have to take their claims on faith – and who promise to deliver some rigour to the claims to social responsibility and transformation made by corporations, co-operatives and other denizens of the moral marketplace.

Social impact

Recall for a moment Vinod Kapur and his chicken farm in Gurgaon. When I asked him to talk about what measures he used in the course of conducting his business to work out whether it was actually making a difference, he looked somewhat puzzled.

"Look, the chicken is the thing," he said. "We research and develop the chicken. If women villagers buy its eggs and raise it, we are making our difference. If not we go back to the drawing board. That is what we measure."

And so it is. With Keggfarms, there are reams of research, independent studies and peer reviewed data and more are being produced all of the time. There is the work they do on the ground with the people for whom they care. They capture it on video. It is recorded in their books and ledgers. They live the experiment with the Kuroiler and they see the good they do face to face. From there the economics of the enterprise is delicately constructed, iterated over years, so that economic and social outcomes, like lovers after a morning tryst, are completely intertwined.

At one end you have interventions like microfinance, which comprises inclusive community bank lending, often to women. There is a high degree of unity between the social and economic purpose here as the lending and recouping of money is itself a proxy for the wellbeing and financial sustainability of the person or business being assisted.

Other social enterprise types, such as the political activist or the public service enterprise, tend not to have such a high degree of unity. For such social enterprises a different approach to measuring their impact is required.

Some try to measure the difference they make by way of cost to the state of their not intervening. They measure forsaken economic activity; costs to the local health service and so on in the hypothetical situation in which the social enterprise does not do its good work. This is at times useful to make a certain kind of public policy argument but it tells us little about what is truly good and which interventions we should value.

It is central to the development of social enterprises, the success of social entrepreneurs and the competition that tests them, that encourages them to adapt and innovate and that makes them strong and supportive, that proper assessment of their work be made that takes into account both the economic and social worth of what they do. This is where social impact measurement comes in.

The measurer of social impact – let's call her an 'impact hawk' – is a true iconoclast. She is a social entrepreneur who has spotted a great deal of value that can be added by getting these organisations to think differently. She asks tough questions of socially minded organisations, from soup kitchens to cancer research outfits. She asks: how many people did you help? How effective are the cures? How well do you work with others to provide something genuinely different? To what extent are you doing that which you claim to do and that which you set out to do? And so on.

These questions form the bedrock of various social impact methodologies. In this chapter, we'll consider a few. A widespread method is to use a so-called *theory of change*. Here the organisation looking to measure its impact articulates a series of social outcomes, against a statement of how the intervention has been designed to work in the first place.

The data that is generated thereby is most often in the form of a flow chart with headings such as 'vision', 'outcomes', 'outputs', 'measures', which can also be subdivided by sub-goal or which might give more detail on who will deliver and how they will be assessed individually on a project basis.

It sounds cumbersome and it can be. From experience it does seem to yield a lot of pieces of paper with boxes and words of seemingly dubious value. Is it the most efficient of effective way of conceptualising impact in a professional, proactive way? I have my doubts.

But this sort of thing certainly does create a framework in which more ambitious, scientifically rigorous impact measurements might be discerned and tested. Randomised controlled trials (RCTs) are one example of where an organisation might go next in their sear. RCTs are a form of medical or scientific trial, adapted to use by those attempting to identify the effectiveness of social interventions. In order to establish the difference made by a given intervention, the RCT process involves observing a second similar situation which in which no intervention is occurring. It is then possible to ascertain the difference in outcomes between the two situations.

One of the best known examples of an RCT being used within international development is the study by Dr Kevin Croke, of Harvard, into the impact of deworming on long-term health outcomes. Dr Croke carried out a large scale randomised control test in Uganda, looking at the impact deworming had on various health and education outcomes. His findings indicated that children in areas where interventions were occurring scored around a third of a standard deviation higher on numeracy and literacy tests than their equivalents in other areas.[2]

I saw an excellent example first-hand while I was a director at Impetus Trust (now rebranded Impetus-PEF), which funds and supports social entrepreneurs. We worked with a grassroots organisation called Teens and Toddlers, to encourage an RCT for a project aimed at reducing teen pregnancy. The trial would eventually set up a so-called 'matched-pair individual-allocation' RCT, and used this to evaluate the programme's success.

The findings were that, while the intervention was not sufficiently successful at its primary objectives, it had a great degree of success at obtaining its secondary objectives, which focused on turning around low self-esteem, poor knowledge of sexual health and difficulty discussing contraception with medical professionals. From this, the organisation was able to adapt its procedures: to learn and measure again.[3]

Impact hawks and sceptics

A movement of social entrepreneurs campaign for the adoption of these tools on an ever wider basis. US organisation Charity Star is a non-profit that aims to establish greater transparency within the work of international development charities. It is an advocacy group that encourage social impact measurement and reporting in order to develop greater trust, which in turn maximises the good work that can be done by these charities.

Part of this process involves encouraging charities to provide, and make open to the public, detailed evaluations of the effectiveness of their operations using measures like those above. In turn, potential donors or investors are able to make a strong business case for investing in their activities, and between investing in the charity sector and other pursuits.

Charity Star appears to have no business agenda; it is not setting up these organisations to make investments itself; it does not buy and sell the organisations that it reports on or have financial interests in their reform.[4]

It just believes in the idea. It believes that ordinary charities and social enterprises can benefit from this activity, as will the people such organisations serve. Charity Star makes no attempt to measure effectiveness itself. It is an impact advocacy group, set up to spread and share the idea of a more internationally rigorous philanthropic movement.

The UK is home to several such impact advocacy groups who love this idea with the zeal of a Gurteen. They develop a variety of approaches to the challenge of measuring for or reporting on social impact. A key player emerged in 2002: New Philanthropy Capital (NPC).

New Philanthropy Capital: the name has the air of an under-the-radar venture fund. I went to its offices in Southwark, London to find out what it was about and I was greeted by the CEO, Dan Corry, who was disarmingly frank about the possibilities, but also the challenges, of the impact hawks' ideas when applied to modern social entrepreneurship.

"NPC's own history is instructive. It began in a very different place to where it finds itself today," said Corry. He continued:

> "It was aimed at rich donors, city types ... trying to get them to improve their giving and take as much care with it as they would take care of, say, an investment of theirs. And basically after a while they discovered

a number of the premises on which it started were incorrect.

The founders had this idea that you can get people to give better. So you could take a city person and say, okay, let's think about the money you have to give. Put some of it in high risk stuff that may or may not help people' – like a new drug that may or may not cure a far off tropical disease, but if it comes off it will help millions – 'and put some of it in low risk stuff that you know will help people, a traditional charity that has been around for ages, say. And you can identify sectors that are high risk and low risk, based on the kind of people that the philanthropist wants to help and give them a sort of basket of investment propositions. And in this way you can ensure that their giving is going somewhere."

He leans back in his chair. "It wasn't very convincing."

Corry has an avuncular manner, a mop of grey-black hair, a nonsense-free open necked shirt. He was a government adviser, first as an economist at the Treasury and across government and then heading the UK Prime Minister's policy unit under Gordon Brown. Many of his contemporaries who also worked at the nerve-centre of government went on to take on foundational positions in the UK's social entrepreneur scene. Geoff Mulgan went on to found the Demos think tank and head up the Young Foundation and the National Endowment for Science, Technology and the Arts (NESTA). Matthew Taylor went on to lead the Royal Society of Arts. Both play key roles in the social entrepreneur movement in the UK. NPC was Corry's move into the space.

"I was interested in public services, in the intersection of society and the state," he recalls. "And that's how I ended up here, out of the state, and in society, but not just trying to connect things and people together, but to improve them."

He joined NPC in 2011. The social impact space was developing at this time and NPC was at a crossroads. Even as recently as then they were "still reaching around for an identity".

NPC has now been repositioned not only as a social enterprise that works with other social enterprises, charities and funders, but as a think tank and advocacy group. It has its fingers in a number of pies: transparency, evidence in public services, non-profit improvement, digital transformation and more besides.

Social impact measurement is the golden thread. Corry is convinced that unless a social entrepreneur knows what she is trying to change, how she is to go about doing it, and then how she is to create results which show that she is achieving what she aims to achieve, it is easy to miss the reality that she may not be doing that much at all.

> "We've worked with charities in prisons, music charities, arts charities. They think they are making a difference. But when they try to evaluate what they do, they have realised that actually they are not doing what they thought they did at all. Prisoners aren't learning. They aren't picking up skills. They aren't becoming better rounded citizens, no matter how many instruments you fling at them. And that should give these organisations food for thought. Often it does. Not always."

NPC's favoured tool is the theory of change. Corry stressed that this document differs in size according to the size and complexity of the organisation but it generally takes into account factors such as the target group it is trying to help, the kinds of intervention it might make to help that target group and the other players in the space – and is then used to create frameworks against which the charitable organisation's performance is measured.

Over time, with the organisation becoming more disciplined, focused and attuned to its primary purposes, a picture of improvement should emerge when that organisation is doing well – or the reverse if not.

Collecting data, improving the quality of programmes within an organisation, bringing better people together, not to fulfil the ego of the charity's owner or leader or a particular donor, but because this objective, written-down, evaluated approach should help the organisation to help more people that much more effectively and show it to be doing so.

Often, an organisation undertaking this journey will release details, say in its annual report or on its website, to show how well it is doing. And these details could in the future be used to improve the social impact of the organisation, attract further donations, contract funding from government to deliver particular services or investment to scale their operations. Or it could just let people know what is going on under the hood.

Despite the apparent logicality of this position, it has been relatively difficult to sell. Governments are interested, charitable foundations too. Forward-thinking social entrepreneur movements are fascinated by this stuff. But what about donors and charities, the two constituencies NPC was originally set up to help?

Not so much. So why does it remain the case that charitable organisations are not lining up to submit themselves to these rigours? To put it slightly mischievously: what does this lack of uptake in the charity sector and understanding in the world beyond say about the success or otherwise – the impact, if you will – of the impact hawks' approach?

Dan Corry sighed when I asked him this.

> "Look, if you ask me if the bulk of charitable organisations are doing this, I'd say no. But we certainly have more than we did. And that's good for them, it's good for us too. Sure, most people who are thinking about giving won't read a charity's annual report or go on their website before giving to them. Generally you just choose the cause and run the marathon with

a logo on your back. But maybe that's something that could change. In any case, transparency is the key thing. The more information they offer, even if it isn't in the absolute perfect form, the better for everyone, especially for those we are trying to help."

One of NPC's longest serving clients is not an organisation but a philanthropist, one John Stone, whose family foundation distributes its funds the NPC way. Since 2004, when he sold his business, he became concerned with "getting the biggest bang for his buck" as Corry puts it, and especially that his philanthropy led to outcomes and organisations that were sustained over time. In other words, the good that would continue to be done once his initial donation had been spent.

Over his time working with NPC he has not only found organisations that he otherwise would not have thought to give his money to – the lesser known lights of the international aid world – but he also has found a sector that he might otherwise have ignored. "We have worked with (John) to bring a greater focus than he might have had without us. Investing in water and sanitation might not have sprung to mind if we hadn't worked through a strategy with him," said Corry.

Corry has an opinion on another reason behind the relative lack of interest uptake in impact measurement across the traditional charity sector (though in charitable foundations, as we shall see, it is higher). "It requires a reallocation of resources," he says, reverting momentarily back to civil servant speak. "And that's not necessarily something that people are comfortable with when applied to traditional charities."

Corry here is articulating something quite simple but profound: if you want good things done well, you have to pay for them.

For some people, that notion presents such a problem that they wish they hadn't raised the question in the first place. We'll leave this there for now but we will get into this argument in more detail in the next chapter.

The challenges of measuring impact

On the one hand it seems axiomatic that any sort of entrepreneurial organisation needs to have some measure of how it is developing and evolving. In conventional businesses, the measure, primarily, is profit. More money coming in is a sign that the entrepreneur is successful. Social entrepreneurs do not have it so easy. They may measure profits, but their measures are necessarily social first, money later. They ask how their beneficiairies are helped and how their care evolves over time, as well as how strong their balance sheet looks on the page. Social impact is, therefore, the defining idea of social entrepreneurship, and is the guiding concept that sets it apart from conventional business 'as usual'.

Nevertheless, the idea that a charity or social enterprise should seek to measure its approach against a single measure or set of measures still irks many. Such organisations exist not only to deliver a particular service well, but to provide a pivot for community action; to be on the ground and form that layer of hope between the individual and the state. Targets and measurements are about as far from the language of community and change and control as one can be. There is no doubt that this is a problem.

There are more challenges besides: let us consider some of them.

The fad argument

Consider the fate of a relatively well-known impact measurement called social return on investment (SROI). First developed and applied by REDF (formerly the Roberts Enterprise Development Fund), SROI was a strategy that entailed identifying measurable outcomes such as the number of hours that children attended school as a result of a particular social intervention.

The output was seductively clear: invest US$1 in the intervention, the algorithms and suppositions monetise the impact and show that you save, for example, US$10 by preventing the need for those children to go to remedial class in later life. You put a dollar in, you get so much money out – from welfare costs saved, or services not having to be used, or general good vibes making people more 'productive' (to take three examples).

It might be compelling superficially but is it compelling up close? Apply it to, say, an organisation that seeks to get vulnerable people into work and we encounter difficulties of measuring social values similar to those above.

We can monetise the amount saved in out of work benefit. But can we monetise the improved family situation from a job-creating business that sometimes follows; indeed do we allow that as a 'social' effect? As NPC themselves said in a well-received intervention in 2009, 'omitting these benefits from an SROI calculation can actually result in negative social returns for work which is socially valuable'.[5]

A social entrepreneur said in 2010 that SROI was 'Shoehorning [social value] through another frame that was created to do something else (which) I don't think is right. The frame of SROI was created for efficiency, and the people in charge of it are given authority based on effectiveness in that area, not on moral leadership.'[6] SROI, it seems, has few remaining well-wishers. Other forms will surely follow. Will there come a point at which the wider social impact movement comes to be seen as something of a fad also?

The take-up argument

There remains the fact that reporting for social impact remains relatively exotic. "That is absolutely the case," Corry said when I put this to him. "And you know what, when we first started up and we worked with donors, even city people didn't want to think about their giving in the way they thought about their investments. They wanted a holiday from all that."

> "The thing is [NPC's] original founders weren't wrong
> to want something better. They weren't wrong to

want to try to make people's giving work harder. Why shouldn't we insist that charitable money helps as many people as possible? There's little enough of it as it is about. That's what we're into now, that's what we do."

But is Corry a social entrepreneur version of Canute fighting the tide? Is it the case that applying measures to gifts does not go with the grain of human emotion and action? The lack of uptake among the charitable sector – let alone the giving public – to date might be cited in evidence. After all, who requires that the impact of their donation is measured before signing a sponsorship form or ticking a gift aid box?

Just because things have been done a certain way to date does not mean it is the best way or the only way. In the UK, in a recent poll, 94% of the public believed that charities need to demonstrate *how* they benefit the public.[7] Now, there is no indication that this means people engaging in measurement-based giving or charities and social enterprises using these measurements at industrial scale. *Do as I say not as I do* may well be the tacit message from the public. But it is unlikely that a result as comprehensive as this would emerge from a public completely averse to the idea of measuring for social impact.

Measuring the penetration of social impact-driven philanthropy is a difficult task. Take GiveWell, an evidence-based recommendation service. In 2014, they claim to have compelled US$27,754,698 of donations to be given to charities they recommended. This was up from US$17,410,475 in 2013, and US$8,601,535 in 2012.[8] While this is significant, and heartening, the total given by individuals in the USA in 2014 was US$258.51 billion, up from US$228.93 billion in 2013.[9] As such – and this is no criticism of what is a very promising organisation – while the contribution of GiveWell is valuable, it represents only a tiny fraction of the overall charitable picture.

Major institutional donors, in particular charitable foundations, have been pioneers in this area. Many use evidence-based strategies to ensure that their larger contributions are as effective as possible. The Bill and Melinda Gates Foundation is one such. Its approach to doing good is eclectic but its focus on social impact is resolute. It operates by way of a model in which grantees are expected to measure certain outcomes and report back on them, thus ensuring that the Foundation can continue to make effective interventions.

In 2014, the Gates Foundation made contributions of over US$4.4 billion – a figure that dwarfs that given by individuals through organisations such as GiveWell.[10] Many of the interventions supported could demonstrate their social impact.

The Gates Foundation is significant, and yet even so its disbursements still only represent a small fraction of overall charitable giving, a 'tiny, tiny amount' as Bill Gates put it when addressing the Group of 20 leaders of the world's economies in 2011.[11] In the USA, where foundations are considerable and significant, they only accounted for 15% of total giving in 2012.[12] And it remains the case that for the majority of charity donors such considerations do not figure. Despite the diligence that 94% of the public adumbrate, most people give based on the work they know that an organisation does, their sense of a charitable brand and the public's trust in it, and their belief that their donation will support their objects. They go with their gut, in short. That is quite understandable, but it has little to do with these systems of impact measurement.

To be clear, this does not mean that these things are given with no evidence. Often the numbers and calculations of impact nerds are replaced, consciously or subconsciously, with the 'softer', universally understood and comprehended ideas of story, of instinct, of personal experience. That can be enough. If efficiency is the key, that kind of evidence may be enough for a small-scale donation; more work than this might cost more in time spent than the value of the donation itself.

But, when a donation reaches critical size – when we have large gifts with great potential to make a difference – the importance of engaging with the social impact idea, of giving people comprehensible oversight and entry points into the programme being created so as to increase the possibility of learning from and leveraging their experience, increases in direct proportion to the size of the gift. The greater the stakes, the more numbers we should want to see. You don't have to be a hawk to subscribe to want funding for social causes to do the most good it can.

The super-impact-nerdery argument

Scientific charity was a child of religion as much as money management; a philosophy as well as a practice. Little surprise then that social impact, developing as it has, with the support and successes it has already underpinned, is beginning to develop its own philosophical adherents too. They go by the name of *effective altruists*.

Effective altruism takes the idea of social impact, and turns it, ostensibly, into a lifestyle. Effective altruists seek to take the idea of measuring, applying and analysing the good and in turn they apply these analyses to the interventions on the world made by their life paths. So the question of to whom one gives is joined by choice of career, disposal of earnings – whatever else can be added to the mix – as items susceptible to honest measurement.

Notable figures in the history of the movement include Peter Singer, author of *The Life You Can Save* and *The Most Good You Can Do* (and inspiration behind the previous segue)[13] and Toby Ord, creator of Giving What We Can.[14] A Centre for Effective Altruism sits at the University of Oxford, led by Will MacAskill, author of *Doing Good Better.*[15]

This movement is worth our time as it presents opportunities and challenges. Effective altruists valorise tools like RCTs, contend that the main thing is to support these evidentiary pursuits in such a way as to help make them better over time. Two measures are also much used: Quality Adjusted Life Years and Disability Adjusted Life Years. They quantify otherwise soft outcomes around how social interventions help vulnerable people by relating that social intervention to the amount by which it improves the chances of survival and indeed of flourishing of those subjected to it. And they do all this with impressive application and zeal.

The idea is smart enough and marketable enough to make it worth our time and our criticism. I like these super-impact-nerds; something about their nerding for good resonates. And it does with others too. Today effective altruism is proving itself to be a very useful fundraising tool. It has had tens if not hundreds of millions 'pledged' by virtue of its doctrines for good causes from the salaries of its adherents and all manner of our time's superstars including everyone's favourite Silicon Valley savant Elon Musk professing an interest in its ideas.

So to the problems. Effective altruism, it will not surprise you to know, commits the sins of other social impact measurement movements in triplicate. It has found itself endorsing some fairly remarkable positions in its relatively short lifespan.

The starting point for effective altruism is that any two (human) lives are of identical value. Thus, the philanthropist should not distinguish between saving a life in her neighbour's house in Connecticut and saving a life in rural Bangladesh. This was articulated in 1972, in Peter Singer's work 'Famine, Affluence and Morality'.[16]

Given the relatively low cost of saving a life in many developing areas – which may involve malaria nets, basic inoculation or clean water installation – compared to the cost of doing so in the developed world – which may involve extensive medical care and attention, potentially over long time frames – the most *efficient* use of philanthropic resources, ergo, focuses on the developing world.

In which case: why are we spending money on the destitute closer to home at all?

Perhaps this counter-intuitive thinking is a contribution in and of itself. There probably are tools within effective altruism that get us to a place where we are justified donating to things close to home. But they are circuitous. One way might be as follows. The reality of 'saving a life' through philanthropy in the developing world is that this action is effectively subsidised by aid money given by governments that create a bedrock of infrastructure on which the charitable interventions rests. The same applies to the developed world where such action is subsidised by welfare and public services are delivered through in-turns fraught and harmonious relationship between the public sector, the social sector and business.

Take away these subsidies, the potential for good from philanthropy decreases, in some cases to nothing. And a structure of domestic philanthropy plays at least some part in preventing those public sector systems from caving in, which in turn contributes to the international aid effort. It is all rather long-winded.

Effective altruists tend to find themselves giving to the same causes precisely because of the paucity of other evidence. If malaria prevention represents the 'most effective' to save lives for a low cost, then effective altruism would have the vast majority of funds poured into this, until the problem had been resolved.

But of course, that all depends on the measures being used. Giving to the cause that performs best on an individualised set of metrics seldom helps the whole system; often it skews and harms it.

We should not need social impact measurements to be perfect before we start using them to drive change; but neither should we place on them burdens that they cannot logically bear. This is utilitarian praxis on steroids.

There are other eccentric positions that emerge from this idea. For example, rather than supporting people who devote their time to philanthropy, effective altruism argues for pursuit of maximum earnings, which enable those involved to disburse consonantly huge charitable donations. This is based on the idea that an effective altruist is unlikely to do a charitable job significantly better than the person who was next in line for the job; however, it is highly likely that they would give more to charity than the person who was next in line for the highly paid job. That makes sense, theoretically, if you accept that the harm caused by the job taken as opposed to the job not taken balances the other way. Go and be a weapons distributor, or trade their stocks and drive their share prices they appear to say. As long as you give it most of it away, you're one of us. Even if weapons aren't a thing, is it really the moral choice to avoid engaging in a life of social change, when the needs are so great and the solutions we seek require not only your money, but your ingenuity?

Effective altruists argue that their movement and its current imperfections are not fatal; that they urge innovation and that creates social value.

Ultimately, the thinking goes, this all will take us to a truly awesome place, towards delivering maximal happiness with evidence that is mindful of humankind's emergent complexity and capacity to change.

I suspect that the effective altruism movement has a great deal of value as a fundraiser and repository for a sort of super-impact-nerdery (it was Bill Gates who coined the 'nerd' moniker in relation to it) that appears to be catching the imagination of a growing, predominantly mission-driven millennial group. If it can turn them on to the questions, problems and possibilities of the wider moral marketplace: all the better.

The anti-community argument

One last point on the philosophical side of things. Consider the works of academics like Will Davies and Robert Skidelsky. They are both excoriators of the principle known as 'neoliberalism,' wherein the contentions of capitalism are applied across the whole of our lives.

In their view, 'neoliberalism' is not just an economic approach but a cultural one. They criticise the degrading of our public space at its persuasions, our personal time and our lives at the hands of measurements, and numbers; of the metrics of the market.

Our lives are bartered and chartered, our experiences, our dreams and nightmares are owned by the people that control capital. Neoliberalism is "our greatest indulgence", Davies once told me (while commenting on a Facebook status of mine – talk about fighting neoliberalism in your own time).

Impact nerdery: is this the 'thin end' of a 'neoliberal wedge' applied to social causes? It sounds a little dramatic, but the stakes are high. Important people are arguing for more of this activity, it promises to radically reshape things in favour of a particular kind of rationalism and efficiency making device. Moreover, we have already clocked some of the world's most powerful people lending their support to it. This convergence of money, power and change is exciting but it should also put us on alert.

Social impact measurement was supposed to liberate philanthropic organisations from the caprice of the philanthropist; from the agendas of old-style donors, often the rich and the privileged. If you have a measurement, you can no longer be pushed around by the whims of the agenda-driven rich person to build a statue in their honour or a ward in their name.

The danger, however, is that these tools become misused and abused and captured by those same elites and power swings back their way. The takeover is more subtle. Here, the arena of community action, of hope and co-operation is colonised by the language and mentality of numbers and targets, the people that understand that way of thinking and then impose it on others in the name of efficiency. In time, they come to be owned and exploited by a Brahmin caste that seeks to create more efficiencies, make profitable investments and take control. Charity becomes capitalism; co-operation cedes to competition. All because we decided to let the mentality of the business elite control the way that we discerned and we decided the good in our own back yards.

If social impact is neoliberalism applied to philanthropy, effective altruism is neoliberalism on meth. It doesn't sound great: rich kids playing roulette with the needs of the poor in a secret society of shared measurements.

When I put it to him, Dan Corry was sensitive about the proper province of this activity.

"I'm not an evangelist – even if some of my staff are! All of this stuff requires a sense of proportion, of what is possible and what is desirable. If you're not applying common sense you're going to lose trust. And trust, for a charity or a social enterprise or for someone trying to work with that them, is a big part of what matters."

He goes on, warming to the subject.

"Look we work with campaign groups, small organisations, who just want a little bit of work doing with them. And we work with bigger organisations too. The bigger ones – you can see where a theory of change can really help them get behind the things that do well and ditch some of the things that aren't helping them do what they need to do. But the smaller charities – and let's be honest, that means most charities anywhere in the world – we just have to let them get on with it. We just have to give them confidence to try and do something, because it's difficult and we should be grateful."

As technology develops and new ideas proliferate, who knows where it may lead? And if many of our young citizens want to be socially active by indulging their numerate or scientific instincts, that need not necessarily be an indictment of our culture.

For now, some may know not what they do, others may have the foresight for something better than the best contemplation of most. The needs of the present are the grit in the oyster for the visionaries of the future; it was ever thus.

When impact measurements empower

Impact: an elusive thing that is tough to get right and talk about convincingly. Not for some, though. Consider the social enterprise

Roshan, which was founded in 2003 in Afghanistan, in the maw of invasion and violence. In 2008, it began to offer the M-Paisa (known elsewhere as M-Pesa) money transfer service to its clients. As in other markets where M-Pesa has been introduced, this was realised in partnership with the Vodafone corporation.

By working with the First MicroFinance Bank of Afghanistan, Roshan were able to overcome many of the difficulties associated with setting up such a system. For example, people were inclined to trust M-Paisa as it was presented to them by the First Bank – an institution they already recognised and trusted.[17]

By 2013, M-Paisa had more than 1.2 million users.[18] One of its selling points was that it has removed banks from the equation – a bonus given the potential for corruption within the Afghan banking system.[19] Reports on the launch of M-Paisa centred on its potential to cut corruption; one story in particular is worth noting of policemen who mistakenly believed they had received a pay rise when they shifted from cash payments to using M-Paisa. The reality was that their superior officers had been skimming-off up to 30% of their wages.[20] Today Roshan is one of the largest mobile telephone providers in Afghanistan.

That is what real social impact looks like. Clear, clean, easy to measure and understand. The ideas we have discussed in this chapter may be inchoate and imperfectly formed, but they are here and they have value and we can see where they are trying to go. They want us to get to a point as crystal clear as creating a money transfer service that is so efficient at tackling corruption that it makes everyone a third richer.

Dan Corry is characteristically sanguine when reflecting on the question of how one achieves those clear results – and how one helps the sceptical to keep the faith as this thing evolves.

> "Ultimately, I would say that beneath all of this debate, the basic question behind impact measurement is the right one. It's a valid question to ask: how do you know you are making the difference you want to make? It's

not just a question for governments or for big donors
but for all of us."

The impact measurement space can seem so complex and business-like; so alien to the typical activist that it can seem designed to disempower. How do we turn that around? The answer might lie in a simple concept: ask people.

There is a great deal of energy attaching to the idea of capturing beneficiary experience. Generating 'feedback' to measure the quality of social interventions attracts a new buzz among social entrepreneurs. Approaches are being mapped and analysed by impact hawks. NPC is trialling new funds that use feedback in innovative ways. This is not a new idea – feedback is at the heart of the social entrepreneur experience – but applying the impact nerds' analytical eye may result in something quite new and doubly empowering.

Right at the end of my time with Dan Corry I saw the excitement rise within him when he spoke for the last time about a project that came up two, three times in the course our conversation.

"This charity, they provide musical instruments to prisoners. They aren't preventing people going back inside. They aren't teaching them skills that help them get jobs. They are just providing instruments to people who don't have them. If you run the numbers, they aren't achieving anything relative to their theory of change. But I look at that and I ask myself: Do I want to live in the sort of world where even a prisoner at their lowest point, who might never have even touched a musical instrument, suddenly has this opportunity to play one. Is that the kind of world I want to live in? For me the answer is 'yes, absolutely.' And I'll bet the people who give to that project to keep it going feel the same."

For a moment the burden of all those measurements is lifted. And we are confronted once again with the simple truth of the social entrepreneur that the ear to the ground is as important as the story of the numbers. Even Josephine Lowell with her ration book and her callipers would concede that.

A trip to the favela:

the death and life of traditional charity

WALT: 'But it's *charity*, Skylar.'

SKYLAR: 'You say that like it's some sort of a terrible thing ...'

Scene from AMC's *Breaking Bad*

The original social entrepreneurs

Daniela Barone Soares is trying to remember her childhood in Sao Paulo, Brazil and she alights on her time working at a children's home in the *favela,* a local community of slum-dwellings, in the mid-1980s. She was aged about 12 at the time.

> "I remember that day in the favela. We were there to help these kids. We stayed all day and they didn't know me and I was pretty useless to be honest. I was reading them stories, playing with them, cleaning up after them, just helping out, you know?
>
> And then it was the end of the day and I had to go. I was leaving and a bunch of them surrounded me and hugged me really close and wouldn't let me leave,

they wouldn't let me move even! I couldn't believe it. And they were saying 'sister, sister, stay'. Just holding me really tight."

She pulls her arms close around her.

"I was crying, I was in tears! But I had to go, I was only there for a day. I wasn't anyone special, I was just another volunteer from the school. And that was that. At that time, there was nothing more I thought that I could do about it."

Years later, Barone Soares would travel from Sao Paulo to take a degree at Harvard Business School. From there she moved on to working in the corporate world, before making a big change and becoming part of the senior team at the international charity Save the Children. Then, when the opportunity to lead a relatively new organisation by the name of Impetus Trust came along, she found what for all these years she had been looking for.

Impetus Trust was one of the pioneers in a sub-movement of social entrepreneurs known as *venture philanthropy*, and she would find, in its theory and practice, an idea that would help her come to terms with the bittersweet memory of that occasion, all those years ago, in Brazil.

I first encountered Barone Soares when she received an award from the *Independent* newspaper in 2007 as one of a clutch of people who made the world a 'happier place in which to live'. By then she had been at Impetus for a couple of years.

"Impetus was trying to do something completely different to anyone else in the UK at the time," she recalled. "in a sub-movement of social entrepreneurs working with like-minded people across the world to try and get charities and social enterprises to think more ambitiously … we were part of an international movement, people who believed that business could actually help."

The Robin Hood Foundation in New York was the godfather of the movement. It was founded in 1988 by legendary hedge fund bruiser Paul Tudor Jones, the trader who tripled his money in 1987 when he predicted the financial crash on 'Black Monday'. Robin Hood focused on 'finding, funding and creating programs and schools that generate meaningful results for families in New York's poorest neighborhoods'.

Over the next couple of decades it raised over US$9.15 billion in money, goods and services to help. It found innovative ways to provide donations to New York-based charities which help the unemployed, disadvantaged youth, the hungry and homeless and help them 'succeed through strategic planning, marketing, finance, technology and legal assistance'.[1]

During the latter part of the 20th century and, at the turn of the millennium, similar organisations were set up across the globe. In Ireland, for example, the One Foundation was set up by Declan Ryan and Deirdre Mortell as a privately-funded philanthropic organisation, which helped disadvantaged young people in Ireland and Vietnam. Over ten years it would come to invest in mental health, children and families, social entrepreneurship and integration of minorities. Projects included The Migrants Rights Centre in Ireland (MRCI) in which One and Atlantic Philanthropies made a joint-investment that allowed the MRCI to expand and grow, spreading its community work, and its overall social impact. The One Foundation's venture philanthropy approach involved 'investing core funds over the lifetime of the business plan, and taking a seat on the board' as their literature put it.

This movement recognised a simple truth: that in the existing national and international not-for-profit sectors there lay a generation of social entrepreneurs. Sure, within a sector as venerable as this, 'lifers' abound. Some are frustrated by process and regulations. There are people who pick up a pay check and carry on business as usual. But there were others who believed that they could do more with the platform they have. They were frustrated, ambitious, hungry to do more. These social entrepreneurs, determined to rewrite the destiny of the often staid or arcane charity sector, deserved support.

Years ago, Barone Soares once told me this business of hers was about nothing less than "finding the Googles of the charitable world". Such ideas were revolutionary, terrifying even, to the vast majority of soup kitchens and micro-local organisations that took their funds from the collection tin or the church tombola and who had no paid staff let alone a plan to survive and help people for the next year, or two, three, four, to come.

They were new to the athlete or popstar or politician or magnate who, rather than working with existing organisations in the field, endows a brand new charitable foundation in their own name, and has a bunch of gala dinners to raise some cash.

They were new also to the public, who often see charities through a traditional, somewhat limited lens. And this is remarkable, not least because those who formed the great charities were the original social entrepreneurs. Social entrepreneurship is a restless and relentless attitude to change; an ever-evolving approach to making a difference. Charity is a legal form. But it is clearly the case that this legal form has delivered incredible innovations that, over the years, have helped millions. The first structures for alms giving and poverty fighting were at the time both novel and revolutionary. Surely, then, the future of the traditional charity and the future of the social entrepreneur are one? That is the question we consider in this chapter.

Visionary prisons

The St Giles Trust building is in Camberwell, South London. St Giles was established by a former boxer in the 1960s, and works with offenders in prisons to provide training and education, reducing the chance that after release they end up back inside. Rob Owen, its CEO at the time of writing, was a recipient of one of the early grants from Daniela Barone Soares' venture philanthropy outfit, Impetus Trust. Many of Owen's employees are ex-offenders themselves. The wall of Owen's office is covered with newspaper articles. One in particular caught my eye as I entered: a picture of HRH Prince William talking about combatting gang crime.

"William was very good," said Owen, allowing himself a smile. "We talked about the issues, he was genuinely interested. I was a bit concerned actually. You bring a royal into the poorer parts of South London, into a building full of people who you wouldn't really think would be natural royal family supporters. You should have seen them when he left. They were literally lining the streets to say goodbye."

Owen speaks softly, with a cut-glass British accent. "I actually came from a banking background," said Owen. "I was working on the equities desk at Schroeders. But I wanted to do something that made a difference to people's lives." He recounted those early days as a charity novice, searching for mentors or support as he made his way.

> "I was astonished when I got here. Not necessarily at the organisation, but at attitudes within the industry as a whole, the other organisations and the foundations who funded them. I remember when I was asked along with a group of other charity leaders to go to a funding meeting with a well-known foundation who had brokered a session with a corporate financier. Someone comes in beforehand and tells us that it's important to wear ties and shine our shoes so we can make a good impression. That was their advice. All of it. So damn patronising."

The journey to working with Impetus was short from there. Owen was a fan of its method and ideas and it became a fan of his. He was given one-on-one support, a dedicated investment manager, milestones, personal support and network of top business people who each gave particular skills pro bono in much the same way as they would give an expanding business the benefit of their wisdom for a stake in their business.

"Everyone's journey in life is different," said Owen. "Ours was about saying, we do this really well. How can we do more of it?"

The St Giles–Impetus partnership is one of the most astonishing in modern venture philanthropy. Working together, over a matter of three or so years, they helped St Giles move from providing services to two prisons when they started into 22 prisons by the end of the investment. In that time St Giles increased its turnover by a remarkable 1,500%.

The strategies of venture philanthropists

Impetus refer to a journey like that of St Giles Trust as 'scale up'. *Growing and spreading* more widely the fruits of charitable services is an important strategy for the venture philanthropist. Growth can spread the benefit of good ideas; it can make social action more sustainable as a social organisation's banking reserves are built and a social brand's identity solidifies.

Improving effectiveness and efficiency across the board is another such strategy. Venture philanthropists are keen to remove as much of the chaff from charitable endeavour as possible, often using impact measurements in ever more buccaneering ways to achieve this end. Charles 'Chuck' Harris, a former banker at Goldman Sachs turned social entrepreneur, commented on the relative inefficiency of the charity sector and saw an opportunity that led to him creating his own venture philanthropy organisation. He founded New York-based SeaChange Capital Partners around the time of the 2008 financial crash with another ex-Goldman partner, Robert Steel. His first area of concern was that traditional non-profits are held back by the time and effort it takes to raise funds in small pieces for one project or another.

By raising larger sums of money at one point in time, they could build their businesses more effectively. 'Imagine trying to grow a company with no financial certainty,' Harris said in 2010.[2]

'Companies do not do that, and, it seems to me, well-managed non-profits shouldn't either.'

SeaChange – which received funding from Goldman, the Gates and Hewlett foundations, and others – set out to create a network of donors willing to make considerable commitments over a number of years.

At the same time, SeaChange started scouting for education-focused organisations on the point of expansion. Match the two together, so the thinking went, and you would have something useful.

The first two non-profits that SeaChange worked with were Uncommon Schools, which runs schools in Brooklyn and Newark, and New Teacher Centre, which trained teachers to work in inner city schools. Fundraising goals were in the millions of dollars.

Alongside the money, there came high quality business advice. In each project there were four categories of work: financial modelling, transaction support, restructuring and strategy assessment.

Diversification is the third major venture philanthropy strategy. Trading as an arm of charitable income is an interesting point of evolution for the traditional charity sector, reflected in differences of culture and practice across the globe. Not-for-profit law across the world gives differing latitude to charitable organisations to trade.

Traditional not-for-profit organisations in the US are prohibited from any trading activities that do not directly serve to fulfil their primary purpose. As a work-around to this, many charities set up a separate organisation to run their trading arms, and then provide funds through donations or grants.

The UK, by contrast, allows a relatively wide degree of flexibility, which yields plenty of useful and inspiring examples. As such, as per the latest available figures, more than half of all charitable income in the UK (55%) comes not from donations, but from trading.[3]

The charity–trading nexus

The charity–trading nexus is worth dwelling on a moment; it is one of the richest and most fertile places in which traditional charity meets social entrepreneurship. The largest heritage charities are almost all involved in it in some way. Consider, when my former colleague Lesley-Anne Alexander was chief executive of nationally renowned UK heritage charity the Royal National Institute for the Blind (RNIB) she oversaw a significant growth in the business side of the charity. To accompany her on a tour of the factory where her charity creates millions of braille books on an industrial scale is to be taken on an entrepreneurial journey centred on doing as much good for as many people as possible and learning to do it better than ever before.

Another charity giant heavily involved in this space is Age UK, which provides services to elderly people. It conducts social enterprise activities through its commercial arm, Age UK Enterprises Ltd, which is run under the charity brand.

It develops products for the over 50s, including travel insurance and mobility aids. This resulted in a trading income of £110 million in 2014/15.[4] In the year 2014/15, Age UK Enterprises reached over 1 million customers.

Crucially, the income from trading represents a significant percentage of their £174.6 million total income, outweighing the £55.4 million received in traditional donations.

When a charity does this sort of activity well, the rewards are considerable. It builds the organisation, makes it more resilient to shocks. It generates growth and revenue that are ploughed back into providing frontline services. And so the charitable cause has more than it otherwise might.

The above is not without complications. Age UK had high-profile problems at the end of 2015 when it negotiated poor deals on certain products including hearing aids for its beneficiaries. Its failings were exposed by the press and Age UK issued various apologies and implemented a number of changes of practice.

The question arose time and again: is it not the case that, where money enters the equation, the desire to sell will trump the duty to help? Judging by the discourse around that particular episode, for all the benefits, when charities begin to view people they are supposed to 'aid' as 'customers' also, the concern among the public rises.

Age UK argues that it has been able to compete successfully with mainstream insurance providers due to the strong focus given to these customers; that by offering these products it is brought closer to their beneficiaries and that is what matters. These arguments have merit.

Academic Kim Alter, whose work we encountered earlier, has outlined some useful terms that help us understand the relationship between charitable organisations and their enterprise cousins.[5]

Alter distinguishes between *embedded enterprises*, in which the income generating activity and mission of the organisation are one, from two other kinds.

There are *Integrated Social Enterprises,* where commercial activities overlap with the social programme, without being wholly contained by it. The Age UK and RNIB models follow this approach.

Then there are *External Social Enterprises*, where commercial activities are wholly independent from social programmes, set up as they are in order to fund the central social mission of the organisation, but bear no operational relationship to it. An example of this with which we are all familiar is the high street charity shop.

In the USA, Goodwill – one of the great international social enterprises and the largest operator of charity shops in the country – raises billions from these ventures.

There are many successes and interesting interpretations of the charity-trading concept. There are nuances and fast practices too. Goodwill surfs that line between industrial-strength employer and trusted charitable brand and has found itself criticised on several occasions for allegedly playing fast-and-loose with people's good will. Getting the balance right between ambition and community concern remains one of the most difficult balancing acts in social entrepreneurship.

Challenging the status quo

Charity remains one of our best known – and loved – social institutions. There are 1.6 million non-profits in the US. In the UK there are 170,000 charities employing nearly 1 million people turning over billions of pounds. According to a study I commissioned while I led the UK's social leaders network Acevo, in the UK, 83% of people used a charitable service in 2016, and charities spend £1,500 per second on services.[6]

But today, the rules of this game are changing. Tanking economies, government cuts and public belt-tightening have hit charities hard. Charities like St Giles, RNIB, and Age UK – talented mid-size organisations or venerable diversified juggernauts – remain the exception rather than the norm, a very small portion of the total, who are better insulated against difficulty, for they have incorporated social entrepreneurship into their offer. The rest are overly dependent on government-sponsored subsidies and tax breaks. Who knows how long such subsidies will last? What will be their fate then?

Bringing charity and social enterprise together

The word 'charity', in English, has a religious, selfless import. Charity workers such as Mother Teresa accepted the self-annihilation of serving others as part of their religious observances. Charities beyond the Church existed in spite of the fact that, as the saying has it, 'the poor will always be with us'. They were the vassals of saints, run in spite of the unending well of poverty and doing their best with it.

The regulations that give form to the legal charity most of us know today are based on ancient common law rules, centuries old, which draw largely from that Christian tradition. This gives us charity as we have it, volunteer owned and resolutely not for profit.

At common law – best expressed in the judgment of Slade J in the British case *McGovern v AG* – the purposes and aims of charity are expressly limited. Charity, it was said there, is expressly designed not to change the world. The purpose is to fulfil certain discrete aims, to give virtue to the giver, and offer solace in this vale of tears. I paraphrase, but don't get above your station was the learned judge's advice.

Other cultural traditions view things differently. In Ancient Greece, philanthropists would sponsor a number of community works and festivals and would receive veneration in return. Aristotle wrote of *Eudaimonia*, or happiness, which was dependent on following a middle way, rejecting total charity, neither giving away everything or nothing.

In Hebrew the closest word is *Tzedekah*, which means 'justice', a word that signals not passive, self-annihilatory love in the face of great hardship, but a commitment to creating a better, more equal, more solidarity-driven world. The Jewish philosopher Maimonides argued for a spectrum of fulfilment that lay in combinations of gifts and deals in order to deliver that justice.

Under such rubrics, charities should not be the vassals of the meek and the mild, but should have an urgency and a determination to change the world.

Charities and their workers – whether knowingly or otherwise – tap into these other traditions when they push the boundaries of the form in order to develop their organisations and deal with the problems they see proliferate about them. They adopt ambitious attitudes, aided by enabling regulations of differing kinds, supported by doses of government largesse when the funds are available. These have led to some really promising developments in business knowhow and mission savvy. They have also led to conflict with more conservative forces.

Some have cast this as a culture war with the object of that war being the soul of charity itself. It is true that the charitable form was not necessarily created to handle some of the things that social entrepreneurs ask of it. This creates a tension that puts these forces at odds with conservative elements who are naturally inclined to try to keep the form within the limits prescribed by history.

This culture war manifests in vicious public debates. Issues around executive pay, working with businesses, political action and campaigning are fissiparous; depicted as skirmishes in this wider battle. Social entrepreneurs are clear about the side they take; their task is to bring the more conservative charity elements into their fold.

The limits of giving

Across the world, people are generous, often unfathomably so, relative to their circumstances. The poorest, indeed, are the most generous in terms of amount given relative to overall income.[7]

But even the largest endowments yield little working capital for charities. Bill Gates' endowment, residing in a trust, yields only around US\$3–5 billion annually and trust income represents 8% of the charitable total.[8]

Compare this to the trillions spent on public services by governments or the hundreds of trillions worldwide in managed investment funds. Compare this also the scale of some of our social problems – child poverty is a good example. It costs the USA US\$500 billion a year,[9] and the UK £29 billion a year.[10]

US citizens are consistently the world's most generous givers, yet the American people give some US\$370 billion and counting each year to charitable causes and nowhere near the amount required, in the world's richest nation, to move their kids out of poverty. In the UK, per capita charitable donations are only £165 a year.[11] Even if we were to treble this, the British would still donate less than the cost of child poverty to the economy. And child poverty is just the beginning.

Australians give around US\$7 billion, the Chinese around US\$13 billion. In the latter culture as in several others, much philanthropic activity remains within families. Even if these numbers were to be nudged to US levels, they would be dwarfed by global and national spending on public services by governments

– and very much dwarfed by the trillions flowing through capital markets.

You might suggest that charities should focus on getting people to give more: they are trying. But this endeavour often causes charities a whole new set of headaches as people grow tired of constantly being asked for money. And I think this fair, for we should never have allowed ourselves to create a system where the problems we face must be solved by donations, arbitrary as they often are.

If our goal here is to create a world in which the 750 million people in extreme poverty worldwide have their situations significantly improved, alongside those in poverty right across the globe, the truth is that the institution of charity – or at least the part of it that consists of low-cost money – will only ever be part of the answer.

Intuition and anthropology appear to back this up. It has been noted that in many societies, complex systems of gifting beyond the charitable sphere are available to people or parties at scale. Many tribal cultures offer complex forms of gift and reward relationship with specified or unspecified benefits emerging at various times. One example is termed *upside-down capitalism*, wherein those with higher social status were mandated to give more to maintain that status. They form in total a phenomenon often referred to as *the gift economy*.

In many such cultures, the concept of a pure or charitable gift is or was relatively rare. Generosity, philanthropy, altruism and community regard abounds across many of society's transactions; and this reduces the need for a large scale specified sub-sector of any great magnitude. It is something like academic Marshall McLuhan's observation that 'the Balinese have no art, they say "we do everything well"'; here it is applied to philanthropy. 'In *gift economies,* there is no charity; we do everything with the spirit of generosity.'

If charity is the seed then this gift economy is the strong oak that grows from it. And this, more or less, summarises the relationship between charity and the moral marketplace that I suspect we should aim to develop in order that both have the best chance of reaching their considerable potential.

Seven steps towards the future

Don't forget that traditional charity and social entrepreneurship are far from mutually exclusive: the former is a legal construct, the latter is an attitude. The question here is how charity, with its quirks and nuances and eccentricities, might be best practically reconfigured or reformed in order to make the most of the burgeoning social movements of the previous chapters and the chapters ahead.

It is increasingly clear that we are at one of those moments in the life of our institutions when change is no longer optional but imperative. The institution of charity is no exception. Removing the choke-hold of establishment patronage, throwing away arcane practices and codes, engaging with the burgeoning movement of social entrepreneurs, embracing venture philanthropy and other forms of social support are all part of the great sea-change that is now upon them. Charities are venerable, often beautiful and humble creatures, but now they must reconfigure themselves for our time if they are to take part in the great social entrepreneur-driven empowerment that is under way. Here are some thoughts about what that might look like in practice.

Step one: A grand consolidation

In the US, there are more than 1.1 million private foundations and registered public charities, deploying over US$0.5 trillion of charitable assets. Yet 85% of non-profits operate with an annual budget of less than US$100,000. In the UK, 200,000 charities access around £100 billion of income and endowment funds; more than half of the sector are micro-charities with an annual budget of less than £10,000.[12]

Consolidation is a word used by many; they see these figures and say 'let's have fewer charities'. There are some who take this further and say, in effect, that efficiencies of scale mean that large charity = good and small charity = bad.

But this is the wrong way of looking at this principle. We live in a time where small charities with the right attitude can make a bigger difference than ever before. Where the scale of large charities can aid innovation but also creates bureaucracy.

In any industry, a new, small organisation with a social entrepreneur or two at the helm can shake things up. Consider the fantastic drug rehabilitation charity in Leicester, UK, The Carpenters Arms, which was named after the pub in which it was set up. It has a turnover of less than £4 million annually, but in 2017 it has created a unique social enterprise arm: a high quality boutique hotel, managed and serviced by recovering drug users. It has done this the right way, inviting the sceptical local community to see for themselves the service on offer. The fruits of diversification are not just for charities with turnovers in the hundreds of millions.

Attitudes to the contrary often represent a peculiar kind of protectionism; a cartel mentality that rears its head from time to time and is ugly to behold. Often those who say such things are stuck in their ways, protecting their wages or terrified of the competition.

One way to think about the grand consolidation challenge is to use a concept I refer to as the 'charity credit'. As we noted above, charities are blessed with low-cost capital, massive tax breaks, and a load of public goodwill to sit atop the moral high ground.

This credit can be compromised by legislation and tight regulation, and it often is. But it should encourage us to ask the question: how do we use the charity credit to achieve the things we need?

Pooling voices is one thing; understanding business functions and capabilities and consolidating them, not just within the sector but outside of it too, can be genuinely transformative. Larger charities opening their supply chains to new social enterprises can give a vital leg-up. This kind of exercise is much talked about, but few have the gumption or vision to see it through.

We have given examples throughout this chapter of medium or large (US\$1–10 million or US\$10 million-plus turnover respectively – certainly not large in conventional business terms) charitable organisations engaging in what for charities are fairly cutting-edge techniques. But it must bears repeating that they remain in the minority; most charities are far smaller, without professional staff, underserved, under-resourced and insufficiently capable of staying on top of their businesses.

Just as we should not fetishise the large, we should also not fetishise the small. There are a great many small organisations worth nurturing and saving. There is also a great deal of room for sensible deal-making in the sector to leverage the charity credit to greater degrees. Impetus Trust has merged with its competitor, the Private Equity Foundation; the best example that I can find of such a merger between equals, with similar capital bases, shared values, and a vision and funding base more enhanced at end than at start.

The idea of smaller organisations partnering up, sharing facilities, entering the supply chains of larger charities, or creating interesting joint ventures in their areas of impact makes sense. The point here is that charity should be the smaller part of our valour – though a really efficient and ideas-rich part. Maximising that charity credit is the thing.

Step two: Embracing 'the golden rule'

I first articulated the idea of 'the golden rule' of charity, the substance of which is by no means particularly new but is certainly true, on BBC Radio 4's Today Programme in response to news that a famous but badly managed children's' charity, KidsCompany, had collapsed. The charity had attempted to expand in concert with generous government largesse but had not put adequate commercial safeguards in place. Allied to a lack of good governance and a reliance on the whims of an all-too-powerful leader, the result was disaster, most notably for the children the charity was supposed to help; they were left without support when the organisation went under.

The golden rule, as I put it there, states that *charity is delivered at the front line but it begins in the back office.* This means that we must require charity funds, charity donations and charity investments to go in part towards securing that back office, and indeed towards contributing to that charity's overheads.

There remain several who maintain the idea that every penny donated to charity should go towards its frontline programmes. Sometimes they are not wrong. Where overheads are concerningly high without adequate explanation, there may well be a problem.

But if overheads are too low, this too is a concern; it suggests that this cause will not make it. High is bad and low is bad: think of it like blood pressure.

The golden rule debate is fissiparous. It is played out in various forms all over the world and indeed online. Charity Navigator is a website that purports to give power to donors to choose their charitable causes by reference to a number of measures including, among other things, the proportion of their money spent on salaries and other overheads relative to what goes to the 'front line'.

For some these measures are the rudiments of transparency for a charitable organisation. Yet for other organisations and charity effectiveness websites, including GiveWell, which we first encountered in the previous chapter, this information represents transparency done badly. Charitable overheads and salary, so the argument goes, while apt to make news headlines, do not indicate the social impact of a charity; of its ability to do well the things it claims to do. The media and popular fixation on these matters suggests bad faith on the part of those providing such information. This viewpoint culminated in an entertaining and somewhat acrimonious debate in the *Stanford Social Innovation Review* where Ken Berger and Robert M. Penna accused detractors of being, among other things, 'elitist'.[13]

Bad faith or otherwise, many charities collude in the narrative. 'All of our money goes to the frontline,' they proclaim. This approach is not sensible, nor, I suggest, is the approach that seeks to keep this information under wraps. After all, if you cannot explain why you do what you do, if you refuse to talk about the rudiments of your business, why should we trust you?

If you do not demonstrate how your pay is linked to performance, how shifts in performance influence remuneration policies, how are we to know that good practice has been followed?

The public deserve not to be patronised and to be told that we will process information incorrectly if it is put our way. Public conversation about the golden rule and how various expenditures of a charity are designed to satisfy the requirements of a highly efficient back office should be part of the culture.

Step three: Diversification and the donations dilemma

We have discussed different techniques of diversification already, and the myriad ways that social enterprises and charities intersect in the common interest. We have also discussed the difficult economics of giving. There is a further challenge that covers both topics and that represents one of the most wicked problems of charity economics.

Economist Tim Harford got it right when he said that, in a complex world with several opportunities for leveraging even the smallest advantage, the value of tapping opportunities – and the opportunity cost of not tapping them, of not having the scale or capital reserve or back office smarts to make those moves – rises higher.[14]

But charities have a unique problem. Organisations that create social benefits require good will, be it on the part of donors or governments, to survive. As soon as they grow, however, the perception among donors may be that they no longer require that generosity. And so donations tail off or those donations are simply no longer enough to sustain the charity's infrastructure.

Thus we have a situation where charities may well make conscious decisions to remain small. And this in turn might mean that their goods reach only a limited number of people; they remain marginal.

Where this is a conscious decision based on mission, it is fine. Where it is a reaction to coming up against a financial wall of this type, the system is at fault.[15]

Conventional wisdom suggests that all that can be done for such organisations is to solicit more grants; to look elsewhere for new sources of funding. However, the bigger such a grant-dependent organisation grows, in the absence of diversification, the bigger its potential to become more bureaucratic and less resilient.

This particular Catch 22, the balancing act between the desire to grow and the need to stay small in order to stay alive, is what I refer to as the *donations dilemma*.

It is a hugely corrosive idea that, in order to live, you have to help fewer people than you otherwise might.

It bears repeating, but diversification is crucial, because it is the best answer to the donations dilemma that we have. This involves not only diversifying modes of action, but diversifying beyond the traditional realms of funding and support. It allows charitable organisations to erupt from the straitjacket of the traditional paradigm.

Business, argued godfather of social entrepreneurship Bill Drayton, could not have succeeded as it has without the 'highly responsive, creative, diverse financial institutions that serve it'. Whether so-called angel investors, venture capitalists, investment bankers, commercial lenders, advisers, brokers, business evolved the capital institutions it has for good reason.

We all know what happens when the resources run out or the donors move on and the organisation and the people who benefit from it are left in peril: charities cut back services and vulnerable people are left more vulnerable. Drayton argued the resulting gap, growing wider as great change-making innovations outpace financial innovation, is probably the single biggest threat to the long-term existence of projects that do good.

He called for a new financial services industry, one that serves the growth needs of the social sector of charities and social enterprises and co-operatives and a thousand social forms in between.

Drayton wanted to coax a range of investors to support new ideas, provide 'medium- to long-term investments to test and refine ideas, learn how to market them, and build institutions and movements'. The answer, he argued, is that non-profits, charities, social enterprises need a system of funding, support and financial services as rich as the systems of support available to standard businesses – but amended for charity.

The social investment entrepreneurs of chapters to come, supported by the venture philanthropists of this, have spent a great deal of time working on this particular wicked problem.

Step four: Professionalise from board to ground

In my time working with the charitable sector, I saw some amazing things. Great acts of kindness and care; people who really make the difference in their communities. I saw leaders agonise over supporting the families of children with cancer (during a visit to the excellent CLIC Sargent charity) and help struggling families put their kids through school. I saw some rubbish practice too, and all of this good and bad, for the most part, was conducted by organisations legally owned by groups of amateurs.

Many charities have directional leaders. Many do not; they are driven by their boards, who in many jurisdictions are compulsorily voluntary. I have come to the view that this is a problem.

From my experience, amateurism breeds conservatism. A board's conservative interpretation of its fiduciary duties can be damaging. This conservatism is exacerbated by their voluntarism; they may not wish to compromise their professional careers by the hand of their voluntary activity so may be less likely to take risks with their philanthropy.

If this was only my experience we could leave it there, but unfortunately it is not. Such concerns and such conservatism are cited by a wealth of professionals as to why the sector continually hits a brick wall. It is part of the reason why technological development and conversion of services in the sector has been slow; why diversification fails; why investment opportunities of the kind in the previous section go unrealised; why great CEOs have their hands tied, or 'potted plants' are appointed or endure in post.

Often it is said that this is prudence, or wisdom. Sometimes it is an honest voice making a sincerely held case for conservatism.

Sometimes it is remarked that training is key and more resources should be available to this under-supported role. That too is fair; it is not as if charity infrastructure support is terribly useful or professional. Chambers of commerce, umbrella organisations, all are locked in conservative patterns and struggle to visualise the future or communicate it.

Too often, however, this conservatism is little more than carelessness, or negligence; the privileging of personal interest by refusing to accept risk or invest in experimentation. The trustees of KidsCompany were society's successes and luminaries; hardly in need of a business education. They got it wrong. There have been and will be several others who get it wrong and I fear that this conservatism in the face of change will see the charity movement murdered on the operating table.

It is regulation that creates the necessity for amateurism. Non-profits often receive considerable tax breaks; regulation and oversight comes with the territory. A highly regulated, tax-efficient form of business is one way of creating social outcomes. It is unlikely to be the best way and certainly not if amateurs are in the driving seat.

The argument is made that loosening regulations and enabling payment of trustees will not of itself change the culture of amateurishness. That is a reasonable argument and an assessment of the extent to which this is a problem should be made in each jurisdiction. There will be grumbles that this undervalues or scorns the wonderful work of volunteers but that is craven virtue-signalling, no more. Volunteers are often lovely people, but that does not mean they should own serious change-making organisations as a matter of law. It seems to me that any puritanism around board pay is at odds with the relative largesse of senior executive pay. It is one of the vestiges of our fractured relationship with charity, where the movement has shifted and evolved without proper organisation or thought.

In 20 years' time, we may look back on this period, where social problems multiplied and charities were in freefall. We may hold the current generation in contempt if they continue to insist that the people tasked with owning and setting the strategies for the organisations that solve our biggest problems be volunteers and amateurs, for fear of overturning centuries-old practices.

It may seem as if we were never serious about using this medium to its full potential and helping people in the direst need in the first place. Is that to be our legacy?

Step five: Embrace feedback and community voice

The idea that the voice of those on the ground – and the feedback of the people a charity serves – should condition its approach is simple and powerful. In the previous chapter we noted movements that seek to better understand the social impact of differing charitable interventions and how these movements are beginning to analyse the role of ground-level feedback in shaping these interventions. Charities of all kinds, but especially those stuck in years-old practices, should embrace these ideas as a route back to the people about whom they care.

The path is not always straightforward. One dilemma in particular is worth nothing. Sometimes scale can bring distance.

Consider fast-growing East London community bus service, HCT. We will learn more about this landmark social enterprise in chapters to come; for now suffice to say that it enjoyed a period of rapid growth during the 1990s and 2000s. This era of acceleration saw its board change considerably. In the early 1990s, it was made up exclusively of the users of HCT's services, who were some of the poorest and most vulnerable people around. Now, the board is much more professional and business-minded. "We needed people who could bring something to the table about how we could keep this organisation going," their CEO, Dai Powell, told me. When I challenged him on whether he felt this made HCT less democratic, he agreed, with qualification:

> 'Yes, probably. But look, more important than having lots of people talking was having a group there that could get things done. And ultimately what we're trying to do is really spread our services to places where otherwise people would be left behind.'

These are the trade-offs, where commercialisation and user voice must be carefully played against each other; where the necessary drive to professionalise is tempered by the authenticity and insight of the communities we exist to empower.

Step six: Campaign and argue for the moral marketplace

From getting seatbelts put in cars to taking cigarettes out of clubs to ending slavery, campaigning is what charities do best. There is no greater force to change the world than when a coalition of charitable and social organisations come together and make change happen.

If charities are to take their rightful place in the global movement of the moral marketplace, they must be more vocal and ambitious with their campaigning than ever before. Charities must constantly harangue legislatures for more action. They must agitate for more action rather than resile. They must never 'let government off the hook'.

Working with government is key. One of my rules of thumb when leading charity leaders' network Acevo was to advocate for positions while at the same time conversing with the relevant officials in order to check against delivery. In this way, we helped raise £30 million in funding through a local sustainability fund. We achieved commitments to close modern-day 'lunatic asylums' that housed people with learning disabilities. We crushed government anti-campaigning clauses, raised awareness about loneliness, and drove public service reform. In each case we had direct, engaged contact – meetings, coffees and cakes, countless strategy documents and diagrams and even some legalese – with government while developing our ideas. Charities have those connections: the virtue of their establishment is that they can support the social entrepreneurs and encourage others to do so. Let's see more of that.

At a time of great change and possibility, when faced with a groundswell of well-wishers ready to unlock human potential as never before, it is the sacred duty of charity's everywhere to raise their voices in unison.

Step seven: Fit for the future

Technology is a tool, a culture, a set of learned behaviours. It involves a willingness to experiment, iterate quickly and share. Charities that don't already get this need to learn these behaviours and learn fast. Charities must use tech – especially free social tech – to improve their offer in every way possible.

For technology is the tool that helps build the partnerships and connect the coalitions that take charities forward. Technology can help charities connect with those on the ground. Technology can break through layers of decades-old bureaucracy or cast off the yoke of disempowering patronage. Technology can help charities rediscover their rightful place among the radicals. We will delve more deeply into these ideas in chapters to come.

The heart of the movement

Working at Impetus enabled me to see first-hand the motivations that drive many of the people who made the trip over from the high profits of the finance industry into the not-for-profit space, and dedicate themselves not to putting their name on the wing of a hospital or having statues wrought in their likeness, but to the anonymous and relatively thankless process of building business capability in the charity and social enterprise sector.

I remember the day that we made a film with a series of voxpops with some of these people. We lined them up, put them on a chair and had them do their spiel. The answers we got fell into a few groups.

Waste. Frustration. The sense of lack of ambition when considering charitable activity.

Opportunity. Hope. That was another.

Scoping the future. Making things better. That was yet another.

Some of them of course, just wanted to get away from the day job for a bit and didn't fancy an evening in with the wife or hubby.

The last thing the charity movement needs at such a difficult, existential moment is a bunch of louche city types on a summer holiday.

But one could hardly make that claim of the tireless Rob Owen in his South London office or Daniela Barone Soares as she looks back on her career leading the venture philanthropy sector.

And there is no doubt that the skills and purchasing power of the business elite can be of inestimable service. Consider the Robin Hood Foundation: billionaire hedge fund manager George Soros pledged US$50 million at its annual Gala Dinner in 2009. Former NBC news anchorman Tom Brokaw is a Robin Hood Foundation board member. The Robin Hood Foundation also partners with thinkers such as Goldman Sachs Group CEO Lloyd Blankfein, and TV personality Jon Stewart. Not a bad supporter cast list for an organisation that is essentially dedicated to building infrastructure.

You might suggest that the changes they advocate are too onerous; that my own seven steps are too great a burden for this sector of fragile saints to bear.

Actually my prescriptions are relatively 'vanilla'. Advocates like Dan Pallotta in the US want a sort of venture philanthropy double-plus; argue that charities should become even more entrepreneurial, hire the best people, spend much, much more on their back offices.[16] Let the cream work at solving the world's problems rather than creating new ones, he argues. Let us have the best people in society working on the biggest issues we face.

We don't wish to be remembered as 'the generation that cut charity overhead', he tells us. Spend our money on solving social problems. After all, on what else should our money be spent?

Some concern is justified. Venture philanthropists can be bruisers, brutal with the organisations with which they work. The story is told of a venture philanthropy outfit that lobbied hard to remove a charity chief executive from position, as it would be better for the charity and its growth plan and got him kicked out. It does leave one in a questioning frame, when financiers are radically changing the character of charities in order to meet their own measurements.

There is often a visceral reaction – honestly felt, it must be said – from charitable folks to the ingress of the city into their work. 'If I hear another person say what charities need is lessons from the private sector, I shall scream' said Lesley-Anne Alexander in one of her more colourful speeches, referring to the unfortunate pronouncement of a politician that had come before her.[17] "The charity funders refused to speak to us when I started, they were very suspicious," Impetus co-founder Stephen Dawson once told me, referring to his earliest experiences at Impetus.

Yet it is not the case that ne'er the twain shall meet. And at the vanguard, both sides work tirelessly to find ways to treat. Charities have recognised the brilliance of venture philanthropists. Many understand that the context in which they operate changes and they must change with it. They are both, after all, different forms of social entrepreneur: the ambitious charity leader and the venture philanthropist are on the same team. With this knowledge in mind, venture philanthropists have evolved their approaches too.

The postscript to the story of Impetus, the tale of its own evolution, is instructive. When I first joined, the organisation was obsessed with scale, making things bigger: those Google charities I was told about.

It was only on my arrival that it began to think about linking up with other organisations, using advocacy as a tool to do so (indeed that was the reason for my joining) – and making the offer more about people rather than organisations.

I played a small part in that journey. But long after I had left, Daniela Barone Soares had completed a much bigger journey with the organisation.

By the time she stepped down, no longer was the organisation obsessed with scale but its efforts were focused much more on learning the chapter and verse of the actual work of the organisation it was helping, getting to know the life stories of its beneficiaries. User voice. Feedback. These were all the right noises. 'Caring better'; 'giving even more of a shit'.

Impetus merged with its main competitor in the UK, the Private Equity Foundation, in 2012 and would be renamed Impetus-PEF. Impetus-PEF's work and investments then focused on improving the lives of disadvantaged young people, via two main campaigns: the school-to-work transition and the problem of young people becoming 'NEET' (not in employment, education or training).

The story of Impetus's evolution is one example of the journey that it encourages other ambitious non-profits to take. There is a process of maturation, refinement, aligning business and social outcome taking place that makes them more ready to contribute usefully to society.

The new Impetus-PEF organisation is larger, leaner, more agile and able to travel deeper into its areas of social impact. This is venture philanthropy in action, going to work on the venture philanthropist.

Barone Soares remains engaged with this area; and was as energised as any time I've seen her before when talking about evolving the measuring of social impact as part of the development of her own business.

"Whatever you call it, ultimately it's about feedback," she said. "If a donor gives to a charity, there's usually no way of them knowing if they're getting a good deal, that is a deal that actually helps people, because there's little contact between those being helped and the donor."

She was scribbling on a piece of paper at this point as she spoke, in that high-tempo manner of hers, lots of circles and arrows and squiggles and words.

"Impact measurement is trying to create an objective system whereby everyone can try and conform to an idea of what good looks like and then make a judgement. But look," she jabs her pen at the piece of paper. "If we, the support intermediary, are the ones setting the measurement then it's the charity that is telling you what good looks like. The donor is still none the wiser about whether the person supposed to be helped is actually feeling helped as a result of what has happened."

As if to prove the point, the line from a newly-scribed word

DONOR

to a similar word

BENEFICIARY

on her piece of paper remains unmade.

"We use measurements," she says. "But we're more into impact management than measurement. We see it as our job to keep a dialogue going, not only between the donor and the charity, but also with the people being helped as well. And we give the people on the ground space to feedback on the charity's performance. And if they are performing well then that should be it. No measures, no impact targets. Not numbers that mean little. No shared measurements with governments or social investors. Just let them get on with fixing things based on the feedback of their beneficiaries." At this point she began to encircle the word 'BENEFICIARY' with vigorous strokes of the pen.

It begins with seeing venture philanthropy as a means to prepare organisations for Google-era growth. It develops into something more human, a facilitator for needs and aspirations of communities on the ground, in direct conversation with them.

It evolves into the realisation that the purpose of the venture philanthropist is not only to build this or that organisation, but to raise the voice of those on the ground, to empower them to shape the forces that attend their lives. If that is our meme, we will not go far wrong.

Inside the social enterprise city:

when communities together build something amazing

> Cities have the capability of providing something for
> everybody, only because, and only when, they are
> created by everybody. (Jane Jacobs, *The Death and Life
> of Great American Cities*[1])

After the quake

On 3 March 2011, an earthquake hit Miyagi on the east coast of
Japan. It was devastating, yet it was only the beginning. In its wake
came a great tsunami that overwrought much of Japan's eastern
coast. It deluged entire towns and displaced thousands of people.
Nearly 4,000 people were known to have died and it left behind
a trail of horrors.

The nuclear powerplant at nearby Fukushima had its defences
breached, leaving a disaster of antediluvian proportion, which
devastated entire parts of Sendai and the region of Tohoku to the
north. It became known as Japan's 3/11.

Fukuoka was about as far away from the epicentre of the
earthquake as you can be while still remaining on Japanese soil;
almost exactly diagonally opposite to Tohoku. Yet just as the whole
world looked on in sorrow as workers doused the nuclear reactors

at Fukushima with buckets of water with almost certain knowledge of their own radiation-induced sickness, so did Fukuoka.

Fukuoka sits atop the active Kega fault and, though not nearly as devastating as the shock at Miyagi, life there was brought to a standstill by its biggest earthquake in 200 years in 2005.

And so Fukuoka's inhabitants were active in the relief effort for the Miyagi quake victims. They gave their money and time to the American Red Cross, Salvation Army and Japanese Red Cross, among others, as well as giving blood at hundreds of centres across the area to help the sick. The mayor of Fukuoka, Soichiro Takashima, saw the potential in all of this goodwill and began to implement an idea.

Three months after the Miyagi quake, Takashima convened a caucus. Attending was Muhammad Yunus, who led a panel discussion involving founder and CEO of Japanese clothing super-brand UNIQLO Tadashi Yanai, directors of corporate conglomerates Danone and Veolia in Japan, as well as the president of Kyushu University.

During three days of deliberations, those present prepared a number of plans to work with the Fukuoka community to create a hub of social enterprise.

The Mayoralty would devise a building, a hub for these and future enterprises, a 'Grameen House' at Kyushu University campus. During that weekend in Fukuoka, Yunus addressed a meeting with 100 female leaders, delivered a keynote to 60 young 'peace ambassadors' and 400 11-year-old 'junior peace ambassadors'.

Projects included a Tohoku cultural Resurgence Company to present musical and cultural events, an agricultural company to rehabilitate farming and fishing in the Miyagi region and more besides. This groundswell activity was crowned by Fukuoka being inaugurated as a 'social business city'.[2]

Takashima had made a bold statement about how his city was to prosper and his country was to be remade – and a bold statement about the role of the city itself as a platform for social entrepreneurship.

Think of it this way: Takashima knew that a million causes, movements and ideas were there, waiting to be tapped in his community. His role was not to dictate what those movements should be but to platform others, inspire, provide infrastructure.

The idea of a social business city is an idea for our time. They proliferate all over the world. There are other social business cities, which follow the Fukuoka model and which heavily involve Yunus's Grameen organisation: the city of Wiesbaden in Germany and the city of Pistoia in Tuscany, Italy are two.

Most, however, emerge spontaneously and informally. Rather than be designated, they grow into the trope over time. In places, community hubs, large geographic clusters of social enterprises and campaign groups accumulate and learn from each other and thrive. People start making the connections and working the infrastructure harder.

This is a feature of my home city of London's social enterprise scene. Here collections and chains of social support hubs develop a welcome presence. One such chain is called simply 'The Hub', and offers a suite of services for social entrepreneurs.

Lesser known local examples, community owned, unique in character, offer different takes on this idea across the city. As I write these words, I am looking at one, Hackney Co-operative Developments (HCD) in Hackney, East London, a building opposite my favourite local library in Dalston that offers a home for Hackney's social enterprises. There has been interest among London's boroughs to self-designate as social enterprise zones, with councils offering specialised kinds of funding to support social ventures.

Put all this together and you see that the spirit of the city ripens and moves in social enterprise's direction. There is so much happening, perhaps all it will take for London to vie for the title of social enterprise capital of the world is for someone in City Hall to make the argument. Really, this is an open goal.

There are many more examples. Take Bilbao, Spain. Here the world's leading social innovation park hot-houses and shares innovations between groups of social enterprises in a bohemian, cultural enclave.[3] Social entrepreneurs are right at home here.

All of this activity serves to create environments in which optimism and hope are contagious. It creates living laboratories of useful insights and information about how we improve our world.

These social enterprise cities are living laboratories; repositories of useful insights and information about how we improve our world. They are the campaigners' dream; a fertile seedbed for the community activist. Many of London's great social movements, such as the movement for community land trusts and co-operative housing, or the national living wage campaign, were supported by one of the city's social hubs. They were reinforced in pubs and on community stages where activists congregate and share the stories of their struggles.

These are the great untold stories behind social change and community action; the places where the techniques of change are forged and perfected. In this chapter, we will learn more about them.

Swathes of potential: community assets

Consider the work of Jack Rosenthal and Herb Sturz. They established the social enterprise ReServe, which helps older, skilled volunteers get active. ReServe provides volunteer placement services for skilled retirees, matching charitable organisations with older members of the public.[4] The business has subsequently expanded in response to demand, and now has locations in New York City, Greater Boston, Maryland, South Florida, Northern New Jersey, Southeast Wisconsin and Westchester.

The idea that there is hidden potential in our society waiting to be tapped is one of the leitmotifs of the social enterprise movement. *Community assets* is a useful idea that helps the social entrepreneur conceptualise it.

Community assets can be *tangible* such as buildings or produce: the things you can touch. There are many ways in which these assets can be harnessed and redeployed to bring people together or showcase talent. Social enterpreneurs within communities or cities might keep lists and legers of tangible community assets in easily communicable form, in online maps or in blogs, leaflets or magazines. Think spare office spaces, desks. A food social enterprise might have a fine-grained understanding of the drop-off points for wasted food from supermarkets. There are countless other examples.

Community assets can also be *intangible*, involve a community's labour force; their *skills*. These might be volunteers; they might also be skilled workers who are hard-to-reach. Think bedridden folks, immigrants who haven't yet mastered the language but might have several PhDs, or new retirees, as with ReServe. Different roles can be offered and appropriated by community members. Some might become leaders, advisers or volunteer testers. There are so many people out there who are not meeting their potential; there are so many quanta of hidden energy. The social entrepreneurs seek to sniff them out.

Community message boards and skills exchange websites or workshops can help bring these skills to the fore for social entrepreneurs to leverage. This was used to great effect by legendary social entrepreneur and urban regenerator Dick Atkinson, whose work turning around the Birmingham district of Balsall Heath remains a landmark example.

Atkinson placed simple community newsletters and quite mundane examples of social entrepreneurship at the heart of his method. There were projects as simple as 'Two Men in a Van', which comprised a vehicle that drove around the community offering to repair things, thus demonstrating that this community was *worth* caring about. An area notorious for crime and anti-social behaviour slowly began to regain its dignity and identity.

Targeted legal changes can assist the tapping of community assets, especially on the tangible end of the equation. In the UK in 2010 I was part of a think tank advocating for legislation that would become the UK's Localism Act, which conferred rights on communities to bid for the running of local buildings or facilities, take them over, turn them into something useful or beautiful.

There are many such potential centres of insurgent community action, from unloved museums, to dilapidated lighthouses; from empty shops to tumbleweed thoroughfares. Social entrepreneurs bring in volunteers, community workers, and create a buzz: this is regeneration Dick Atkinson-style, from the bottom up.

These ideas spread and are replicated by savvy social entrepreneurs all over the world. Social entrepreneur Gareth Potts' New Barn Raising movement in Washington provides tools, 'webinars' and resources for community asset transfer. I first met Gareth when discussing the implications of the Localism Act. *New Barn Raising* is his rather snappy term for the repurposing of community assets. His organisation, he told me, is about getting these tools "to an international audience".[5]

When we think about intangible community assets, we can be as high- or low-tech as we need to be. There is the Dick Atkinson or Betty Makoni approach. All it takes is a community space and a kind ear for people young and old to begin to realise their potential.

Consider an insightful project from Muhammad Yunus' Grameen Bank in Bangladesh. Here, the bank leased cell phones to its female borrowers. The phones were mostly used for exchanging price and business and health-related information. The results were very interesting indeed. Phone owners shared social information that resulted in better prices, easier job searches, reduced mortality rates for livestock and poultry, and better returns on foreign-exchange transactions. The women who held these phones were also able to earn additional income from providing cell phone services to others in the community. Research showed these cell phones were not only good for business but also improved the social status of women who used them: they became significant community assets because they owned these tools. Phone-envy as a way of building social capital: who would have imagined that?

The ReServe example highlights a slightly different but related point about such operations. ReServe hinges on two very familiar sources of funding for traditional non-profit organisations: philanthropy and government. Here we might make the observation that while social enterprises often sell services or goods to the general public, in places where regeneration is the game especially, philanthropy and goodwill can form a significant segment of the whole.

This puts social entrepreneurs in an interesting, at times invidious, position of managing the expectations and contentions of the marketplace and its investors but also the expectations and contentions of philanthropists, and of governments who they have enjoined as partners – and, most importantly, the communities who vote those governments in and out of power. This keeps them honest, for sure, but it also gives them something of a very real democratic responsibility. It bears repeating: these social entrepreneurs are not just social leaders but civic and public leaders too. They might not thank me for giving them this moniker, but social entrepreneurs are the people's politicians.[6]

A culture of social design

Social enterprise cities are not only places where members of the community are engaged and enthused about social change; here, community members are in fact an integral part of the process of change. The distinction between these two concepts – and the role that citizens play in each – is at times quite subtle and is worth considering in more detail. At the heart of a social enterprise city is something akin to a culture of social design, of care and love for where one lives allied to a strong grasp of behaviour change and allied disciplines. It begins, in its simplest incarnation, with *listening*.

Two kinds of listening

The PlayPump was once considered to be the next big thing in social innovation.[7] It was a roundabout, a children's toy, connected to a well that drew water. Children would play and water would emerge from that play. That was the theory, anyway.

It sounded clever. Organisations and foundations stepped forward with increasing vim and vigour with the aim of erecting PlayPumps across the developing world. Yet an investigation in 2009 concluded that the PlayPump was actually one of the least efficient methods of getting water out of the ground. The *Guardian* newspaper calculated that children would have to 'play' for 27 hours a day to meet PlayPumps' stated targets of providing 2,500 people per pump with their daily water needs. The PlayPump supplied only 2 litres, per child, per day, of drinking water, a tiny amount compared to that generated by more traditional hand pumps.

A later investigation suggested that in the communities the pumps was supposed to aid, many older women, who were not consulted prior to the installation of the PlayPumps, could barely operate them. When there were no children around, and resorted to the indignity of having to go round and round the roundabout themselves just to obtain the smallest quantity of water. The pumps continually broke down after a prolonged lack of use, with no way for villagers to make expensive repairs.

In response, let us start with the obvious. Nobody listened. Those who had this idea didn't even think to start a proper conversation with, or listen to, people from these communities.

Government agencies and academics, especially those working in development, have had a real problem with this. Bureaucracies have instantiated arrogance and hubris. It is here, in this vacuum of leadership, that the work of social entrepreneurs has made such a difference.

Social entrepreneurs like Vinod Kapur listen in at least two ways. They have as much interest in understanding and tracking the economic habits of their customers and partners as they do in understanding their social situation. For tracing both helps them gauge what needs to be done next with that much more accuracy.

Indian author C.K. Prahalad in his book *The Fortune at the Bottom of the Pyramid* studied the unique behaviours and consumption patterns of those who were very poor in order to learn more about them.[8] He made the case that the very poorest folks should not be considered outside the global economy but a unique part of it. They must be engaged with and understood, not only as social actors but as people who make trammelled choices, just like anyone else.

Author Michael Sherradan conducted similar studies and advanced the idea that the poor were often more assiduous and thrifty than the middle classes but even they could accumulate savings and assets with help.[9]

The point is that listening really, really matters. Social entrepreneurs gain their advantage from listening in two ways: both with an ear to the ground but also by taking the pulse of the community in which they are based. For any social design intervention to work, it must be rooted in a culture of listening, of feedback, of democratic empowerment. These two kinds of listening are the foundation on which most of the best innovations of the social enterprise city are build.

Social design

Sophisticated listening techniques yield insights into people's aspirations, habits, ideas and dreams. They tell us what will work and what will be scuppered by everyday reality. Interventions can then be *designed* more creatively to fit with the lifestyles of those they are supposed to aid.

'Social design' is a fascinating discipline within the social entrepreneur movement and it has found many champions within social enterprise clusters, hubs and cities. Social designers encourage us to note not only the *effect* of the services we provide to a community, but also the *means* through which the very poorest access those services. The type of question they will ask is: how is does the service look and feel from the point of view of the user? What is their lived experience of it? They consider 'touch points' at which the community, the service user and the service intersect and how these can be used most effectively.

It is a bit like designing the rooms in a house by understanding how the people who live in that house will use them. This might mean a separate toilet and bathroom for a house designed for a busy family. It might mean a connected kitchen and lounge to create an open plan entertainment space. It might mean no more PlayPumps in areas of famine and water shortages where children only have the energy to play for a few hours each day.

So how does it work? One of the first orders of business of social designers is to map and understand 'touch points' when designing services. They might capture this information in a number of ways. The process can be as simple as holding a public forum. They might make and study films shot from the point of view of a user which shows the journey through a service.

If the service involves sourcing materials or building things, the designer might articulate principles on which the selection of such materials should be made. Perhaps they are locally sourced or the wood comes from sustainably managed forests.

The hotel industry is a place where designers of all kinds let their imaginations loose. Social enterprise hotels have become arenas for social designers show the best of themselves and their art in the service of others. Good Hotel is the archetypal example. The first of these was set up in Amsterdam, a boutique floating hotel with great views that provides tailored training and employment for those who find the route to the job market difficult, while reinvesting its profits in entrepreneurship programmes and education.

The design of the intervention and the design of the hotel itself are two sides of the same coin. The materials for the hotel are locally sourced. The staff are drawn from legions of long-term unemployed, with jobs found for them within the local networks after their placement is up. The whole business, including the furnishings used in the rooms, reflects the simple, professional and ethical ethos of the company.

Hotels are places of community, where the local and the other meet. The Magdas Hotel in Vienna takes this concept and does something quite wonderful with it. On its staff are refugees from several different backgrounds; more than 20 languages are spoken among them. The design ethic here is quirky and eclectic. It reflects the patchwork of cultures; its website is similarly quirky and eclectic. It mixes information about the hotel with hard-hitting but jauntily presented information about the hoops through which asylum seekers from different countries must jump in order to make a living in a host country. The process of staying with and being cared for by refugees is a very effective way of building empathy and understanding while providing proper employment at the same time.

Furniture in the hotel is upcycled and creatively sourced. It all fits together into a very cool, very socially conscious whole. As a piece of social design, it is in every way opposite to those rusting, unloved, unimaginative PlayPumps.

A story about cell phones highlights the possibilities of social design thinking. In the early 2000s, conventional wisdom was that there was little market for mobile phones in developing countries; they were luxury devices, not goods to be found on a poor person's shopping list. There was no hope of multinationals taking their wares over there.

In reality, the developing world has been a success story for mobile technology; it has enabled businesses to flourish, and conferred status on individuals. In Africa, millions are already paying for goods on their cell phones as electronic payment systems become more reliable, safe and secure than cash.[10]

Latest estimates suggest that Africa has over 600 million cell phone users[11] compared to the mere 50 million that have access to computers.[12] They are sources of information. They enable goods to be bought, services offered, or employment sought often at cheaper prices. Indeed half the world's population are now cell phone users and growth rates are currently fastest in the poorest regions.[13]

As a result, successive generations of social entrepreneurs have a new arena with which to reach members of their community; a new swathe of touch points. An array of pro-social mobile services such as online money transfer services, health check-ups, language courses and more are made available that base themselves in resources already in rural areas, such as the local stallholder or shopkeeper. Incorporating these new touch points into the nature of our proposed interventions and testing them with an engaged community has yielded innovations galore that have changed livelihoods and improved lives, M-Pesa and Roshan, which we have already encountered, being but two.

Drishtee's rural revolution

Social design disciplines have become influential enough to help us analyse why some social enterprises succeed and why some fail; why some community movements are successful and others do not take off. The Drishtee example – and the failure of its counterpart CareShops – shows how.[14]

Drishtee is a major Indian social enterprise; a network for rural shops, stalls and kiosks that offer a variety of goods, online or e-money and small loans, microfinance, distance learning and education support.[15] Add computer education, English education, e-governance, health check-ups, as well as a wide range of fast-moving consumer goods (including groceries, cosmetics and mobile phone recharge coupons), rechargeable torches and batteries, and you have a hi-tech, flexible community resource with a purpose that offers livelihoods and training in one package in some of our planet's poorest places.

It sounds great and it is. And so others tried to replicate it. CareShops was an endeavour launched by the Ghana Social Marketing Foundation, after the manner of Drishtee. The plans seemed good. Many Ghanaians, particularly in rural areas, had limited access to health-care facilities and didn't know where their next prescription might come from, let alone non-medically sanctioned drugs like aspirin. Licensed chemical sellers were the port of call for those who could not reach a doctor, and there was a considerable black market trade in prescription drugs. CareShops was to fill a niche.

Like Drishtee, it was a franchise. It provided its franchisees with a distribution network, a delivery service, extensive business training, a strong branding scheme and some renovation opportunities for their stores. The idea was that CareShops, like Drishtee, could enable several community businesses to move from moderate success to profitability and in time provide their owners and workers a route out of poverty. In return, CareShops charged a fee, received a significant volume discount from suppliers, and took a profit.

The result? As much as Drishtee has been a lifegiving success, and a movement that has lifted the aspirations of thousands of Indian stallholders, CareShops was a turkey.

Social design allows us to see why. Franchisees found that in reality there was not a great deal of sustaining money in prescription drugs. CareShops only accounted for 15% of franchisees' product purchases during its best year, while supporting all of the costs. The black and grey market stuff was actually what customers wanted. And even those prescription drugs that were sold often came from other sources, who sold them to store holders at lower unit cost, or were more flexible than the somewhat bureaucratic CareShops central office.

There were real difficulties also on the ground. Too little effort made to understand the touch points, the principal actors, how things worked; to establish trust between central office and the new franchisees within the communities themselves. Shop owners – an obvious touch point here – were barely listened to or bought into the system; often goods were left without payment.

Drishtee's challenges were actually very similar to CareShops': a fast-moving market, unreliable franchisees and a relatively disorganised workforce. Yet they sought to minimise these risks directly, by understanding their target community: rural dwellers.

They created a web-based inventory tool that enabled kiosk managers to order supplies online and helped central office better manage and aggregate orders. Drishtee's focus on perishable goods like razor blades, as requested by stallholders, helped it to reduce costs as the frequency of sales was higher. This created a variety of incentives and rewards that encouraged franchisees to stay loyal to the project instead of trying to game the system.

To do business in certain countries is to run the gauntlet of capricious governments, corruption or lax regulations. In many countries, a recurrent problem is the inability to enforce contracts in certain situations, where the lack of proper legal recourse meant that people created a culture where they 'just did not pay'.

Drishtee, run by people who understood that culture, listened out for those signs and devised work-arounds. It operated, for example, a revenue share model that meant loyalty was rewarded and up-front costs and risks were minimised too for both the social enterprise and the franchisee. Conferring ownership strengthened the bond between entrepreneur and community member, and made all the difference at the narrow margins on which success and failure are founded.

Social R&D: embedding a culture of adaptation

This process of learning from failure is that much more successful when it happens hand-in-glove with communities on the ground. A social enterprise community or city can be thought of as a sort of living test-bed or laboratory for social innovation ('social labs', I once called them). Come and do your thing, they say to the social entrepreneur, we're ready to give it a go, and make it a success – eventually.

Professor Muhammad Yunus will forever be associated with one of the great social enterprises: Grameen Bank. He started his journey in ethical credit distribution to the world's poor by giving to the male of the species. This didn't work. The men would often run off with the money or would spend it not on the homestead or their business, but on entirely unhelpful pursuits.

That is when Yunus realised that he actually had to give the money directly to the women in the communities he cared about if there was to be change. Given his centrality to the spread of microfinance across the globe, the world – and the lives of hundreds of millions of people – changed on that revelation.

That is not as simple in practice as it seems it ought to be on paper. It often means negotiating a series of fairly tricky and complex community sensibilities and relationships. Few wish to see their neighbourhood as a laboratory.

Governments are often loath for their interventions to be seen to fail – after all, what would the political consequences be of that? Thus they throw bad money after bad. Charities too are often loath to discuss failure for fear of losing donations. This culture of not wanting to 'lose face' is very corrosive indeed.

Creating a culture that embraces and broadcasts failure en route to success in our efforts to change the world is one of the great insurgent endeavours of the social entrepreneur movement. Trusting a social entrepreneur to learn and fail is a tough manoeuvre to make. But social entrepreneurs are finding innovative ways to garner community consent for their experiments. These are the basics: good communications, personal charm, honesty, optimism and a propensity for partnership.

There is the formalisation of the testing process. A culture of so-called alpha and beta testing – encouraging key communities to test software before it comes to market – is a key plank of the internet industry. These ideas have been used by social entrepreneurs to test interventions across the piste. Local universities or trusted institutions with a social enterprise department may partner or lend their support to such projects. Universities indeed are excellent connectors of social entrepreneurs and communities. Examples are diverse; a particularly interesting one is that in Elizabethtown, Kentucky, where the local university has gone out of its way to bring the student and the local populations together through social enterprise, its development and experimentation.

Updates on the trial are part of the process of conversation with the people whom the social entrepreneur cares for and represents. They appraise community members of their progress, hold regular question-and-answer sessions, take ideas and discuss the future. Getting popular and political support for this activity, as well as the support of local social entrepreneur support hubs and individual entrepreneurs, is the only way the social entrepreneur can fulfil her mandate and improve what she does.

On London buses: the power of civic pride

Let us alight once more in Hackney in East London. One of its greatest sons is an organisation known as HCT, formerly Hackney Community Transport, a part of the fabric of the place and a symbol of its past and its future. HCT is a fascinating example of a social enterprise that has grown and flourished in striking parallel to the community from which it springs; a community that has historically been associated with countercultural movements but which in recent years has become more affluent, more gentrified and also more unequal.

I wanted to learn about its story and understand quite how it had come to be so revered within the locality I call home. And so I went to see its leader, Dai Powell, to find out more about the power of place in the work of the social entrepreneur.

Powell arrived in London in 1987 with little more than the shirt on his back. He was a miner in his native Wales before his pit was closed. From there he moved to Glasgow in Scotland, which was similarly bereft of opportunity. London came next, "the obvious choice for someone who didn't know what he wanted to do next and had nowhere else to go", as he put it to me.

Hackney became home and there he volunteered as a bus driver for HCT.

The story of its beginnings is telling. Five years earlier Hackney's council shut down a lot of its bus services; HCT emerged from the wreckage, the brainchild of 30 community groups which existed to ferry those the council no longer would. For its first few years it rested on the goodwill and grace of volunteers like Powell; a cottage industry of minivans that gave Hackney's poor or disabled residents and many little groups a way of getting about.

Places like Hackney are the sum of such parts. Today these cottage industries have been redefined as part of the 'hipster' scene. Artisanal wares, local food pop-ups, freelancers, skateboard parks that sprout in abandoned truck depots: that was all part of it and Hackney was this one of this culture's prime movers. Before all that, there was HCT, one of the original and the true, part of that do-it-yourself concord that formed the beating heart of the community. Powell saw this and threw his energy behind it. Within a couple of years he was organising his fellow drivers on the ground. Only a couple of years after that, he was leading it.

People needed this help, often those who were immobilised and couldn't get to bus stops due to infirmity. HCT soon acquired a smorgasbord of clients, and some 300 local community organisations, including the Hackney Pensioners Project, the Stoke Newington swimming club, Hackney Greenham Groups and even the wonderfully named Consenting Adults in Public.

HCT by now was a clutch of minibuses, a few paid staff and some community volunteers. Like many local charities, it relied heavily on donations and grants. The council provided it with some money and there was the occasional gift too from the odd well-wisher. But this was always an uncertain position. And as the boom of the 1980s was exposed to the recession of the 1990s, even this goodwill, honestly meant though it was, started to wane.

"We needed to expand," Powell said, as he spoke to me in HCT's breezy offices.

> "If we were going to continue provide the services that mattered to people, we realised that we needed to do more with the knowledge we had. We would have to expand our understanding of how the business of running buses properly actually worked and somehow try to use it to help ... We had arguments, some of them quite vicious. Our supporters didn't see us as a business.

We weren't a business in the way that people understand it, we were there to help people at the margins. But it's difficult to get that message across."

Powell is softly spoken – since childhood he has had a slight speech impediment – and he measures his words, tinged with a soft Welsh accent, with care. He has a bulky frame, a slightly leonine face.

"There was one meeting we had, we couldn't agree on anything. Everyone was getting so pissed off that we had the meeting on Regent's Canal [which passes through Hackney] on a barge. It was the only way we could be sure that people wouldn't storm out."

HCT's brand was a community asset in itself, a symbol of self-reliance and defiance; a source of pride. It had tangible assets in its vehicles, routes that were all its own and the knowhow and hunger to acquire more. Winning new routes would help it multiply the number of services that it could provide to the marginalised groups it had been set up to help – and increase the quality of its services at the same time. "People worried we would forget where we had come from." For a moment he looks troubled, as if recalling difficult conversations of years past. "But you can't forget that. That's what makes you unique."

Ultimately, "Nobody stormed out, nobody drowned. There was a lot of shouting though." And HCT's board agreed that it would compete, not for donations or grants, but for business, in open competition against the transport market's giants.

HCT would win its first London red bus route – a mainstream route that mainstream providers left behind – soon after. By 2004, it had added two further red bus routes and a second depot at Waltham Forest in East London to deliver transport services for children with special educational needs. In 2006 it expanded into West Yorkshire, way up in the north of England, beyond its beat, with contract wins to deliver school transport.

The business flourished. Mergers with other organisations with similar values like Islington Community Transport and Leeds Alternative Travel would follow. The London 2012 Olympic Games brought a new sort of opportunity. HCT established a joint venture with Ealing Community Transport (ECT) – a similarly forward-thinking local community bus service organisation, which, inspired by and working in complementarity to HCT, pioneered recycling routes and alongside its community transport services helped to make the prospect of sorting recycling, which today many of us take for granted, a mainstream proposition. Together they would deliver transport to and around East London's Olympic Park.

For those who were in London in 2012, or who saw it on the television, this made perfect sense. Those Olympics would be characterised by an enormous voluntary effort; a spontaneous blossoming of goodwill across a usually grey, curmudgeonly city. And by now the HCT group, as it was called, had buses working across London, in Yorkshire and Humberside in the north of the country and in the southwest too.

> "It's very different thinking about your work when you're an enterprise, trying to win contracts rather than making applications for donations or for grants. The whole idea is different, you need different skills. We didn't bring in huge consultancy firms. We muddled through. But I'm happy about it. For all the difficulty, it does make your service better. You're holding a sort of mirror up to your organisation and saying – are we reaching the people we say we are reaching? Are we really any good at running buses? That's the key thing. And you find out – you're not just helping people, you are actually good at what you do, better than these commercial types. And that gives you confidence."

The HCT Group now has hundreds of employees, depots, a fleet of hundreds of vehicles and a 2013/14 turnover of over £40 million

– compared to £202,000 in 1993. It runs several key bus routes in London and delivers tens of millions of trips each year across the UK.

Its community services are similarly diverse. There is low-cost minibus hire; YourCar, a low-cost alternative to minicab hire, especially for people with disabilities or mobility difficulties that regular minicabs cannot cater for. There is minibus driver training; Route 812 is a community-designed hail-and-ride route that helps older people and those with disabilities get out and about; and it even provides mobility scooters. A little resistance movement in a once-forgotten part of London has come a long way and still continues to deliver so much for the communities from whence it came.

Throughout, HCT has been hungry to find new ways to help people. The combination of reach, knowhow, history and leadership makes HCT a powerful force for good. Dai looks about his office to his windowsill and spots a small glass award shifted to one side, a rectangular shape almost invisible in the sunlight that streams through his large square window. "I was thinking about how to describe what we do. And it was only when we got this, in 2004, that I realised what we were." He reaches over to pick it up. "I'd never heard of this before and then this came and look what it says here. BEST SOCIAL ENTERPRISE 2004. So that's what we are, I thought. A social enterprise."

So it is. Its home, once one of London's most deprived boroughs, is now home to a mixed community with an upwardly mobile core who both live alongside and at odds with the poor who occupy vast disappearing estates. It was just south of here that television chef Jamie Oliver's Fifteen restaurant emerged, encouraging kids who lived on estates on the Kingsland Road, which connects Hackney to the money-hungry City of London, to leave those estates and move into the kitchen of a chic restaurant with smart leather sofas out front.

At the same time, warehouse spaces host everything from gardening clubs to industrial designers to upcycling classes. This is a highly recognisable, highly stylised version of modern urban living, for better or worse, and it is sorely unequal.

Much has changed about Hackney and much has changed about HCT. Their stories are intimately connected, a sort of urban economic parable that is part of the living fabric of the community. Social entrepreneurship is that process of creating stories from the fabric of cities and communities, stories of hope and indomitability; ingenuity and love. They belong to the places from which they spring.

It amounts in sum to a determination to harness the singular beauty of where you live, wherever that is. Walking past Hackney's identikit new luxury developments makes the knowledge that enterprises like HCT and HCD exist that much more comforting. If your goal is to help your fellow citizens in the community or city you love, goodwill is like gold dust.

Pirate stores, robot supplies and more

As I was finishing this book, I got into a conversation with social entrepreneurs in Manchester in the UK, who wanted to create a social enterprise city there, who were soliciting ideas and undertaking conversations within the community. Great idea. Social enterprise cities are on the march. What each new project will look like, how it will reflect that community's unique identity, its population, their touch points, their learning centres, their assets and their pride: this is to be discovered.

Creativity, artistry and design: all of these things make successful social enterprise cities places we want to hang out and be part of. Someone who understands this is author and activist Dave Eggers, best known as a bestselling novelist. He is also a social entrepreneur, who set up an organisation called 826 Valencia.

826 Valencia is a really interesting public service social enterprise[16] that began when Eggers was looking for a venue to house the fledgling tutoring centre he wanted to create for schoolchildren This was one project in his wider campaign to increase the quality

of literary education across the entire socioeconomic spectrum of young children in the US, a campaign which was no doubt influenced by his own experiences as a twenty-something raising his younger brother Toph.

Eggers saw this as a place where he could link together writers he knew who worked flexibly and needed a space to work with children who needed some help with their reading. He and his friend Ninive Calegari found a space at the eponymous address that his small publishing company and tutoring centre could share. But they were told that the space was appropriated for retail use. Instead of looking again, they pivoted. They decided to turn it into a pirate shop, by which I mean a shop that sold items and accessories that could help you look like or act like or get with the general vibe of being a high-seas voyaging pirate.

A pirate shop – with its skull-and-crossbones dice, copious supply of eyepatches, apothecary that sells scurvy cures – was one thing. But this was a pirate shop with a further twist. It offered tutoring classes behind its facade.

Eggers and Calegari retained the idea of using the space to help with their social endeavour. Using the pirate shop as their hook, they built a social enterprise that would draw children in. They connected their network of writers with teachers and parents and set it up so that remedial students could be referred. The pirate shop in time would become more than a remedial class, it would become a hang out.

When a New York chapter of 826 – 826NYC – opened in 2004 it had its own spin on this story. It was built with the Brooklyn Superhero Supply Co out front. The shop sold photon-shooters and invisibility potions, and the reading group was hidden behind a trick bookshelf. Other 826 chapters each had a unique storefront, from the 'time travel Mart' in Los Angeles' Echo Park to the 'Liberty Street Robot Supply and Repair' in Ann Arbor. Each centre, each place has an identity all of its own.

Social enterprise sits at the heart of the city. Travel from one social enterprise city to another and you find distinct ways of connecting industry and community; culture and design. Each comprises thousands of diverse, constant conversations between social entrepreneurs and the metropolis.

Movements for good make their homes in these places; take time to rest there, recharge, reinvent themselves anew. Then they get up and go to work reforming our institutions and improving our lives all over. They show us the wonders of spirit and generosity that are right on our doorstep, the good things that emerge from the most unexpected places. From the hotels that give back to the café on your corner that employs your city's disaffected and dispossessed, it's all happening here, right here in the heart of the place we call home.

The bull market of greater good:

fact, fiction and the rise of big-money activism

... knavish in its practice and treason in its publick. (Daniel Defoe, under alias A. Jobber, writing of the stock market[1])

If Coca-Cola can sell billions of sodas and McDonald's can sell billions of burgers, why can't Aravind sell millions of sight-restoring operations? (Dr Govindappa Venkataswamy, Founder, Aravind Eyecare[2])

One per cent for God

Accompany us now to the middle of the 15th century, to Perugia, Italy, where a crucial moment in the history of the moral marketplace is about to take place.

This is a time of great energy and learning and development in the human condition. The renaissance of art and culture, driven by the invention and dissemination of the printing press, is underway. Vestiges of the medieval persist. At this time 'usury' – the lending of money at interest – is forbidden. But the many contradictions of this time are about to yield a fascinating instance of financial and social innovation.

The Church is one of the main money lenders here and creates a loop hole for rich Christians, whereby they would seek 'indulgences' from the Church by giving money to the Church directly as part of their transaction. *Per Messer Domeneddio,* they called it: 1% for God. The poor have no such provision. Then, around 1460, orders of Franciscan monks began to preach a new idea, sparked from experiments conducted in England. They argued for the rich to give into a series of financial funds that could in turn help the poor. The *Monte di pieta* or 'Mounts of Piety' were born.

The *Monte di pieta* offered cheap loans for nominal pawns – a hat or a knife were typical – paid for by a network of levies on larger loans to richer Christians. A manageable interest rate was agreed with those who received the loans. Any profits from the resulting scheme went to the church and paid for the *massaido* – the clerks that would administer the system.

The *Monte di pieta* quickly spread and were soon adopted by other orders. Here was a very simple example of an almsgiving institution doing something more than simply giving alms.

From obscure beginnings in the distant past, this technique ripened into the modern microfinance movement. The parallels with the *Monte di pieta* and the small loans of microfinance, which are often made to village-dwelling women whose farm or craft work barely raises enough for an evening meal, are immediately clear.

Many pioneers in the microfinance field remixed and remade the idea. On the ground, activist networks gave the movement access to some of the poorest areas ignored by traditional providers of financial services.

Investors like eBay founder Pierre Omidyar and Mexican Carlos Labarthe saw the potential, were buoyed by the promise of access to new markets and interesting solutions to serious social problems. Microfinance pioneer Professor Muhammad Yunus's robust advocacy kept microfinance at the top of the lucrative development agenda. A steady stream of research and development saw the whole movement balloon.

From the holy yet humble beginnings of the *Monte di pieta* in 15th century Italy, through the incubation stage created by Yunus and others, these swells of interest and innovation in our time means that microfinance is worth tens of billions worldwide.

You start with an idea, you develop it, you nurture it and you help it grow to some sort of sustainable point, in pursuit of some ambitious vision of the way that the world should be. The next stage, that of expansion and growth via financial markets, has historically eluded social revolutionaries and community movements despite the injunctions of its deepest thinkers.

No more. A social movement slouches our way that promises the assistance of capital markets to any organisation that wants to take its wares to the world. It comes from the boardroom, the trading floor, the connections of the world wide web. Its scope is truly massive; perhaps unnervingly so. It promises expansion and growth for the greatest social causes of our time, but for a price. This chapter tells its story, the story of the place where the high-minded treat with high finance.

Microfinance in focus

One of the first modern microfinanciers was Accion in South America. Its lofty aim was to use a bit of credit and a 'handful of seeds', as its supporters evocatively put it, to enable the poor to become entrepreneurs.

Muhammed Yunus's Grameen Bank was the first truly well-known global microfinance brand. At the time of writing, Yunus's Grameen Bank has thousands of branches in Bangladesh. There it lends out more than US$100 million a month, from loans of less than US$10 for people in its 'Struggling Members' programme, to small business loans of some US$1,000.[3]

Even today, these banks' clientele remains the opposite of most others: those with no chance of credit. They are found most often in rural or very poor inner city areas, and are sought out and helped by Grameen outreach workers.

For many providers, microfinance would become more than just a way of distributing money. Yunus and his peers soon found that through the distribution of capital, social norms could be changed. Yunus crystallised the behaviours that he contended were most positive to enforce in what he referred to as '16 decisions' by which his borrowers would be compelled to abide (see Figure 7.1). The cultural frame of reference remains the rural Bangladeshi women that were his original clientele. Still the decisions give fascinating insight into the moral mindset of the Grameen approach.

Development and debate

Over time, new financiers would enter the microfinance space with different ideas and priorities. eBay founder Pierre Omidyar was particularly enthused by the model and the potential for for-profit microfinance institutions to grow and be sustainable while helping those without access to financial services at the same time.

A division formed. One part of the industry remained resolutely non-profit, adhering to the community development principles of Yunus. Another moved resolutely towards the idea of delivering a service and making its delivery sustainable: the left and right of the social entrepreneur equation dividing an industry. Different balances of these two persuasions could be noted in any number of different shades in hundreds of institutions in many of the poorest countries in the world.

At base most microfinance approaches share common characteristics. They charge far more interest than a standard bank account or credit card (typically from 10 to 120%) and far less than a loan shark (whose interest rates rise in excess of 200%), largely because of the unpredictable nature of those to whom loans are made.

Figure 7.1 Grameen Bank's 16 Decisions

1. We shall follow and advance the four principles of Grameen Bank: Discipline, Unity, Courage and Hard work – in all walks of our lives.
2. Prosperity we shall bring to our families.
3. We shall not live in dilapidated houses. We shall repair our houses and work towards constructing new houses at the earliest.
4. We shall grow vegetables all the year round. We shall eat plenty of them and sell the surplus.
5. During the plantation seasons, we shall plant as many seedlings as possible.
6. We shall plan to keep our families small. We shall minimize our expenditures. We shall look after our health.
7. We shall educate our children and ensure that they can earn to pay for their education.
8. We shall always keep our children and the environment clean.
9. We shall build and use pit-latrines.
10. We shall drink water from tubewells. If it is not available, we shall boil water or use alum.
11. We shall not take any dowry at our sons' weddings, neither shall we give any dowry at our daughters' wedding. We shall keep our centre free from the curse of dowry. We shall not practice child marriage.
12. We shall not inflict any injustice on anyone, neither shall we allow anyone to do so.
13. We shall collectively undertake bigger investments for higher incomes.
14. We shall always be ready to help each other. If anyone is in difficulty, we shall all help him or her.
15. If we come to know of any breach of discipline in any centre, we shall all go there and help restore discipline.
16. We shall take part in all social activities collectively.

Source: Grameen Bank, **http://www.grameen.com/16-decisions/**

Yunus mitigates his risk by lending in groups, so that every member of the group is responsible for ensuring every other members' payment and if one group member fails, the entire group is said to fail. This has been touted as pioneering in some quarters, a model of civic and community engagement.

At other times, a darker picture is painted. As film-maker Lorian James Delman's 2007 microfinance documentary *Easy Money* put it,

> The women leave the same way they came: single-file, silently, orderly, obediently… To achieve the high repayment rates the MFIs [Microfinance Investment Vehicles] target, the ethos of self-help groups needs to be one of compliance and conformity, and not one of social empowerment and transformation.

Yunus's opponents, including the Mexican microfinancier Carlos Labarthe, criticise the former's 'cultural agenda' while Yunus criticises Omidyar and his fellow profit-seekers for seeking profit. The objects of his ire include Indian for-profit microfinanciers SKS, now renamed Bharat Financial Inclusion, whose vehicle floated on the stock market at the same time as protests organised massed against it in Andhra Pradesh for some of its heavy-handed practices for '(making) money from the poor'.[4] Huge payouts to executives following the stock market float were accompanied simultaneously by media stories of suicides and tough regulations.

In December 2009, the Centre for Giving and Philanthropy (CGAP) organisation named 91 active microfinance investment vehicles. By 2015, gross loan portfolios stood at US$65 billion.[5] And it is not as if microfinance has reached its limit: billions of adults still lack access to financial services.

From debate to data

What we know is that data, analysis and hard research are crucial. A whole body of knowledge has been created that seeks to contribute to these debates beyond the headlines and the anecdotes, to create arguments for and against, and create useful tools for analysis.

Take the profit question. Are for-profit microfinance organisations like those of Omidyar or Labarthe's highly profitable Banco Compartemetos by definition less trustworthy than not-for-profit microfinance organisations? How are we to tell if something has become a thing merely of exploitation, which can produce such burdensome interest repayments that poor and vulnerable borrowers have gone as far as to commit suicide to avoid the mess in which they have found themselves?

Several models have been proposed that seek to answer this question, most notably by Yunus himself. They take into account operating costs, interest rates and local conditions to create a scale for microfinance institutions.

The Yunus model was quite simple and ran as follows: if you are a real micro-lender who cares about the poor, then your interest margin (the difference between the rate you charge when lending to your clients and the rate you have to pay when you borrow from your funding sources) should be no more than 10%, *a green zone*, where true pro-poor micro-lenders operate. If your interest margin is 10–15%, a big warning sign is flashing because you're in the yellow zone. Anything above 15% is the red zone, where you've left true microcredit behind and you are nothing better than a loan shark.

Apply this analysis to the field and the results are eye opening. A study conducted by Adrian Gonzalez at the Microfinance Information eXchange (MIX) suggested that most of the world's microfinanciers at the time were in the red zone. The average interest rate spread for microfinance institutions (MFIs) in 2008 was over 20%.[6]

Grameen didn't fare a great deal better. In the same survey Grameen's microfinance partners were tested and came up short. The study's convenor describes:

In 2007, for instance, 33 MFIs (representing about two thirds of the Grameen Foundation recipients) reported to the MIX. The only one in the green zone that year (interest spread below 10%) was Grameen Bank itself. Seven were in the yellow warning zone (10–15%). All the other 25 were up in the red zone (above 15%) and most of them way up in the red zone (between 30 and 55%). The three preceding years looked pretty much the same.

Interestingly, non-profit MFIs were more likely to be in the red zone than for-profit MFIs. Whether this was because not-for-profits invested in more inefficient loans in poorer communities and so are forced to raise their interest rates was unclear, though the study did find that the average loan size in the non-profit variants is about a third of what it is in for-profit MFIs, which may provide some explanation (smaller loans will often be taken by those who are greater credit risks and so will have higher interest rates attached to them in order to mitigate that risk).

MIX gave balance to the findings as follows, 'The Grameen partner MFIs that looked so terrible on the green-yellow-red test actually appeared quite strong—in fact, well above average—on indicators normally thought to be associated with commitment to the poor, such as average loan size.' Nor did they appear to be inefficient: their overheads per borrower were far lower than the other MFIs in their countries. Yunus's test alone, without explanation, without story, was a blunt instrument. A richer debate is always a better one.

The big picture

The movement as a whole remains the target of critics and here we see a foreshadowing of some of the criticisms of other social investment movements. Economists Milford Bateman and Ha Joon Chang characterised microfinance as 'a neoliberal fairytale' in a hard-hitting critique that attacked the 'hubris' of its purveyors, whose metrics for success, in some quarters appeared to rest upon turnover as some sort of proxy for life change.[7]

There is something to this view. Consider: a microfinance organisation in Bogota referred to a very poor client living in a bedsit in a slum, whose home-based business had gone from defaulting regularly on the loans the microfinancier gave her, to paying on time, every time and appearing increasingly well turned out as a result. A huge success until one realises that her business was supplemented by her own prostitution. The increasing success of one had led to more time for the other. The business did indeed last longer, but we need not be excessively prudish to realise that these entrepreneurs were getting their definition of success wrong. Paying back a loan is not evidence of success; life improvement is. Getting someone to pay back a loan is only evidence that you've got them working for you. The had committed the cardinal sin: forgetting about the beneficiary.

Bateman and Chang suggest that microfinance has indeed left behind the people it was supposed to help. The movement, it is said, has followed the inexorable logic of the market, forsaken the ear to the ground and the primacy in all of this of its social purpose.

At is best, microfinance is a social cause, a philosophical debate, a rich conversation, infused by data, philosophy and practice; finance and field work; and people's life stories first and foremost. We have targets and measures, the ledgers of finance and they are a crucial part of the picture but they are not the only part.

It is not 'the answer'. Muhammad Yunus spoke of his 'Museum of Poverty' which by the year 2000 would contain the artefacts of a bygone time when people were once poor, where now, through microfinance, they were saved. Microfinance was never the single silver bullet that would puncture the heart of the problems we see around the world today and it was never going to be.

Yet, it continues to grow and diversify. It is found online in variations like kiva.org. It still has potential as billions of the world's poorest remain unbanked. It has its contradictions but it has given us a heck of a lot of data with which to develop our knowledge – and solve other social problems besides. This is a useful approach for proponents and critics of other such social finance innovations to adopt; innovations pertaining to ethical, responsible and social impact investment that form the substance of our inquiries in this chapter.

The rise of ethical and responsible investment

A short story for adults, written in 1968 by Roald Dahl, tells of a food critic of grotesque disposition and physique who gets into a tasting competition with a stock 'jobber' over a lavish meal.

The narrator of this contest is a fellow guest. Despite the odiousness of the critic, he gives both barrels to the financier, 'He knew in his heart of hearts he was nothing more than a personable, infinitely unctuous bookmaker, and he seemed almost embarrassed that he had managed to accumulate so much money with so little talent.'[8]

The financial exchanges were just about always regarded as the domain of spivs and scoundrels. The stock exchange in the UK began when in 1694 King William III first allowed government borrowing to be transferred from one person to another. Stock jobbers, who operated in Sweetings Alley in London and in a nearby café called Jonathan's, made money from these transactions. *Robinson Crusoe* and *Moll Flanders* author Daniel Defoe, using the alias 'a jobber', referred to this trade as 'knavish in its practice and treason in its publick'.[9]

By the time of the stock market crash of 1929, it was sufficiently powerful to bring the world economy to a standstill and with it ruin millions of lives.

Alongside this persistent narrative another lesser known trope has emerged: that of the *good banker*.

By this, I don't mean the 'banker to the poor' image that microfinance icons like Muhammad Yunus cultivate. I don't mean the archetypal successful banker who makes a great deal of money and then gives a portion of it to charity. There are more subtle ideas and more convincing ideas that sit behind this 'good banker' trope.

One such goes something like this. Bankers deal with unimaginable sums of money in complex ways. So, if we have not talentless scoundrels, but thoughtful, ethical types at the helm, the disciplines of banking might be capable of doing real good. The ingenuity and engineering that yields money from money might help social causes too.

And even if we do not have thoughtful, ethical types at the helm, what if financial incentives could be engineered in this direction and so impel capital towards the grass-roots causes that matter?

If to Dahl or Defoe – or indeed to any number of us – this idea might seem like Alice-like in its unreality, the history of such investments provides at least a pause for thought.

Many religious groups, including the Methodists and Quakers, have travelled this course. They are prolific investors with strong moral purposes attached to that investment, and they created significant financial institutions to pursue those ends.

The Quakers were responsible for the foundation of Friends Provident in 1832 as a mutually owned 'friendly society' providing life insurance for its members. Over the next 140 years, Friends Provident refused to invest in or have anything to do with the arms industry, alcohol, tobacco and gambling. Methodist churches followed a similar approach when they established an investment fund in 1960.[10]

By the late 1970s and early 1980s, this type of finance found a new generation of champions. There was rising awareness about the parlous state of the environment, labour conditions in the developing world, a willingness not to support repressive regimes, for example apartheid era South Africa, and opposition to the damaging health effects of tobacco.

Companies that supported these ills were targeted for 'divestment' by the socially conscious rich and investing middle classes. More investors demanded more information on who was involved in parts of the financial system and the investment chains that bring it together. By this time, there was even a catch-all term for this activity: *ethical investment.*

Ethical investment has been the object of study of a number of practitioners, analysts, academics and authors. Briefly, it involves a screening process. The investor sits down with her manager and together they create a strategy that 'screens out' investments in things that they find objectionable.

The line is walked between filtering out things that do social harm – but which are often very profitable, such as weapons manufacture – and ensuring that the overall portfolio is stable and not prone to ups and downs in value and return, or 'volatility'.

The infrastructure around this industry has become extremely sophisticated. It has been aided somewhat by government edict, such as the UK government's edict that managers take some heed of ethical and responsible investment principles from the 1990s onwards.[11] But its spread is also a direct consequence of a heightened awareness among the public of the existence of such funds and their willingness to support them.[12]

In 2014 I helped lead an inquiry on behalf of the UK's charity leaders, chaired by UK pensions supremo Martin Clarke, into the ethical investment market for charity investments – far smaller in volume than the funds of businesses but significant nonetheless – following a British documentary that suggested that anti-arms, pro-development charities such as Comic Relief had funds invested in other funds which had investments in arms.

Similar concern was raised when the Church of England was found to have invested in funds that drew profit from payday lending loan sharks – while at the same time the Archbishop of Canterbury in public denounced some of the practices of online payday lenders. The point is that even charities are expected to be on top of this area; certainly that was my recommendation.[13]

As the ethical investment idea grew, the associated trade in ethical information grew with it. A number of industry associations and social research organisations began to publish ethical performance information on companies. For example in the UK, the UK

Social Investment Forum (UKSIF) was established in 1991. The so-called Ethical Investment Research Services (EIRIS) began to expand significantly after its creation in 1983. During the 1990s, companies that voluntary reported on social and environmental issues became more commonplace. A number of new ethical investment funds emerged and the UK's first ethical 'unit trust' – the Friends Provident Stewardship Unit Trust – arrived in 1984.[14]

Financiers over time sought to create separate, objective indices of companies that conformed to certain ethical principles. Thus the ethical counterpart to the Financial Times Stock Exchange (FTSE) was born as the FTSE4GOOD, an exchange consisting of companies that conformed to certain ethical criteria. FTSE4GOOD allows investors and managers and even traders and private customers who care about ethical concerns to find kindred companies.

There are codes and practices for managers who work to these themes. Government legislated to normalise these ideas and urged their application to UK pension funds; not everyone through that was a good idea; not everyone trusted it.

Said one trustee,

> 'I think it entirely wrong that government should try to make pension funds into the social conscience of the financial community. If government thinks something is wrong ... then it should have the guts to legislate and not leave trustees to do it for them.'[15]

Similar concerns that managers pay lip service to this rule with boilerplate statements of ethical or responsible practice abound.

At the same time, parallel developments have sought to make an alternative claim: that adhering to 'responsible' practice is not only good in a moral sense, but also good in terms of its shareholder performance.

A note, at this point, on the jargon. 'Responsible' in this context means something slightly different from 'ethical'. A scruple-light investor may wish to purchase a particular stock in a polluting industry in a particular country, but if that country is about to pass legislation to limit pollution, then the value of that stock might be about to plummet.

So while an investment manager screening 'ethically' does so primarily on the basis of the investor's choices, a 'responsible' investment manager will assess for these sorts of concerns, not necessarily out of moral obligation, but good practice. If 'screening' requires positive moral choices, then responsible investment offers a vanilla version that allows, so its protagonists contended, the incentives of society and the investor to be aligned.

The United Nations Principles of Responsible Investment are designed to encompass and crystallise that idea. By 2009, 881 companies were signatories of the principles, up 30% from 2008, representing US$22 trillion assets under management, a significant proportion – though much less than half of all the world's managed money. By 2015 it was up to around US$59 trillion and considerably more than half.[16]

Perhaps most importantly for the funds' continued longevity, it could be argued that investing in ethical funds did not necessarily mean losing money. In the UK, for example, through 2012 the top ten ethical funds achieved annual gains between 13.6% and 19.4%, compared to the FTSE, which rose by 14.3%. From 2009 to 2012 the top ethical funds rose by between 33% and 57%, compared to the FTSE which rose by 28%. Ever increasing public awareness and interest in ethical and environmental issues such as climate change, organic foods, ethical behaviour, pollution and renewable energy have undoubtedly influenced would-be investors.

All of this development is very interesting, subject to a few concerns. The biggest: is all of this actually making a positive difference to the world around us? Does this industry actually have a social impact? Or is all this endeavour and effort, with its ledgers and its funds and its consultants, more mirage than genuine force for good?

The industry has many fervent advocates; yet some experts are not so sure. I spoke to Catherine Howarth, who remains unconvinced by the whole thing. She advocates for an alternative approach of active dialogue with companies, as the boss of ShareAction, an organisation that attends annual general meetings (AGMs) on an investor's behalf and argues for pro-social and environmental practices.

She lamented the reluctance of large fund managers to turn up at AGMs to raise such issues. "Investment managers have an interest in being cautious rather than radical so you need to look to others to put these concerns on the agenda," she told me. "You need to look elsewhere then if you want to make a difference."

Her approach has many admirers. There are organisations like Howarth's placing strategic questions on behalf of campaign groups or consumers, lobbying directors to change behaviour and insisting on reports against environmental or social targets. The practices of oil company Shell have been among those targeted by shareholder activists in recent years.

"It's a democratic approach to investing," said Howarth. "We're saying that you can make a difference to these huge corporations. You don't just have to worry about whether your money is improving the world but you actually see that you can play a direct role in 'civilising' – if you like – a corporation."

Howarth is an energetic and infectious social entrepreneur, not five and a half foot in height, with a shock of red hair. She has seen the investment space – and what she refers to as the conservative figures within it – up close. Her approach requires a radical sort of rhetoric because the subject matter is so apt to be confused and shrouded.

The space is awash with contradictions. One fund manager's 'ethical' is the devil itself to another. One person's investment in sustainable agriculture is another's investment in a crop-producing regime that legitimises institutional hatred: think Outspan oranges in apartheid-era South Africa. Palestinian olive oil competes with vegetables from Israel: in which do you choose not to invest? There is no end to the potential for discomfort.

Investing in fracking is pillaging the countryside to one, but guaranteeing the national energy supply and security to another. And that is before we begin to get on to private investments in abortion clinics or other frontiers of various culture wars, for which different investors and fund managers will have different criteria, each of which they may refer to as ethical or responsible – or not.

To some investment managers it remains a question of what one can 'get away with' while fulfilling the fiduciary duty to make as much money as possible. Any dialogue with communities, any sense of popular empowerment is conspicuous in its absence from the conversation, save for when people like Howarth have the microphone.

Given all of this, ethical investment was only ever going to be the smallest of starts on the journey towards bringing the markets and morality into alignment; was indeed only the broadest of fields from within which truly radical financial and social movements might emerge.

Impact investment

Where ethical investors sought to do no harm, *social impact investors* (there are many interchangeable terms for what they do: social investment, impact investment, social impact investment: it is all the same) went further. They sought *not only to do no harm, but actually to do good*.

Their idea can be expressed in even more simple terms still: as an investor, all you have to do to make the world a better place is invest in social enterprise.

Arthur Wood of the Ashoka Foundation explained it me as follows:

> "With conventional investments, you make returns of around say 4–5 per cent, a 'market return'. With philanthropy, you make returns of negative 100 per cent, in other words you give it all away. There is rarely

> a middle way between these two grounds. But why should that be so? Making social impact investments, low return, sometimes no-return deals over longer periods of time in uncertain marketplaces may overall yield you less than 4% but you are likely to at least get your capital back and a little bit more and that may make it attractive."

Renewable energy companies are examples of commercial concerns with vast investment potential often backed by public subsidy of some kind that seek to make the world a better place. They are ripe for investment. Housing co-operatives and associations, with obvious bricks and mortar asset bases, are other areas that offer huge potential: that make solid and sometimes spectacular social impact investments. Companies like social enterprise transport juggernaut HCT, too: it owned a fleet of buses, a host of contracted routes and the infrastructure to support them, all of which was eminently investable.

HCT's West London counterpart, Ealing Community Transport (ECT) also has an interesting story to tell in this regard. It went through a similar process of growth to HCT but at the same time diversified hugely, notably into recycling services, which encouraged people to separate their waste themselves (revolutionary stuff in those days). Another one that was ripe for investment, with the assets and also the subsidy offered by local government as solid collateral.

Social impact investment is not completely new. The Commonwealth Development Corporation in the UK, established in 1948, invests in the poorer countries of the developing world and attracts other investors through their track record.

The International Finance Corporation was created in 1956 to foster private sector investment in emerging nations. Prudential, alongside its ethical investments, has a long tradition of making investments that attempt to support and improve communities. It established a formal social investments programme in 1976 and invested more than US$1 billion since then.

The fundamentals were there. And then came the great recession of 2008–09. A gently rising interest in social enterprise and the social impact investment that might support them suddenly found a new gear.

It is not difficult to see why. Picture the scene: banks are going under, governments are struggling to pay bills. A new way of paying for good causes at scale emerges. A report from a respected bank says that investments like these will be worth US$1 trillion over the next ten years and are cited as having a profit opportunity of about 70% of that: such was the value placed on the sector's head by JP Morgan in a 2010 report.[17] The assumptions of this report have been tested and found wanting since then; the hype it created at the time was undeniable. Even the *Economist*, usually relatively sanguine about such matters, heralded its arrival as 'the birth of a virtuous new asset class'.[18]

In a relatively short space of time, social impact investment began to engage in a huge variety of change-making endeavours. Investors, analysts, academics, charity leaders, and even politicians began in no small number to question the extent to which complex kinds of finance reserved once for companies could enter the domain of the social entrepreneur. Equity investments – buying up chunks of social enterprises that have entrepreneurial promise – special loans with decent interest rates, overdrafts for social enterprises and entrepreneurs that allow them to bridge and expand, a thousand interesting variations in between would all be possible.

Today, big banks, major charities and large metropolitan authorities enter these waters. There are investments in healthcare in developing countries where corruption may be endemic and government sponsorship of public services remains fraught as a result. A private investment can make all the difference here.

We see clusters of investment in particular areas. The UN states that almost 1 billion people worldwide do not have access to clean water, despite annual global expenditures in the hundreds of billions. Yet the economics and logistics of water, especially in hot places, places ravaged by climate change, are hard. Humanitarian disasters of increasing scale and frequency can only be avoided by a concerted investment over time and social impact investors have found a niche here, not necessarily in building large infrastructure but in helping understand which fixes work and which do not.

Monitor Inclusive Markets, a think tank dedicated to this space, studied the market in India in particular, and found that filtration units attached at the tap can often be too expensive for poor populations. According to Monitor, filtration attached at the water source, often a well, provides access to purified water at about half the price of – and at about a third of the cost – of boiled water.

Different forms of social entrepreneurship require different kinds of investment. For example, investments in bottom of the pyramid social enterprises have been aided by simple finance, easily available and comprehensible, offering investors access to new markets in the process. Investing in social entrepreneurs of other kinds yield myriad financial and social opportunities. There is finance for expansion, premises, programmes or equipment. There are more complex forms too that social entrepreneurs work into their models.

What does this all look like in practice? A great example of this involves one of the seminal names in social enterprise: Aravind Eye Care.[19]

The ascent of Aravind

Aravind began in India, when in 1976 a retired ophthalmologist named Dr Govindappa Venkataswamy, or 'Dr V' went to work for the last time. After a long career helping the sick, he was saddened by the enduring blindness that blighted his rural clientele. He believed that one's sight should be a right. His vision was of an alternative healthcare provider that would allow most of the very poorest blind people to access the operations they needed for free, with only a minority paying based on ability to pay.

Aravind Eye Care was born. Its beginning was difficult. Eye surgery is complex and expensive. A US expert named David Green, then a fundraiser for the Seva Foundation, successfully raised large volumes of in-kind donations of intraocular lenses (IOLs) from the USA. With this ingredient, Aravind grew at low cost. Meanwhile, it worked at improving its processes, succeeded in redesigning the surgery process, creating a 20-minute low-cost eye operation that worked.

The problem came when the gifts ran dry. IOLs dried up in the late 1980s. The high cost of IOLs in the market, in excess of US$125 each, threatened everything.[20]

Green's response to this new problem was to help establish a non-profit organisation, Aurolab, as the manufacturing division of Aravind Eye Care. After months of research, Aurolab discovered a way of manufacturing high quality IOLs at affordable prices at about US$5 a pair.

Since 1992, Aurolab has supplied millions of lenses to its customers in India and to over 120 other countries worldwide. It uses a cross-subsidy social enterprise model. Charging higher prices to wealthier patients makes subsidies to the poor possible, offering them care at low or no cost, connecting rich and poor in one action. Indeed in 2009, Aravind centres treated about two thirds of their patients for free.

The process was designed to ensure that this price structure kept the business solvent. Every patient receives the same quality cataract operation; however, patients who are treated for free are placed in lower-quality accommodation than paying patients. To get access to better post-operative facilities, those who can do choose to pay the full rate. Given its low cost base and secure access to core components, the Aravind cataract model is sustainable and indeed in theory very profitable.

David Green had found his niche. Instead of retreating back to the USA, he began to consult with other eye care systems around the world. In Egypt, Green was introduced to ophthalmologist Akef El Maghraby; together they developed what became the largest eye care programme in the Middle East, The El Maghraby Eye and Ear Hospitals and Centers.

Social impact investors would add another chapter to this story. The Deutsche Bank Americas Foundation would work with Aravind to create a US$15.8 million 'Eye Fund' established in collaboration with the Ashoka Foundation.

The Ashoka Foundation introduced the bank to a network of frontline organisations and hospitals, operating in sync with Aravind. The bank started this fund as means to raise capital for hospital equipment and expansion. It did so with a relatively small outlay; with just US$1 million, Deutsche Bank was not the largest investor in the fund. But it created an infrastructure that allowed many similar investors to jump in, multiplying the fund value in turn. Deutsche took a profit; its return at this stage, according to then CEO Gary Hattem, was 1%, a relatively small price to pay for such a large injection of capital.

This was a seminal, easy to understand example of a major bank getting involved in social impact investment, with one of the great social enterprises of our era.

The Aravind network today performs hundreds of thousands of eye surgeries each year.

There are broadband connections in rural telecentres that call doctors in city hospitals who can provide instant diagnosis to villagers affected by difficulties. Camps in rural areas screen thousands of patients weekly.

There are eye specialists who are trained in one form of eye surgery, which means that more surgeries can be delivered without the costs of training a high volume of doctors for the decades it usually takes.

The opportunity for further expansion, with this experience banked, is considerable. "We are going from village to village to provide eye care to the unreached," said Aravind's chair, Dr P. Namperumalsamy in a recent interview.[21] Dr V's mantra was even more simple. As he quipped once to a journalist: "If Coca-Cola can sell billions of sodas and McDonald's can sell billions of burgers, why can't Aravind sell millions of sight-restoring operations?"

Aravind today is a *bona fide* centre of excellence. It is an international training centre for ophthalmic professionals and trainees who come from within India and around the world. It is an institute for research that contributes to the development of eye care and to the training of health-related and managerial personnel in the development and implementation of eye care programmes. It is a manufacturer of world-class ophthalmic products. And social impact investment helps it reach its goals.

It is a much-loved social enterprise, and the social impact investment Deutsche Bank put together for them is but one in a burgeoning 'bull market of the greater good'.

Capitalist criticisms

It is 2012 and I am watching Sir Ronald Cohen speak at the London Business School about the potential of social impact investment to fix big social problems, not only in developing countries, but in developed countries too. His message is clear: if we build the social impact investment market and push it to expansion using the tools and strategies of venture capital finance we can create hitherto unthinkable sums for social good.

Softly spoken Cohen is a significant figure in the history of this movement. He was a founder-director of the British Venture Capital Association, a founder-director of the European Venture Capital Association. He was chair of the G8 taskforce on social investment, an academic, an advisor. Of Egyptian descent, he is a one-time liberal political candidate, at home in the worlds of politics as in the world of finance, with his bookish glasses, white hair, svelte frame and sharp suit.

In 2002 he was appointed to be the head of then UK Prime Minister Tony Blair's so-called Social Investment Task Force. He believed community development finance, microfinance and other kinds of social impact investment could help bridge widening inequalities in advanced economies by working hand-in-glove with governments. He drew on several examples in his report,[22] notably from the USA. Specialist community development finance had grown considerably there, aided by legislation such as the Community Reinvestment Act, which mandated commercial finance institutions to meet community needs, which in turn encouraged financial innovation. Community real estate investments were eligible for tax credits from the state. There were Calvert Community Investment Notes, which offered a range of community-based options for would be investors. Investors chose the profile of investments underlying their notes, targeting specific geographical regions and programmatic areas.

Similar innovation stimulated by government action could be seen in the Netherlands. Triodos Bank's strapline is 'not greed but green' and it has another variant on how government and specialist intermediaries work together. Its green fund has levered hundreds of millions of dollars into Dutch social causes, thanks to a combination of careful pricing and government sponsored tax breaks that increase the incentive for would-be investors.[23]

One of the recommendations of the Cohen report was that the UK find its own way of bringing together these ideas, getting government to stimulate this space, and build something pioneering to make the running. From here sprang Bridges Ventures, the UK's social impact investment pioneer.[24]

Bridges used public money as a catalyst in order to raise new private capital for businesses that operate in the poorest 25% of communities in the UK, investing around £10 million a time in socially beneficial businesses with strong profit potential. £20 million of government money was used as cornerstone investment for its first fund, which was focused on regeneration. Another £20 million was raised on the back of public money in the private sector. A second fund successfully raised £75 million from the private sector alone on the back of the track record of the first fund. This work was directly responsible for creating a network of community development finance institutions across the UK to lend to the poorest people.

That was only the start of the journey, a proof-of-concept, if you will. Now Cohen conceived of a new body, with government weight behind it, that would take the market further. It would bring all this work together, incubate ideas and new financial instruments take them to the wider financial markets, pumping them with capital and creating something genuinely world-changing: the first complex financial marketplace in the world that supports ambitious social action, the counter-intuitive idea first envisaged by Ashoka's Bill Drayton.

Today that body exists. It invests in intermediaries or collaborative projects, which funnel capital to projects on the ground. In return it takes a chunk of each. It is based in a smart set of offices in the heart of London. It is the world's first social investment 'wholesale' bank, and it is called Big Society Capital (BSC).[25]

I must confess a slight interest here as I was one of the researchers who worked up the early versions of its plan. Things have moved hugely since my involvement. The BSC of today is a fascinating organisation, truly one of a kind.

I was there as politicians discussed this idea and its implementation, taking notes as part of the research team, ruminating on Cohen's vision. His advocacy was high quality; his ideas were impossible to dismiss.

BSC was to be an independent body, drawing assets from dormant UK bank accounts, money resting in people's old pocket books unclaimed for nearly a generation.

The vision was dynamic and innovative. Take this money (about £600 million), 'pump' it into the market, make it available to social intermediaries who work with social entrepreneurs and watch the investment vehicles they create deliver social and economic value. That £600 million would attract further money, there would be co-investment deals and all sorts of other products that as yet were beyond our ken. We just had to take a leap of faith.

Some of the nooks and crannies of this marketplace were known to us then. Property was always solid. Specific kinds of property, such as property for people with learning disabilities – 'supported housing' as it is known – are rare and if offered can make a tangible difference to a person's quality of life. This is social impact investment material.

Sure enough, the BSC of today has several such investments. Supported housing needs certain tweaks and modifications, has certain services attached to it, may be close to family and friends. Charities can provide supported, serviced housing close to the families and friends of those in need – as long as they have the money. In the absence of such capital, the bricks and mortar of supported housing make excellent collateral.

An organisation called Golden Lane Housing took this idea to market. In 2015 it issued a bond listed on the London Stock Exchange which it used to buy land to adapt 30 properties for people with learning disabilities. It raised around US$15 million initially and would use rental income to take care of management costs and pay interest to those who invested. The bond was convened and capitalised in the first instance by a range of investors including an outfit called Threadneedle, local government and private banks. The project was boosted by money from BSC. Its money aided this project and incentivised others to enter this market and scout for projects like it.

The multiplier effect of working with intermediaries like these creates a wave of innovation. Organisations and relationships are made that endure, track records are created. The result, the promise of BSC and its 'flood' of capital is a 'big bang' for social impact investment. "Supply creates demand," as Cohen put it in his characteristically clipped way.

The idea, as expressed here, had at first many disputers. The original plan for BSC was far from perfect. Practice has refined its model over time; it will continue to do so. A flood of capital is only one part of the puzzle that attends the growth of social organisations; a 'flood' of expertise and support is just as important, as are many other things beside.

Cohen had been here before and rode the criticisms as he worked to get BSC established. He had experience at the forefront of the 'flooding with capital' that created the venture capital market in the UK in the 1970s, which created a boom in investing and supporting start-ups and entrepreneurs. He was clear that the technique really could be repeated here, in the arena of the good. It just needed political will to go with the vision.

Social entrepreneurs like Professor Muhammad Yunus and Sir Ronald Cohen are as adept at pitching their wares as they are at devising them. And so, with just less than a decade since that plan's submission, it is right that we look back at and behind the claims, check against hype.

There are many enduring questions. Would not only the very biggest organisations and businesses – most probably large businesses venturing into the impact arena rather than grassroots charities or social enterprises – benefit from this sort of investment? Do we really want a raft of huge institutional investors skewing the market for social goods by bringing large chunks of capital and taking their cut? How exactly would the voice of the people and communities we are supposed to help be represented in all of this?

Those are just for starters. And it is right, when money and power converge to significantly change something that belongs to the people, that BSC wrestles with these questions.

Commentators have intermittently questioned the ideas that underpin this movement. Polly Toynbee, the British social affairs journalist and commentator, in a fiery radio debate with Cohen raised a practical objection to all this social impact investment: government can borrow and spend in a far simpler way than these complex instruments with their middle men taking out a chunk of cash at every layer. So why bother doing things in this way?

Indeed, you do not have to be a radical lefty, or one who regards bankers as 'knavish or fraudulent' to feel profoundly uncomfortable at all this. Using taxpayers' money as profits for private investors, putting the onus on charities and social enterprises to deliver profits, using 'social targets' as performance indicators that unlock profits as some social bonds do (a positive exam result for a poor kid is just the sort of thing we might see performing this task in future years) seems cold at best, a bad bargain at worst.

It risks placing undue pressure on the imperfect impact calculations and ideas that drive social impact reporting, and even the work of the venture philanthropist. Our mind is cast back to the microfinance experience, the problems vulnerable beneficiaries faced at the hand of overzealous loan administrators hitting financial targets; or the overworked prostitute in Bogota who was doing fine because she repaid her microloan on time. These are problems that destroy lives.

As social impact investment proliferates, so does the risk of people falling under this juggernaut and that is why we need eyes on this movement.

Thus far, there has been very little room for thought or reflection. Few commentators have offered sustained criticism. Those who have followed it have given it room to develop, and this is to the credit of people who may otherwise be uncomfortable with the direction that BSC and its Fellows articulate, but who genuinely want to give it a chance to do good.

Social entrepreneur David Floyd over at the wonderfully named Beanbags and Bullsh!t blog has attempted to do this; to form a sensible counter-narrative in the public interest to the hype that surrounds the new wave in the corridors of power.

Rather than question the entire basis, Floyd in particular has sought to accept the case for social investment while bemoaning the unduly positive narrative and inquiring forensically into the practices of social investors.

At the same time he has attempted to offer services as explainers or translators of the often arcane financial language in which their activities are expressed and renegade thought leadership like The Alternative Commission on Social Investment, co-chaired by Floyd and Dan Gregory of Social Enterprise UK, which reported in 2015, and of which I was part.

Let's heed the call for criticism and take on some of the greater objections here.

Exploitative

We wrote earlier of investments in water. JP Morgan, in its seminal study, estimated the potential market for this particular investment to be US$5–13 billion. Reaching 273 million households over the next ten years resulted in potential revenues of US$29–71 billion.[26] Interesting to a would-be investor, but how accurate were these numbers, how academically rigorous were these models? It is one thing to use the market as an additional source of information to academic data, but who is to hold accountable those huge financial institutions that run their own numbers, enter the space and flex their huge muscles accordingly?

Indeed, should we feel horrified that we are so happily allowing financial elites to wade in on the biggest questions of social justice and poverty alleviation – with a free pass to producing profit-making investments in such interventions?

Analysis is one thing; delivery another. There will be many who will continue to argue that it should not be for private firms to offer such services – water is a right not a commodity. Its provision is the government's job and that is that.

The other side of this urges pragmatism. Many poor communities lack access to government services and often pay a premium to procure basic services from second-rate private sector providers. The opportunities here for innovative, 'first-rate' social businesses to make a difference are immense.

It was academic C.K. Prahalad who compared prices paid in a shanty town outside Mumbai with prices paid for the same products or services in a higher income area of Mumbai and uncover the 'poverty premium' paid by so many in the lower income community.[27] The role of social investment may be to compensate for this so-called 'poverty premium' that many in poor communities pay for their substandard services. Paying a higher price for lower-quality goods is the lot for many of the poorest of the poor. In such situations, waiting for academic or government approval is tantamount to hanging poor people out to dry.

Social impact investors have a genuine interest in garnering community consent for their wares. They should not wish to expose themselves to revolt or protest. We may be concerned at the capacity of the most vulnerable to resist, but then maybe the very poorest aren't the target market here.

The services in question may not cater to those who are the absolute poorest, but rather those just above: those in poverty rather than severe poverty depending on where a return may be gained. The most vulnerable and disadvantaged can then be targeted more effectively by scarce government funds.

There remains a value judgement about the extent to which we are comfortable with private interests entering the social space at all. The question of propriety is closely tied to the question of morality, but also to the question of voice.

Our pragmatism here should urge vigilance, but where caution stifles opportunity and potential to help people, it may be up to us to reconsider our perceptions or shift our prejudices around where the private sector begins, where the philanthropic sector ends – and vice versa.

And there is another way of looking at this: the private sector benefits from tax breaks, venture capital funding and educated labour from the public sector: why shouldn't we seek to diversify and maximise, beyond tax, the benefit we get in return?

Exclusive

The big social investors of the present and near future are boutique specialist financiers, NGOs, foundations and government funds. Pierre Omidyar's Network has evolved from focusing only on microfinance to social impact investments in several organisations.

Private wealth managers such as Capricorn Investment Group and New Island Capital in the US integrate social impact investments into their portfolios. Commercial banks such as Charity Bank in the UK tap into retail customer interest in social impact investment and lend to charities. Companies such as General Mills and Starbucks are diversifying their supply chains and expanding their fair trade operations through social impact investment too.

However, beyond the pioneers, at the moment there are not many out there who 'get' the idea that investments and charitable giving can mix in this way. They prefer, to recall Arthur Wood's terms, to make money from investments – and there are enough companies in the world that do not sell tobacco and weapons to make lots of money even from ethical investments – and lose their money on their gifts. There is a current sense that social impact investment remains the perverse plaything of the investment set.

There is evidence that those with private wealth, finance, business assets, or interests are slowly being brought into the fold but there are interrelated issues that need to be overcome if more social impact investors are to emerge.

The first is the cost of social impact investing and the extra knowledge investors need to navigate such investments.

Measuring social impact remains a hard art, but in the investment space, a helping hand is given by organisations such as the Global Impact Investing Network (GIIN) that was set up to 'remedy the lack of basic investing information'.[28] GIIN launched a comprehensive impact-investing database where potential and current impact investors can obtain materials to educate themselves about this nascent sector. GIIN also collects data from early-adopters so that it can create industry standards and reports.

It has created a standardised taxonomy for impact measurement called the Impact Reporting and Investment Standards (IRIS) so that social impact investors can assess the social impact of their investments in the same language and save time and resources when evaluating social enterprises and funds.

A number of other initiatives to lower the costs of social investing have been established, including special kinds of ad-hoc community networks or clubs that pool deal search and transaction costs.

One example is Toniic, which aggregates capital from impact investors across the world to co-invest in social ventures. Members of Toniic can share their deals with others, and potentially co-invest in deals together, all of which helps to lower the high search and transaction costs of deals.[29]

More recently, a non-profit organisation called ImpactAssets released a list of the 50 most reputable impact investment funds called the 'ImpactAssets 50' to help new investors, including retail customers.[30]

Another potential barrier to new investors will be that of emotion. It is one thing to be provided with the numbers, with projections of a sector's potential, positive examples and inspirational deal-chains but does it have the sentiment, the feeling of being directly involved with and empathetic to the grassroots?

Social impact investment, the apotheosis of the social impact movement, rests on the most rational, the coldest assessment of the potential of a given social intervention than any we have considered thus far.

Early research into the new wave of social impact investment conducted by NESTA, polling company Ipsos MORI and New Philanthropy Capital in the UK suggested that people's response to the idea of social impact investing, relatively new as it then was, tended to be broadly positive, impressed as they were by some combination of return and philanthropic virtue.

More practically, there is a long-term project funded by the Rockefeller Foundation and NESTA, among others, that aims to make this all more accessible to more of us: a Social Stock Exchange, which only lists social enterprises, in the manner of the FTSE4Good.[31]

The project has a way to go before it forms part of the everyday lived experience but the promise is that it will give more people

– anyone in theory, even the beneficiaries of those enterprises – a direct stake in the movement. That is a powerful idea.

Expensive

At this early stage of the social impact investment industry, it is said by financiers that there are relatively few social investment-ready organisations. The process of discovery, of both the social and financial sectors learning about each other, and also of supporting an infrastructure without a significant investment pipeline, is expensive.

Sir Ronald Cohen remained unfazed throughout BSC's early development about this, arguing that things would take time to get going but the public profile and financial power of BSC would bring about reform.

This may be true, but for its first few years, BSC struggled to justify the public's considerable investment. The public have been and will continue to be patient. Will there be time enough to see the mission through? BSC remains vulnerable to changes in the political wind.

There are other moral challenges around pricing, however, that require more thought.

For example, venture philanthropists and charitable trusts support social entrepreneurs and build them up as part of their mission. Then BSC comes in and invests in intermediaries that support them and takes profits from those investments.

In the business world, there would be some mechanism for the BSC equivalent would pay the original venture capital investors who supported the entrepreneur in her early start-up phase, perhaps through the latter having taken equity in the company. There is no mechanism for that here.

The idea of the financier coming in and taking a cut from the good work of others may wear thin the donor's patience in the absence of a more diverse set of incentives delivered by the burgeoning social impact investment set for those who support organisations at the start of their growth journey.

The objection from the public may be simpler: change your definition of 'investment-ready' and start investing in the causes that matter ; in the movements driving real change on the ground, in our communities. There is probably some truth to both prescriptions.

Millions of social investors

It is true that, in its most harmful form, we are confronted by the spectre of awful practice. When financial engineering meets shady practice masked as community regard, we enter the realm of so-called 'sub-prime mortgages', large-scale secured lending to the poor, and we see housing bubbles, global market crashes, recession, panic and misery. We say 'never again' and we are tempted to shut it down.

But it is always worth considering the risk, not only of engaging with it, but of placing it to one side. For this arena, and the scope and ambition of its philanthropy, never ceases to surprise.

Social impact investment sits is at the heart of the Global Action for Vaccination and Immunisation (GAVI) alliance, perhaps the most complex example of philanthropic, public and social impact investment in human history. It is worth considering its incredible scope as we assess the future of this movement.

GAVI sprang from humanitarian need. Campaigns targeting childhood diarrhoea in the 1970s and 1980s scaled the use of so-called oral rehydration solution (ORS) to prevent dehydration. However, in the 1990s the situation began to deteriorate once again.

Experts argued that the most effective way to treat diarrhoea was through a combination of ORS and zinc tablets, which decreased the severity and duration of an attack. Both treatments were cheap and simple to administer – but were unavailable to millions of children in the developing world.

Meanwhile, 88% of diarrhoeal diseases worldwide were attributable to unsafe water, inadequate sanitation and poor hygiene.

As of 2006, an estimated 2.5 billion people still had no access to sanitary facilities, and nearly one in four people in developing countries continued to defecate in the open.[32]

Then there was the rotavirus. Experts argued that accelerating introduction of the rotavirus vaccine in Africa and Asia – where the rotavirus has most impact – would be the most effective cure. Years of trial and error produced the accepted treatment. The question was how it is to be paid for in sufficient quantity, to sufficient scale.

Diarrhoea is not the only relatively simple illness for which vaccination can be a lifesaver. Pneumonia, eminently curable in the young, is another where poor resources mean the world's poorest children face the spectre of death. Hepatitis C, malaria. It was to battle them in places ravaged by civil war, apathy or ignorance that a group of social entrepreneurs from finance, business, government and the foundations linked up.

GAVI was their creation. Targeting the poorest countries with a gross national per capita product of less than US$1,000, the GAVI Alliance was created in 1999 with an initial grant from the Bill and Melinda Gates Foundation. GAVI was a partnership: WHO, UNICEF, the World Bank, industry representatives, the GAVI Fund, and donor and recipient governments played important roles.

GAVI acted as a global stockpile and distributor of cheap vaccines. It set priorities through its board – on which sits at least one pharmaceutical manufacturer – and aimed to secure low prices for vaccines, especially those for hard to commercialise tropical disease vaccines, which were then supplied to poor nations at a fraction of their cost. At the time of writing GAVI-funded vaccines had reached more than 250 million children in the poorest parts of the world and had helped avert 5 million child deaths.[33]

The GAVI programme asked that countries who were helped paid some of the cost of the vaccines. Critics such as Princeton's Donald Light argued that this sorts the very poorest – and by extension the very poorest children in these countries – out of the GAVI programme.[34]

Fellow – or rival – aid organisations bemoaned GAVI's effectiveness at colonising the aid budgets of western and eastern countries. Substantive objections have been raised by the Poor Economics academics, Duflo and Bannerjee, who argue that purchasing such treatments is not the same as ensuring that the clinics that stock these treatments operate conscientiously, so that mothers who travel miles to get their babies inoculated do not find the duty nurse has taken the day off and they dare not lose the income from venturing forth again.[35]

For such a grand design – indeed because it was such a grand design, complementary to but removed from the work of grassroots social entrepreneurs – GAVI was not universally loved.

Yet GAVI remains a global brand that can bring finance and support to its mission. GAVI's financiers are adept at developing methods to finance its health programmes; to leverage governmental influence but also the capital markets, social investment, impact finance.

The International Finance Facility for Immunisation (IFFIm) was one of its innovations.[36] IFFIm raised funds by issuing bonds in the capital markets, using long-term government pledges as a guarantee and to pay back interest. Between 2006 and 2011, IFFIm raised more than US$3 billion by tapping the capital markets, and effectively doubled the funds available for GAVI's immunisation programmes.

France, Italy, the Netherlands, Norway, South Africa, Spain, Sweden, the UK and Australia came together and in this way protected 500 million children in the 72 poorest countries in the world.

GAVI's Advance Market Commitment (AMC) was another. In an AMC, donors commit funds to guarantee the price of vaccines once they have been developed. These financial commitments provide vaccine manufacturers with the incentive to develop or build manufacturing capacity for urgently needed vaccines.

In exchange, companies sign a legally binding commitment to provide the vaccines at a price affordable to developing countries in the long term. In March 2010, the first supply agreements for the AMC against pneumococcal disease were signed by GAVI and two pharmaceutical companies. The AMC was launched with a US$1.5 billion commitment from donors.

Bill Gates, whose foundation was one of the masterminds behind GAVI, was especially bullish about its potential. He argued that companies – especially those in China and India– had demonstrated an increased appetite to produce suitable vaccines for developing countries and competition among firms could increase, leading to cheaper vaccines.

Other criticisms are discussed. To wit, GAVI is a programme that seeks to inoculate babies, a cause that is easy to support; true transformation would help les newsworthy beneficiaries.

Critics further suggest that having a drug company on the GAVI board represents a conflict of interest given the vast sums at GAVI's disposal.

It is true that those who invest in GAVI invest in a flagship project that could in theory be delivered elsewhere – and leave other causes aside in order to do so. On the private sector angle, GAVI's supporters insist that the numbers inoculated have only been possible by this massive partnership between governments in the developed world and so 'buy-in' from drug companies is essential.

One may argue this either way. GAVI's scale, its board structure and its distribution may be subject to doubt; but the undoubtedly unique way it brings its various elements together is not.

From the healthcare centres and social projects on the ground, to the financial instruments up above, to the governments that work to supplement these impacts, GAVI is a new kind of transnational, trans-sector social movement designed to solve a huge public problem by using the marketplace, philanthropic investment and government muscle to flood the developing world with medicine.

It is an archetype for the good that can be done when we link the great forces of our time together: government, finance, technology and social entrepreneurship.

It also raises questions of how social entrepreneurs on the ground respond, how the voices of communities are to remain paramount when faced with such momentum. It is impressive in size but that does not mean that this is the best intervention of its kind or that the medicines are being delivered in the most optimal way. When it is not quite right, who do we tell, how do we pause the juggernaut and put it right?

It is tempting to suggest that, in the face of financial markets, great transfers of wealth, large institutions, the idea of the primacy of a social mission, the notion that people on the ground will be involved in any way other than as a PR exercise is delusional.

As financiers find new ways to leverage the social impact investment idea, create new kinds of philanthropic intervention based on such evidence, the potential disparity between the data and between real change on the ground becomes a matter of ever-greater concern. We must be clear: the beneficiary matters more than anything; the principle of its primacy and its protection through feedback generation must be at the heart of all of this.[37] An ever more benign regulatory environment works in combination with an emerging community of fellow investors to make social impact investment on ever-grander scales part of our international philanthropic architecture.

Over the next few decades, projections suggest that some US\$40 trillion will move from private to ethical funds in the US alone, to be made available in what Arthur Wood called 'the biggest voluntary transfer of wealth in human history'. We can look at this transfer another way: as one of the biggest potential economic emergences of mankind's collective capacity to do good our world has yet seen. Social impact investment can help us leverage this opportunity. We have to use the tools at our disposal to ensure it does this in the right way.

What are these tools? In part they are the tools of advocacy, campaigning, scrutiny, public debate. In part they are the tools of finance; the power of our wallets. Here we see something really interesting emerge.

Sir Ronald Cohen initially cited the interest of big 'institutional investors' as the prize when devising the social investment marketplace. Incentivise big finance into the social space to tackle huge, intractable social problems, he reasoned, and the sky would be the limit. Get foundation endowments into social impact investment, and you will have huge amounts of capital (this is actually a very good idea; we will return to it). As we write, there is some of that, but actually the more interesting developments are taking place on the ground, at grassroots level.

In our time, institutional investors are rarely interested in anything that is not worth several hundred millions or indeed billions. In most countries, such sums are beyond the purview of all but the most successful social entrepreneurs. And so into this space have stepped grassroots communities.

In France, one of the most interesting social investment innovations is the Solidarity Fund. Here ordinary people come together to pay into group pensions for a defined community. The approach has gained popularity over the last decade, raising more than US$5 billion.[38]

Similar to an ethical pension fund, the solidarity fund packages social impact investment with other socially responsible stocks. It has proven popular with people of all backgrounds.

In sum this represents a movement of ordinary people, led by social entrepreneurs, raising huge sums for social causes through their own financial investments; rewiring the everyday to 'create real change in their communities. And Today's France is home to more than a million grass-roots social investors.

Solidarity funds proliferate across Europe and represent the social impact investment idea remade as a tool for empowering people. Such vehicles are put to work supporting new housing co-operatives in Germany – and helping entire communities, citizens young and old, rich and poor, come together in common concourse thereby.

There remains hope for a non-elitist, community-centred vision for social impact investment. Crucially, the people with their hands on the levers of investment agree. As CEO of Big Society Capital – and former CEO of social entrepreneur support hub UnLtd – Cliff Prior told me in 2017:

> "In social investment, the assessment of social impact has a powerful role, and yes it can become cold, calculating and misused. My view is that we need impact measures designed by the beneficiaries – it is they who should determine what good is. If we get that fundamental right, the rest – while still imperfect – is greatly improved."

As BSC approaches its first £1 billion worth of invested projects, there is reason to believe that we might yet create a financial movement that supports practical yet radical change on the ground.

Bringing capital back to life

A final, somewhat sideways thought on the opportunity presented by social impact investment.

In *The Mystery of Capital*, economist Hernando de Soto put forward the theory of 'dead capital': that in too many countries the barriers to legal ownership result in informal ownership that then inhibits the owner from later being able to realise the value of her assets.[39]

De Soto points out that many transactions in emerging markets are not legally enforceable transactions. The 'obstacles to legality' include the sheer wall of bureaucracy that can face business or asset owners, and the cost of legal registration.

For example, in Peru, he cites that it took his team 289 days working six days a week to fully register a garment workshop, which then cost them US$1,231 – 31 times the minimum wage. According to de Soto, 4.7 million people in Egypt chose to build their dwellings illegally rather than face the 77 bureaucratic procedures that could take anywhere from 5 to 14 years. If the scale of the business is small, the time and resources required to obtain approvals and secure legitimacy for the business can be very onerous. The potential size of dead capital? Some US\$9.3 trillion.

Social impact investment could well make a difference here. Perhaps social impact investment could bring investors into hitherto 'uninvestable' places by examining uncatered human need. Perhaps such investment could incentivise cultures of property rights and effective titles.

It could help local people to leverage their own community assets through useful market interventions, even simple loans or overdrafts.

It could change the local economic profile and strike serious blows against poverty and for equality. It might help unlock the power of such assets and give that power to local people.

The processes are arcane, the language is opaque. The people are not quite as colourful as the social entrepreneurs who work on the ground and there are many contradictions and issues outstanding. But at the heart of this there is a radical social project.

Social investment experts ClearlySo's Rodney Schwartz has argued that one day *all* investing will be social investing; he even has a name for this: *three dimensional investing*, where business takes into account risk, reward and social impact in each and every one of its investments.[40]

Our job is to ensure that it realises this promise, but at the same time that it helps those who needs its help.

We are talking about those who do not have clean water, those without a roof over their head, the sightless of rural India and Egypt, the destitute across Europe or the USA, the isolated elderly, the billions of children who might die of diarrhoea before knowing anything of the joy of life: they should be our guides.

The task for the social impact investment movement as it finds greater voice is not only to develop new financial instruments, but new feedback instruments that run alongside it; to leave the space for us, the people, to be the ultimate arbiters as through this movement, grand decisions are made on the biggest social issues of our time.

8

The digital device in the wall:

#peoplepower meets the block-chain

It has become appallingly obvious that our technology
has exceeded our humanity. (Albert Einstein)

The Indian experiments

In 1999, Indian scientist Sugata Mitra placed an internet-enabled
computer behind a glass screen in a wall of his office building,
which looked out to a piece of land occupied by street kids. The
difference between the sleek piece of equipment, the sheer glass
pane and the uneven road that sat before it was stark. And the
computer and the many worlds of the internet it offered became
an instant object of curiosity, a rabbit hole that led to wonderland
for wide-eyed children.[1]

It became known as the 'hole in the wall' experiment. The
children, who were at first curious and then shy, very quickly began
to use the equipment and with minimal outside guidance learned
an impressive range of computer skills, from typing and website
and program access to rudimentary coding.

As one child learned something new from experimentation, he
or she passed it on to the next child with a speed and alacrity that
impressed those who looked on.

The right technology at the right time transforms lives and it alters realities. One needs only to look out of the window or to the screen of the nearest device to see the impact of social technology and the internet on our social and political lives. In the parts of our worlds that are mediated through the feeds of our Facebook or Twitter pages, we see the causes, ideas and politics of those we know and those beyond. These are our own holes in the walls, and from here voice of the grass-roots and the networks that move them to action are ours to behold and access.

In India, there is a grand tradition of using technology in this way to the end of development. In the post-colonial era Prime Minister Jawaharlal Nehru had the first ever computer to be located in Asia, a Hollerith Electronic HEC-2M brought from England, placed in Calcutta in 1956. The Indian pioneering of 'tech-based development' began there.

It continues to this day in the form of organisations like Drishtee which, as we saw in Chapter Six, uses technology to aid rural businesses and do it rather well.

Fads come and go. In the early 1990s, the tele-centre came to occupy the attention of practitioners. This was a sort of public internet café that was to bring the fruits of the internet revolution to Africa. Yet, despite a major academic push and a significant amount of goodwill and resource behind the idea, it never stuck. During the 1990s and early 2000s, fewer than 0.5% of African villages were connected through these centres.

Of more interest have been developments like that suggested by the hole in the wall experiment; insights that emerge from the ground up. Academic Richard Heeks, a leading British academic in the field of tech-development, wrote of a project in Pondicherry, India, where a huge barrier to local use of technology was the difference in script between the Tamil language and English.[2] Working collaboratively, locals and project workers developed Microsoft Office applications in Tamil script using a western script QWERTY keyboard.

The operators were mainly semi-literate women who learned the keyboard codes for Tamil characters. Together they produced a huge amount of local information. At one time there were close to 100 databases of information, including rural yellow pages, a benefits database and more.

Each database was linked to data collected from government departments, the Tamil Nadu Agricultural University, and even the local Aravind Eye Hospital and the US Navy's website. Armed with all of this new information, they were able to build new structures for learning and sharing.

They held health camps in the villages in co-operation with local hospitals, used multimedia and loud speakers to interest those who could not read, and published a fortnightly Tamil newspaper called *Namma Ooru Seithi* (*Our Village News*).

This kind of co-creation, as it is often called, is happening all around us in this era of social networks and mass connectivity. The spirit and energy that drives activists working on the ground – communicating through messaging applications and social networks to change our political dispensation – are harnessed in ever more practical and ingenious ways by digitally minded social entrepreneurs. And so in this chapter we consider the possibilities that emerge at the intersection of social tech and social entrepreneurship, where the needs of the many are logged, shared and galvanised into a considerable force for good.

The playground of digital social entrepreneurship

A relatively early application to riff on this theme was Pledgebank.com, set up by MySociety founder and social tech entrepreneur Tom Steinberg. This website enabled people to pledge to do good works – provided that a requisite number of others join in. 'I will start recycling if 100 people in my town will do the same' was the format.

Notable pledges on PledgeBank.com include, for example, 1,000 people in India who donated books to set up a library, or pledges in the USA to save books from landfills.

It was utilised to solicit global support for online protests, including by Freeculture.org to boycott CDs with anti-piracy rights management encryption on them.

When former UK Prime Minister Tony Blair started a pledge himself – that he would become patron of a community sports club if 100 notable figures would do the same, the site gained huge notice and traction and the pledge was carried with brio.

Pledges sprung left and right, back and forth, covering countries, communities and enhancing the lives in individually very small, but collectively very large ways of people in towns, villages and streets.

From there it is but a short step to using the power of the crowd in ever more radical ways. Social entrepreneurs have been quick to harness this goodwill of others in very practical forms.

The tech industry often sets its sights high when it comes to solving any problem. Social change is no exception. Consider the scientists at IBM who produced the IBM World Community Grid. The Grid applies the unused computing capacity of individuals and businesses to help address global problems. Thousands of computer run years have been harvested to date.

It is the really big problems that scientists are looking to solve here: the first project of World Community Grid, the Human Proteome Folding Project, hoped to identify the proteins that make up the Human Proteome and, in doing so, improve our approach to diseases such as malaria, still a major killer in the developing world.

Not all of the interventions in this area are quite so space-age – and indeed they need not be. When individuals or groups of people are brought together in the course of their everyday lives who would not have been able to connect any way other than by virtue of social technology, good things happen. You see it in online dating and you see it other kinds of social application also.

Take a social enterprise like the Good Gym. I met with Good Gym's founder, Ivo Gormley, for coffee in Shoreditch in 2009, when it was but a flicker in his eye.

You could tell it was a great idea straight away. The Good Gym enables people to plan a local jogging route with stops at the home of an elderly or immobile, isolated person. The jogger gets fit, the beneficiary gets, say, a paper and the company of a young person for some time and it is all brokered through the internet.

Good Gym, over the years, has gone from strength to strength, incorporating a number of crucial regulations and checks into its service, becoming approved by governments which work with it offline, and even at one time striking a deal with corporate partners New Balance, the training-shoe manufacturer.[3]

Bringing people together is the bread and butter of the social web; linking people to create massive political change is a natural next step. Here too, Tom Steinberg was an instrumental figure. For example, his website theyworkforyou.com allowed people to search political speeches and interventions and so keep tabs on their representatives. Another of his applications enabled people to simply and easily get in touch with their democratic representatives.

In time, the social enterprise he founded, MySociety, developed into a suite of applications and a global network that reached out to people in politically oppressive regimes and kept open, democratic debate alive.[4] His efforts in digital social entrepreneurship were supported at a relatively early stage by UnLtd.

The potential of big data, freely available, has begun to offer new possibilities for socially minded organisations. Governments have investigated new ways to share data (for example via Nationalservice.gov in the US, see Chapter Nine for more on this). Newspapers, such as the UK's *Guardian*, on their data blogs invite amateurs to scour and represent entire chunks of socially minded data on a bewildering use of topics and make them fit for everyday consumption.

Private sector companies like GlaxoSmithKline have released details of certain patents online and invited anyone and everyone to use them to develop cures for obscure illnesses.

We have seen, in Chapter Seven, the online MIX databank used to analyse the fairness of global microfinance institutions. The increasing prevalence of such information is not only of use to the writer or the academic; the social entrepreneur too leans on this data as she develops her products and services.

Social impact investors benefit too. Alongside GIIN and Toniic, information sharing agencies that cover deals and prospects and potential impacts, you have Mission Markets, an online marketplace for impact investing that facilitates deal sourcing and due diligence by providing necessary materials of listed social enterprises.

The dream of open data is that together we create a sort of digital commons that gives social projects the sort of leverage and insight that corporate giants find in their expensively assembled research and development units.

Amazon and Google's engineers are able to call on unparalleled banks of data and sophisticated products as they track our trillion little interactions and gestures on an ongoing basis and offer us things they think we will like.

Such developments are not always in our best interests; there is a well noted 'echo chamber effect' where the more such companies only show us what we think we will like, the more closed off we become to new ideas. The digital commons for development gives social entrepreneurs a fighting chance to overcome the negative effects of the market fundamentalism that gets us to this point – and break open that echo chamber.

Online political action in focus

The first politically significant instances of social network-based political action were perhaps the social media messages that helped Egyptian protestors in 2011 organise in Cairo's Tahrir Square to overthrow their government. Even before this there were online organised 'flash mobs' – impromptu or quasi-spontaneous demonstrations – protesting autocracy and despotism in Eastern Europe. And then there was the story of Neda in the aftermath of the Iranian election of 2009, a story saturated with symbolism and tragedy.

Neda was 26, a music student from the suburbs of Iran's capital, Tehran. One summer in 2009, she was shot at a political protest in the City. The perpetrator of this attack, a man on a motorbike, was a *basij* – one of the 13 million-strong force of volunteers who were loyal to the Iranian government. She died around two minutes later and those two minutes were crucial.

We know what happened in those two minutes because it was recorded. A witness who was an acquaintance of the Brazilian author Paulo Coelho, whose works include the bestselling *The Alchemist*, shared the video, and Coelho published it on his blog. Later, somewhat sanguinely, he would write, 'After I published the video … it seems that it spread worldwide.'[5]

One of the lesser-known aspects of this viral message spreading was the secondary battles and skirmishes that took place in cyberspace to keep the message alive. A particular kind of pro-dissident tech social entrepreneur emerged to join in this battle.

A community of online activists came together to understand and repel the attacks. Papers were created and shared on how state-sponsored hackers in the Iranian government were believed to be hacking those who helped the protest.

The methods included blocking data from going to or from certain websites, and 'packet fingerprinting', a technique which allowed the government to filter 'good data' such as money transactions, from 'bad data' such as an email about government.

People across the globe registered their support and helped the Iranian protestors by donating stick drives to help protestors get back online securely. Sympathetic websites and blogs shared useful projects through their own mini networks and started up new streams of their own.

Freegate was another similar project, first developed by Chinese dissidents to get around Beijing's heavy internet censorship. The Tor project has been co-opted too for this purpose, a protocol that it is often used to access the 'dark web' with its array of forbidden and at times illegal activities.

Videre est Credere and the citizen journalism revolution

As the power and knowledge of authoritarian regimes has grown, the ingenuity and diligence of the community movement that offers hope and resistance has metamorphosed with it. As the internet develops, more of our information migrates online, ready to be bartered to the unscrupulous. This information we willingly give in return for free services. There is great potential for abuse, especially from rogue political elements.

In this environment, raising awareness, messaging, keeping people online is not enough; you have to give them more tools to produce better-quality, more professional interventions.

Enter Oren Yakobovitch. He is one of dissident video's most innovative purveyors, part of a new wave of social entrepreneur citizen journalist.

When he was a child, Yakobovitch's mother and father emigrated from Eastern Europe to Israel. At 18 he joined the army, serving in Lebanon, West Bank and Gaza, witnessing armed conflict and working in intelligence. As a young man, he became concerned that the struggle of which he was part was actually part of the problem. He was further concerned that the reality he saw at the front line was not the reality that made it into mainstream discourse.

He quit the military and was jailed. On exit from prison, he decided to become a filmmaker. He started by making on the ground documentaries about the Bedouin, education for Palestinians and the treatment of psychiatric patients. The real radical moment, however, came when he realised that perhaps the most difference he could make was by taking the camera and not holding it himself but giving it to others.[7]

In time he would found Videre est Credere.[8] Videre exposes human rights abuses in remote areas, bringing justice to victims who would otherwise remain unheard. It builds networks of local human rights activists proactively capturing human rights abuses on video, allowing patterns of abuse and violence to be detected.

Videre then distributes footage to media, policymakers and indeed gets it wherever else it needs to go.

Videre sits between the citizen journalism that accompanied Neda's passing, on the one hand, where information flows are completely open, can be of low quality and impact, and has questionable lasting effect, to the highly impact, high production value traditional media. By putting technology into the hands of the oppressed, training them in its use, linking in communities and decision makers, Yakobovitch is making the difference.

His networks are anonymous, closely guarded and secure. He uses his military knowhow to provided up to the minute training, data encryption and counter-surveillance techniques so that they stay safe and stay active. This combination of technological and media knowhow to push the boundaries of change make Videre an archetypal social tech enterprise.

A range of NGOs encourage citizen journalism, but the footage they produce is often reactive and scattered, lacking the strength to truly change abusive practices.

Oren Yokobovitch's innovation lies in building constant, grassroots monitoring networks of local activists, who proactively gather unique insights and information. As with all good social entrepreneurs, Videre's work is grounded on the principle of constant communication with the people it is trying to help, that produces learning that enables it to track its social impact. These include things like decreasing election manipulation, political intimidation and violence against women.

The future for Videre, and its hybrid real media/citizen journalist movement, is filled with projects, for there are so many atrocities and flashpoints across the globe and we live in a place of rising conflict between the powerful and the powerless, the brutal and the democratic, those who share information honestly and openly and those who abuse that trust for personal gain.

At least we have hope that these battles will be fairly documented, there will be witnesses and we will, in time, be able to learn.

Production values increase, cell phones become entire post-production units. New iterations of wearable camera tech will help too. We are watched and scrutinised ever more closely, take liberties with our own security without a second thought. The role of the social entrepreneur in this wild west of personal information is as a last line of honesty – and the spark that sets new activist movements on their way.

Fintech and the future of social money

From raising voices to raising dollars: the intersection of tech and money is one of social enterprise's most fertile grounds.

Financial tech ('fin-tech') innovations involve evolutions in the way we share and distribute money. So-called crowdfunding is a simple example of this. It often uses a pledge mechanism, bringing a critical number of people together to get particular initiatives off the ground, often in return for various rewards or incentives.

Kickstarter and CrowdCube are crowdfunding companies that help countless projects develop each year.

What began as a niche operation now funds all sorts of causes from scientific research to unsigned bands – and helps campaigns and social innovations get off the ground.

Peer-to-peer lending

Peer-to-peer (P2P) lending is a more complex fin-tech movement. P2P lending allows one person or a group of people to lend to another without the need for a bank; it all happens through the internet, aggregated through the lender's online network.

Think of it as a cyber variation on microfinance and you see the social potential of the movement. Impelled by the high-profile work of organisations like Kiva.org, whose online microfinance loans go to developing world entrepreneurs, these organisations have been interesting analysts and practitioners for some years. The *Harvard*

Business Review included P2P finance on its list of 'breakthrough ideas' for 2009.[9]

P2P lenders have gone some way towards meeting that early promise. Take Zopa, the leading British variant. When it first began, the form was simple. Log on to Zopa and you have names, profiles and pictures. You see them on your computer screen, an ordered list of people wanting to buy a new car, wanting to get that garage extended or wanting to consolidate their debts, asking for a certain amount of money. Zopa offers you a pool of borrowers. You set your own risk, and split your money into chunks.

It continues to claim very few actual defaults and contends that if such defaults were totalled, they would amount to 0.1% of Zopa's combined loans: a far lower rate of default than conventional banks. Borrowers benefit from the competition to lend at increasingly competitive rates of interest.

For years now it has been the UK's leading P2P service; at the time of writing, it had lent more than US$1.5 billion over its lifespan.

The P2P lending space today is full of interesting organisations, many of which have social purposes. CommonBond is an interesting example that offers new ways to finance US college educations. It wraps into this a social enterprise model that funds a less privileged school kid for every education funded through the platform.

Abundance is of special interest too, a social enterprise P2P platform. Its funding projects are exclusively pro-social in character.

P2P lending has well and truly established itself as a part of the financial mainstream. Governments are keen to back this new form of finance and in the UK popular government sponsored savings products are offered by specialist P2P financiers. This is no surprise to Zopa's CEO Giles Andrews, with whom I spoke about Zopa in those early days.

As he put it, Zopa is about money, but it is also about a whole series of relationships that form around money. Financial crises, in his view, highlighted another key attraction of Zopa's operation – 'tangibility'. It is easy to see exactly what is going on. People are borrowing and lending between each other, with Zopa making it much safer and easier to do … There's no highly paid City Slicker buying and selling futures, derivatives, Bizarre Bonds or whatever to make Zopa happen.

The next stage will be for more of these organisations to demonstrate layers of social impact; the relatively early signs are promising.

Enter the blockchain

A free-to-access encyclopaedia (wikipedia) entirely by collective endeavour; computer and mobile operating systems (Linux OS and Android OS) by globally connected teams of independent developers. In recent times, mass communication and open collaboration have created much and even the most detailed set of despatches can only give us a flavour of the possibility.

The future promises yet more radicalism and more opportunity. So let us for a moment indulge in some soothsaying.

Alongside P2P lending, Bitcoin and Ethereum are two key projects of our era. Bitcoin is a decentralised currency that requires the presence of no issuing central bank, merely the historic and future computer power of the network to survive.

It is volatile but potentially radical – after all, the money is in theory capable of being produced by any one of us. The ledger of how that money is spent – the blockchain – is validated democratically, by the network.

Ethereum offers to do something similar for contracts and legal agreements, based as it is on a blockchain that is a perfect record of the actions of the community, which means that contracts can be effected 'smartly', with minimal human intervention.

The decentralised nature of these protocols is in theory transformational as is the way in which these transactions are validated.

Just as P2P lenders in theory removed the need for loan guarantee institutions, so Bitcoin in theory removes the need for central banks, and Ethereum in theory removes the need for systems of contract law.

In place, they substitute forms of democracy across their network to validate such transactions. And they provide fascinating testing grounds for different kinds of democratic action to achieve this end.

If a critical mass of transactions shift to these media, the regulatory and intermediary institutions whose monopoly over such things gives them power may yet begin to wane.

That is interesting enough in terms of where the power lies in a society. But there is more. For example (and this is fairly 'out there', I know): in a world of smart contracts, a trusted intermediary like a charity may no longer be *required* in order to ensure that a service is delivered.

Instead a group of philanthropists can come together and ensure the service happens – be it dropping food parcels or providing addiction counselling – when the contract is delivered.

In such situations, there is no need for an intermediary. There may be need for a social entrepreneur who can help oversee the delivery of many of these contracts at time. But the blockchain itself contains the record and protocols for the effective delivery of the service, completely transparent and there for all to see.

The role of the traditional social sector in such situations would be radically restructured. It might be no more than (a) helping structure such contracts so that they do the most good, and (b) campaigning to help donors, governments and social entrepreneurs of other kinds focus resources.

The blink of a cursor

One last thing on this for now: note if you will an important limitation that could scupper the social potential of these movements. This may be the age of the tech social entrepreneur but it is also the age of the tech social activist, who actively seeks to bring down the digital divide between the 'haves' and the 'have nots' in the world of tech.

Poor hardware, slow connections, lack of local language and locally relevant content is a major barrier to consistent growth. Development may help overcome these divides, but the spectre of them is a constant challenge for reformers.

Gbenga Sesan is a social entrepreneur operating in Ajegunle, Nigeria, a place that a generation ago was wracked by civil unrest. His PIN project helps teach computing skills and use technology to build the kids under his tutelage's belief in themselves.

'Dare to be B.I.G.' (Brightest ICT Girl or Guy forms the acronym) is the name of an associated television show he made to push this agenda further. He is one of many working on the ground in communities, attempting to ensure that they are not left out of this.

Sometimes, with despatches likes these, it feels as if we are a world away from the social change of earlier chapters, the low-tech projects and quirky but effective interventions that characterise the social entrepreneur movement.

But are we really? Remember Sugata Mitra's hole in the wall, the children that stopped to play with the computer in it, the sparks in their eyes as they realised that they could do anything within this virtual world; control anything; make anything happen at the touch of a button. To some this feels alien; to others, especially young people, it is as natural as anything.

I've been there, programming in BASIC on my brick of a computer as a five year old. The spark that gives hope to children is not always so different from the blinking cursor on a brightly lit computer screen – or the fire that sparks dissent, protest or compels a community to find its voice and take control of its destiny. It all amounts to one thing: possibility.

Reclaiming the heart of government:

power in the age of the moral marketplace

> Every nation gets the government it deserves. (Joseph de Maistre)[1]

The President's platform

In 2008, just prior to the US presidential election, a movement of community representatives sought a radical commitment: a pledge of a US$100 million of public money from John McCain and Barack Obama, the Republican and Democrat candidates respectively. It was a big ask but then they had big ideas. They wanted this money to seed a new generation of socially enterprising grass-roots movements.

They wanted a war-chest to help grass-roots organisations become more sustainable; to foster new kinds of data-driven analysis of their interventions. They wanted to enable social enterprises and charities to become ready for social impact investment; to collect evidence of impact that might help these organisations thrive and grow from the grass-roots to the local; from the local to the national.

The candidates got the message. In one of the most successful lobbying outcomes for infrastructure ever procured by the US non-profit sector, a promise from both major presidential candidates was secured that a *social innovation fund* (SIF) would be created by a future Obama or McCain administration.

Paul Carttar was part of the influential group behind the effort.[2] Carttar is a non-profit veteran with a host of initiatives behind him, who was tasked with leading this work from the Office of the US President. I spoke with him towards the end of President Obama's first term about how the SIF came to be and how it was getting along.

Carttar's manner is deliberate and methodical. Straight away, he eased into the detail with barely a pause. "The theme of the initial effort was about being more proactive about society and having an alternative strategy to tackle social problems with federal money," he told me. "There were three streams to begin with: health, youth development, economic opportunity – as well as a fourth, multi-issue pot."

Carttar described the fund as having three further 'layers' that comprised the delivery mechanism of the fund. The first was the grant programme itself, comprising US$150 million distributed through an open public competition. The administrators of the SIF were clear that the programmes funded by their intermediaries should contribute to the administration's strategic priorities. "This," said Carttar, was a "programme for impact".

In return, the organisations received good, long-term funding renewable annually; a quid pro quo, if you will.

The second 'layer' was the benefit that the knowledge gained from the programme would confer on social sector organisations looking to work with federal departments. Carttar hoped at the time to marshal enough evidence to begin to make the case to individual departments to invest in similar programmes in their areas of delivery.

The third 'layer' was the benefit that the evidence from the programme would confer on the social sector itself. Organisations taking part would treat their participation entrepreneurially, seek to become more sustainable, track their impact, innovate and build foundations for the future.

Indeed, Carttar said that he planned to "open source" the evidence and release it for free as a lasting legacy for the movement.

In its execution as well as in its theory, SIF was a grand design that brought together a number of the ideas that we have discussed over the course of this book in a professional, well-judged government intervention.

Its originality lay not in its mechanisms or the thinking behind it but in its scale, its profile and in its emphasis on creating innovative and credible forms of evidence that can be used as foundations for others going forward. Oh, and the fact that this nudge towards the moral marketplace was applied straight from the Office of the President.

It was the Office of the President insisting on this evidence, the Office of the President contending that these entrepreneurial, data gathering and sharing behaviours could be part of mainstream charitable activity.

It was the Office of the President, indeed, creating a structure in which charities and social enterprises articulate the good they do and the social impact that emerged from their work. Sometimes having the support of the Chief can make all the difference.

The programme posed many positive questions and challenges to its participants. Data was collected at the point of selection, collected throughout during year on year evaluations. The SIF administrators created a 'hierarchy of data' that privileged the quantitative (for example, survey data) over the anecdotal (for example, a 'feel good' story). They aimed to create a 'body of evidence' that not only provided internal validity to the SIF and a point of common external assessment, but that could also justify the external validity of future similar uses of federal funds.

The social movements that would come to be supported by the SIF are diverse. The Nebraska Children and Families Foundation was awarded US$1 million over two years. It worked with government and business using a public service social enterprise model to improve the lives of children in foster homes, in juvenile detention units or who have been homeless.

The grant provided by the SIF allowed it to expand outwards from its few existing urban locations to cover the entirety of Nebraska.

The Share Our Strength organisation was also funded, with a plan to expand the reach of the No Kid Hungry campaign. This programme seeks to provide education and support to children at risk of hunger across the USA in the places in which they 'live, learn and play'.

It channelled the grant received from SIF into numerous smaller organisations, each of which targets its own area of the campaign in a specific way which helps meet the goals of the campaign and the broader goals of Share Our Strength.[3]

And then there was REDF, a support social enterprise that creates job opportunities for Californians who face multiple and complex barriers to employment. We earlier briefly encountered it doing interesting things in the world of social impact reporting; it was one of the pioneers of the 'social return on investment' calculation.

REDF was awarded significant grants under the scheme in order to fund and support social enterprises which in turn employ its beneficiaries. Its SIF funding in 2010 allowed it to create more than 2,500 jobs in this way.

The SIF a pioneer initiative; a marker for what active, humane government looks like in our time. As we have noted over the course of this book, our epoch is characterised by powerful, vocal movements, led by social entrepreneurs, driving innovative change from the ground up. The Obama administration made it their mission to place this exhilarating force at its heart.

The statement and symbolism are clear: government by elites for elites is over. The future lies in government embracing the endeavour and spirit of grass-roots organisers, not only during election campaigns, but as an ethos and oath of office.

The final chapter of this book builds on that vision with ideas for reform and reconciliation. There are ideas that bring the voice and activism of communities back to the heart of our often degraded political systems. There are ideas that harness the moral marketplace of social entrepreneurs, community movements and mission-driven millennials, to return ethos and democracy to the offices of state.

1. Get the infrastructure right

The SIF sought to support many aspects of the infrastructure underpinning social and community movements. While it is true that many funds exist to support or fund the work of social entrepreneurs – to 'build capacity' as it is often put – relatively few programmes exist that help build such infrastructure; improve data; improve connections between different agencies; and connect social entrepreneurs with the tools to help their ambitions soar.

We have encountered schemes over the course of this book that develop part of the infrastructure puzzle. Big Society Capital (Chapter Seven) may yet help build a flourishing social investment market in the UK. Other schemes enable organisations to become ready for investment with simpler products or grants. Governments are well placed to deliver or broker such interventions and help ambitious movements use these tools to take their message to the masses.

But there remains a great deal more to do to realise the potential. As we saw in Chapter Two, at the time of writing there are significant gaps in the provision of support to social entrepreneurs. These vary from country to country, but the research, including my own on the subject (cited above), has generally shown similar patterns of wasted potential and missed opportunity. There are many worthwhile start-up funds. Social impact investors waiting to take on high-growth social enterprises at the other end are multiplying apace. The section in between is the piece that is missing. And these are the points where a community movement goes from lone voice in the dark to long-term solution or agitant for change.

Support centres, informal and formal mentors, angel investors, private equity firms and even high street banks are responsible for the success and riches of millions as they support millions of conventional businesses the world over. But this specialist infrastructure for social entrepreneurs, flourishing though it is, variegated though it is, remains incapable of coping with the sheer demand for such services by a generation; mission-driven millennials who wish to push on.

As around a fifth to a third of all new start-ups are social, we need to get on top of this, and fast. Here are some ideas.

Funding

There are several approaches one might take. A 'big bang' *community voices infrastructure fund*, perhaps offered in conjunction with a *solidarity savings product*, or involving a significant central government investment as part of a policy platform, after the manner of President Obama's commitment, part SIF, part BSC, would be a great policy approach for many jurisdictions.

In cases where this method is appropriate (and the funds exist) the programme should be created in concert with groups of social entrepreneurs, commissioning appropriate research, and getting to the heart of the matter.

There are some fascinating examples of even bigger 'big bangs' than this. The South Korean example is one. Recall, in 2007, the South Korean government passed the Social Enterprise Promotion Act. This was subsequently amended several times up to 2011. This Act laid out the requirements that an organisation must fulfil in order to be classed as a social enterprise. It also placed a duty on the Minister of Employment and Labour to establish a basic plan for the promotion of social enterprise every five years. *Ministerial responsibility for social enterprise development* is a positive idea: other jurisdictions should steal it.

There are concerns that this support may be providing a crutch for unsustainable organisations. For example, the South Korean government has provided payroll subsidy for some social enterprises, in some cases keeping the businesses afloat.[4] Yet there seems to be no record of a capitulation of the sector. According to official data, 131 certified social enterprises have closed down since 2007.[5] Given the total number of around 1,600, this is at the time of writing neither negligible nor catastrophic; and in fact represents on the face of it a very good success rate indeed.

Mapping

In many jurisdictions, such an approach would risk duplicating work already happening on the ground. Working with existing foundations or with existing community organisations will ensure that useful networks are properly tapped. There is nothing worse than a new government project to create a new enterprise with a logo and offices that could have been delivered using existing capacity. The key for administrators is to look for the gaps in the moral marketplace in their area and seek to fill in where possible. *Local social enterprise mapping* is a real quick win. They could create open source social infrastructure maps that convey useful information about what exists and where the gaps are. And so they should be good stewards of the marketplace, intervening where necessary. Identify the organisations that map or have the capability to map these sectors, work out who is speaking to whom, encourage sub-sectors to self-organise, consolidate, pool resources and map themselves and get that infrastructure built in concert with the grassroots.

Golden rule approach

There are other, smaller options that should be part of the mix or act as standalone policies. A package of government grants might be agreed that specify that part of any funding given should be used to build back office infrastructure and sustainability, especially in smaller organisations. This *'golden rule' approach to grant and contract funding* has been used effectively by the UK's Big Lottery Fund and the Lloyd's Bank Foundation (through their 'funder plus' model), among others.

Place-based budgeting

The emphasis should be on giving social entrepreneurs the platform to 'do their thing' rather than telling them what to do. Local government might invite social entrepreneurs to take over entire swathes of provision; give them carte blanche and invite them to tell them what they think can be achieved. Can businesses, can foundations, help government create the space in which such experiments might happen? In an era of endlessly bureaucratic audit requirements when working with government, such *place-based' budgeting* and contracting is a fascinating prospect.

Tax breaks and social enterprise cities

Speaking of place: measures to support the infrastructure and creation of social enterprise cities, zones and communities should be high on the list. Social infrastructure and geographic hubs work well together: let's have more of these *social enterprise zone policies*. Specific incentives, tax breaks within these zones, ease of conversion of property to social purposes and other initiatives should be part of the mix. Do you want to set up a social enterprise city? The attitude should be: let's talk.

Bureaucracy and regulation

Our attitude should also be: let's cut bureaucracy that holds community activists back. Regulations around social start-ups should be as light as possible to encourage more of our mission-driven millennials to enter the space. Jurisdictions should encourage innovation and *minimise restrictions on non-profit trading*.

The form chosen at the outset is a particular headache in some jurisdictions for social entrepreneurs. It may be unfit for purpose further down the line, especially if the organisation wants to move from the profit to non-profit space or vice versa. Implementing B Corp style legislation will help. I have previously argued for a *non-bureaucratic 'venture lite' company form* that can be converted easily to any type for a start-up social entrepreneur: this may be right for some jurisdictions. The key is to make the social entrepreneur's journey that much easier, give them room to help and empower their constituencies.

Legislative change

Taken together, what we have here is the bones of an *industrial strategy for social entrepreneurship* and the potential in several jurisdictions for a *Moral Marketplace Act* to enact necessary legislation under one banner. The former should sit alongside the business strategies devised by governments and take pride of place in their economic and social offer to the public. The latter would show commitment to building the field that not only has national impact but will also assist the global movement.

Government can no longer duck the issue of how it is supporting the moral marketplace. Where it does, we should take a dim view – and demand the dispensation we deserve. Let's fight for proper support for the people that make the difference.

2. Social first: public services should be socially – rather than privately – delivered

As we have seen throughout this book, the domain of the social entrepreneur, from community group, to multinational co-operative, is huge. This presents an opportunity for more of us to buy into the social enterprise ethos, to purchase products and services that help improve the world about us. Government should be leading this movement.

This is why I am very much in favour of a 'social first' principle, whereby specific contracts or sub-contracts are reserved for social enterprises and non-profit organisations, in order to resist the remorseless rise of the private sector super-delivery organisation.

With the moral marketplace developing at pace, the social first principle could and perhaps should be extended to large contracts for construction and other services in the public domain. Private sector organisations contracting for public services should know that socially enterprising bids will receive preference; that community activists with a social mission and solid business models will be preferred over those seeking shareholder profit and little else. The rules of the game should be rewritten and rigged, in favour not of the rich and powerful private sector delivery companies as is currently the case, but the community-driven organisations that represent us.

Social enterprise offers us a tangible opportunity to take back control of how public funds are spent and to which sort of organisation they go. Social enterprises, mission focused or community owned, should be front and centre in our thoughts and the thoughts of those who commission our services.

Social first is the *sine qua non* of a new approach to public services. Social entrepreneurs have much to teach us about other, related aspects of public service reform

Building social capital

Researchers Charles Leadbeater and Hilary Cottam in an essay from a few years back told the story of a boy named Joe who wanted to travel on the bus to school, but it so happened that Joe was differently abled and thus was told: no.[6]

Local administrators were not inhumane but had in fact provided a taxi service for him at some expense. They thought they were covering every angle but in fact the whole thing was pretty dehumanising; they were a barrier to poor Joe making friends/ messing around/playfighting with kids his age in his own time.

It seemed that no party was destined to be truly happy until Joe's mother, Caroline, approached a social enterprise called In Control.

In Control was the brainchild of welfare reformer Simon Duffy. It is a social enterprise that facilitates *personal budgeting*.[7] This allows the user of a public service to hypothecate the budget their care would cost and spend it themselves, with support from the social enterprise and family and social networks – this allows multiple forms of co-production as the technology allows new, fine-grained services to be produced and reiterated with ease, without the bureaucracy of re-commissioning a service.

Organisations like In Control pull people through the system and help them identify the support they need to take charge of their own care. In that sense, it is a truly modern, responsive service, which falls under the category of a *'user-driven'* or *'co-produced' service*.

There is a vast repository of energy and good will that suggests that, people are prepared to put 'sweat equity' into collaborating on such solutions when those solutions promise to make significant differences to their lives and the lives of others and when they have the power and the control.

Getting control of Joe's healthcare budget and organising a system of care that involved him using the bus with a minder known to them meant that Joe and Caroline's new system actually cost the government less than the taxi, while making everyone a whole lot happier and more engaged in the process.

A useful way of looking at this problem is to adduce one of our favourite concepts: social capital. Connected with areas of high social capital are behaviours such as voluntarism and the propensity to give more of one's time and effort for little in direct exchange: 'sweat equity'.

One of my favourite examples of sweat equity in action in the social enterprise world is that of Mothers2Mothers. This was set up by Dr Mitchell Besser, a Harvard trained obstetrician, whose work in South Africa exposed him to the horror of HIV and the havoc it wreaks there. In his early years in South Africa, Besser had neither the facilities nor the support to make a substantial dent.

So Besser took the approach was that of any top social entrepreneur: he empowered a community of mothers to organise their own cares. The social enterprise Mothers2Mothers (M2M) was the result of his reflections.[8] The M2M programme uses education and mentoring as tools to prevent mother-to-child transmission of the HIV virus, to support mothers' adherence to medical treatment, to empower mothers to improve their health and the health of their babies, and to combat the stigma within families and communities.

It assigns mothers with mentors who are also mothers, who may have been through the same thing as the mentee, and who facilitate the interaction between mother, baby and clinic. The results of this simple addition to the cycle of care have changed lives.

These bonds are the pith and substance of social capital and they are air-tight. One M2M mother motorcycles across hundreds of miles to be with her mentee. One braves a-four hour walk up a mountain. Simple, low-tech communications, such as text message-enabled phones, open up the possibilities.

A combination of organisation, hard work, social technology and social investment has seen Mothers2Mothers last more than a decade. From the spark of an idea in Dr Mitchell Besser's brain it has become an enterprise that trains a network of amateur mentors all across Africa, in countries as far apart as Namibia, Tanzania and Kenya. Backed by a grant from the Elton John AIDS Foundation and patient investors, an idea that began in South Africa has been replicated and franchised.

In his book *Unanticipated Gains*, academic Mario Small focuses on how social capital is created through our interactions within one another and the organisations with which we work – often in ways that are unexpected, or incidental to purpose. That is a nice way of looking at it: social entrepreneurship is the art and science of creating value from spontaneous or unanticipated gains.[9]

Why shouldn't this art and science be part of the government's approach to service building too? I oversaw an inquiry into the effects of loneliness on young people in 2015 that revealed the levels of loneliness and reduced social capital in our urban centres, or 'grey zones' as we referred to them.[10] Such *social capital mapping* studies can form the basis of good public policy.

It would be very useful to collect hard data on how discrete social interventions lead to a decline or increase in the 'stocks' of individual and neighbourhood social capital: let that be one of the aims of government research.

The goal should be to 'design in' from the outset support for building social capital into the organisations and programmes that people use as a matter of routine. Not coincidentally, that will inevitably mean more services driven by people on the ground, articulated by them and specified by them to solve the problems they see – and more partnership opportunities for social entrepreneurs.

Policymakers have often traditionally sought to build social capital as a separate and distinct activity from 'business as usual'. But social capital cannot be sprinkled about like glitter on a fairy cake. The work of public service social entrepreneurs like Duffy offers better ways. They demonstrate consistent variety and potential that should be considered and considered again by legislators.

Social capital begets ideas, innovation begets yet more innovation. Shop4Support is a social enterprise that has itself spun out of the In Control stable.

Set up by a user in 2003, it has had a significant impact by creating a retail market for social care services. In essence, it arrived as a supermarket that allows personal budgeters to acquire the elements of their social care service needs for the cheapest possible price with the utmost convenience, online.

By logging onto the website, individuals could find and buy support they desire, decide on a support plan, administer their personal budget and even employ their own staff.

For hundreds of care businesses, it provided an online, easy-to-access platform for accessing large retail demand for social care products and services. A number of other organisations follow their lead today and a market that works for care users emerges as a result.

When I spoke to Simon Duffy who, years after In Control was formed, remains a formidable activist and thinker, he was bullish about the future of social entrepreneurship, this sort of co-production and personal budget. "I don't think people have even begun to scratch the surface of what the technology can achieve. I don't think governments even understand it yet."

Often people speak of personal budgets as if the purpose of the exercise is simply bung a wad of cash in a vulnerable person's hands and then be surprised at the horror show when that cash is spent on cigarettes and cosmetic surgery (as happened on a horrifically exploitative television show where a lump sum of cash was offered in lieu of regular welfare payments, go figure).

Needless to say, that is precisely the opposite of the point. The budget is to be managed, not by a remote administrator, but by a group of caring people who are motivated to help the service user get along, are bought into the vision and who give their own sweat equity to see that the money achieves the social outcomes it is supposed to achieve.

There are so many ways to deliver great services and build social capital. One approach that emerged from the US is that of time banking. *Time banking* allows people to exchange voluntary service for credits, which can then be exchanged for other items or even in some places with local currencies.

This kind of entrepreneurial volunteering offers a relatively innovative way of unlocking social capital and getting people involved; in conjunction with government, however, there is the potential to make bigger changes. Relationships are built and countless hours and sums of social value and social capital are yielded.

Local currencies of themselves can be a fascinating model on which to pivot. Encouraging people into local shops, buying local produce, these can all help define a sense of an area through social enterprise. The Brixton Pound is one example of a local currency with national profile. More of them, perhaps aligned with social enterprise cities or localities, is an intriguing prospect.

And there is the simple truth that having more social entrepreneurs involved in delivery will of itself send social capital through the roof. So governments, national and local should give social entrepreneurs and their communities tangible rights to challenge and build social capital, bid for assets, and empower and encourage people to get involved.

3. System change and social investment

'Payment-on-success' or 'social impact' bonds

System change involves reform that seeks to tackle 'wicked' social problems that do not have a simple solution. Often this requires a fine-grained understanding of the relationships at work within a particular community and the different kinds of interactions, exchanges, gift relationships and obligations that make it tick.

Understanding, mapping, engaging with and platforming social entrepreneurs is the key here. And the next set of ideas helps us get there.

In 2008 one intriguing element of the spec for Sir Ronald Cohen's vision first crossed my desk as a young political researcher. It was a paper on a new theoretical social investment instrument, called a *social impact bond* or *'payment on success' bond*.

To understand how it works, consider the difficulty highlighted by Rob Owen of St Giles Trust and others over the course of this book: former prisoners are constantly reoffending, as if drawn by some magnet back inside. The price of such recidivism is high. It costs to re-incarcerate the wrongdoer. It costs to provide reparation, where possible, to the people they harm. It costs the victim their peace of mind or worse. This is precisely the kind of wicked problem, reckoned Cohen, with which the social impact bond can help.

The social impact bond was a partnership between social entrepreneur, taxpayer and investor. It effectively gives taxpayers a break if the programmes paid for by tax money fails.

How did it do this? By encouraging private investors to provide the money up front to pay for those programmes with the fillip of a profit at the other end. If the programme fails, the taxpayer doesn't pay, the investors get no profit. If it succeeds – everyone wins.

In essence, government acted as the 'guarantor'. It is bound by a contract with two other parties and in this contract is contained a payment schedule. Payments are made to private investors – be they foundations, banks, pension funds, or rich people – and are contingent on making savings as a result of the programme.

The savings are the prize. Most of the savings are banked by the taxpayer. In the pilot of the programme, in a prison in Peterborough, England, up to a third of the savings comprised the investors' profit, plus their principal investment plus interest. The bond raised was worth about US$8 million.

For the investors – mostly forward-thinking foundations like the Barrow Cadbury Trust – to get their money back starting in 2014 (with interest) the recidivism rate had to fall at least 7.5%, relative to a control group. If the rate fell by 10%, the investors would receive the sort of return that the stock market historically delivers.

Delivering the savings and reaching the targets set in those contracts is the major endeavour of this thing; and in essence it is the job of the third party, the charities and social entrepreneurs actually offering the innovative alternative that promises to do things better.

Prisoner reform charity St Giles Trust was part of the Peterborough delivery group.

"It's tough," St Giles CEO Rob Owen told me. "But these are early days in the history of social impact bonds. We have to try them out first and see what the limits of the possible are."

The promise of these bonds is that, by rewiring financial incentives, it takes the difficult moral questions of how to prevent reoffending and places them in the hands not of politicians but of prison governors, of social entrepreneurs providing rehabilitative services, and of those prisoners who work with them to make something of their lives.

It is not about *this* or *that* pet project but about what works, as evidenced by the performance of *this* intervention relative to a control group. The market would have to be led by the data and pay on the delivery of a just outcome. And the more value the social entrepreneur delivers, the better for everyone.

Creating such a bond, setting savings levels and calculating the requisite targets for the charities and social enterprises involved is not easily done; in Peterborough it took two years of crunching numbers to generate the right sort of levels for any sort of return.

This is a developing art, one not easily transferred to other social problems where the cost of things are not so readily available.

In order to set a fair level of profit the creator of the bond needs to have a well-developed sense of how much money is saved from the improved social intervention and a saving ratio that allows principals to be paid back from the savings.

Similarly, obtaining savings is a rather simpler endeavour in some areas of social policy than others. We know how much can be saved from preventing someone from reoffending because we know how much it costs to house a prisoner each night. In other areas, such as reaching at-risk families or vulnerable kids, it may be that much harder to calculate 'cashable' savings and the desirability of setting such targets may be limited, especially when it will cost time and money and effort to research in depth the data and so calculate those savings and limits.

Social investment bank Big Society Capital has been a huge supporter of social impact bonds. In its first phase it placed the social impact bond at the centre of its strategy to grow the social investment market in the UK (it has diversified considerably since).

In addition to the Peterborough social impact bond it invested in the social impact bond set up by Bridges Ventures with Teens and Toddlers, the previously mentioned charity that mentored children in order to try and improve academic achievement in under privileged kids between the ages of 13 and 17, which was also funded by Impetus-PEF.

Another social impact bond it has invested in is one set up by Eccles' outfit Social Finance, which, alongside the charity Adviza, created a bond that sought to reduce unemployment among young people by supporting vulnerable 14 to 15 year olds to improve their examination results at 16 and secure work. The saving is generated from a calculation based on how much is saved when young people don't go straight from school onto employment benefit. Each of these carried their own questions and risks, their own moral and practical difficulties.

In the USA, on a larger canvas than that of the UK, these projects have found even greater life.

One of the recipients of funding from this has been the Green and Healthy Homes Initiative, which has received US$1.1 million since 2012. It aims to reduce asthma incidence in low income children, by removing environmental hazards that are risk factors. The Green and Healthy Homes Initiative has distributed the funding received to ten smaller providers, dependent on the levels of success which they achieve in meeting the Initiative's aims.

Another major recipient of funding has been Third Sector Capital Partners. It distributes money to a variety of causes, ranging from Austin Health and Human Services Department to the State of Nevada. Each of these receive funding from Third Sector Capital Partners, dependent on their success in meeting targets which were pre-prescribed within their agreement.

These funds, and others like them, are a major source of funding for many organisations. In addition to the government funding received, they are able to leverage private donations as investment. As their schemes become more successful, the hope is that they will be able to attract more capital, and this expand their operations.

The critical response comes that this is a complicated instrument – and it is. It takes tough calculation to set the levels of profit, success and payout in a way that attracts investors.

The price of failure is always high, but the value of success higher still and the opportunity cost of not giving it a go and learning from failure rather than fearing it has been too great to ignore. Indeed, not engaging in prevention and early action is a game we cannot afford to play.

The USA spends US$190 billion a year on treating preventable obesity-related illness.[11] The cost of not funding mental health prevention could be as high as US$440 billion a year.[12] Public Health England estimates that a failure to engage the public in their own health costs the UK government £30 billion a year,[13] while the charity Action for Children claims that the cost of failing to intervene with 'at risk' children is likely to be £486 billion over the next 20 years.[14]

As such, the social impact or payment on success bond is one part of the equation, but only one.

A prevention revolution

There is no doubt that we need to get behind an international movement that *shifts spending towards preventative services*. Repeated studies show across a variety of contexts that spending a small amount in the foreground prevents a far greater bill from arising in the future. However, economic constraints mean things get tightened the other way.

In the UK, the National Audit Office found that spending on prevention was cut by 45% between 2010 and 2015. And even then preventative spending is a tough sell: government departments don't much like funding the future, especially when their bosses may be completely different in a few years' time.

It is not just a question of will but logistics. Governments are split into departments and the logic of this is that spending on prevention through increased education, for example, may result in fewer in prison further down the line. Here the money is spent by the education department and saved by the justice department. Internal civil wars prevent progress.

Social entrepreneurs are finding ways to resolve some of this tension but we also need reform at the political level.

In 2015, I helped to initiate the UK campaign 'Five for the Future' which attempts to *push government spending on prevention to 5%* of the total (an effective doubling) in key social welfare departments and 'Five More for the Future' which attempts to push it to 10% over the next five years, which closer to what the norm should be.[15]

Making this case requires the work of interventions like the social impact bond, great comings together of philanthropic foundations, government departments and businesses.

Even if money were made available through huge tax rises, the need to gather evidence on particular interventions would remain.

Yet if these interventions can give us the evidence base to encourage more government spending on preventative solutions, the entire system of government thinking might change, billions might be saved and millions of lives uplifted.

4. Welfare, aid and a financial transactions tax

We have made the case for tax breaks and reduced bureaucracy for social entrepreneurs and those who support them. *Investment schemes and incentives to invest socially and innovatively* are good ideas. But what about the bigger questions of supporting socially entrepreneurial action through the national tax base?

Domestic welfare budgets should certainly be used to platform the work of social entrepreneurs to achieve key social outcomes.

International aid budgets too. The Millennium Development Goals (MDGs) were formalised by the September 2000 Millennium Declaration which sought to reduce poverty and improve health and education and gender equality. They asserted that every individual has dignity; and hence, the right to freedom, equality, and a basic standard of living that includes freedom from hunger and violence, and the right to live in an environment of tolerance and solidarity.

There were eight development aims, established by the United Nations at the Millennium Summit in 2000 and a total of 144 areas where the UN measured progress. As of 2015, targets had not been met in most of them; however, only a handful of indicators — 16 in 2015 — saw no progress or deterioration.

The most lauded achievement of the entire endeavour was the success of goal 1A – to reduce, by 2015, the number of people living on less than US$1 a day by half.

This is undoubtedly significant – cutting the number from 1.9 billion to around 830 million (or 30.8% of the global population to 14%). That said, between 1981 and 2001 China alone cut poverty by over 600 million, ostensibly through targeted economic restructuring.[16]

As such, the MDGs have not been without their critics. More mirage than miracle, some have contended. And, following a UN 'My World' survey in 2015, other commentators noted that the aims of the MDGs bore little resemblance to the priorities set by those living in the developing world,[17] instead having the character of development aims imposed from 'on high'.

However fair or otherwise these analyses might be, at the time of writing, the MDGs' time is up. As of 2015, they have been replaced by the SDGs, a collection of 17 objectives, outlined by the UN report *Transforming our world: the 2030 Agenda for Sustainable Development*.

Rather than focusing on the developing world, this latest round – as the name suggests – outlines an ambition for more holistic global development. As with the MDGs, there are sub-targets and indicators: 169 targets, measuring 304 different indicators.

The evolution of the MDGs into SDGs is the key moment of opportunity here. It reflects the increased interconnectedness of our world and the importance of countries in all parts of the globe of adhering to a way of living and working and doing business that enables more of us to flourish.

No one country will have sufficient resources to tackle all 169 targets; there will have to be trade-offs according to the needs and resources in particular areas.

Consultancy firm Deloitte's influential report *Social Progress in 2030* was written in conjunction with the Social Progress Initiative and is a key resource.[18] It reflects on the Millennium Development Goals, on the fact that many argue that the success of the MDGs is the result of rapid economic growth in a few developing nations rather than any magic in the targets themselves (true: China's industrialisation and growing wealth has been responsible for the bulk of the movement on reducing extreme poverty since the early 1980s) and on how we can meet the SDGs.

It argues for the use of a metric referred to as the Social Progress Index (SPI) which tracks quantities, ranging from basic needs such as food to 'higher' causes such as political participation. Of less importance are so-called 'first order economic metrics': measures based exclusively on the disbursement and recycling of money.

So, for example, over the period to 2030, it is expected that global GDP (in the countries measured by the report) will increase from US$14,000 per capita to US$23,000 per capita. When the existing relationship between GDP and SPI is applied to this change, we see it rise from a score of 61 (out of 100) to 62.

This is contextualised as the difference between Cuba or Algeria and Nicaragua or the Dominican Republic. Even a doubling of economic growth rates over the next 15 years – bringing GDP to US$31,000 per capita – would still only see SPI rise to around 63. Economic growth alone, the conclusion goes, will not be sufficient to realise significant social progress over the next 15 years.

The terrain, therefore, is tailormade for social entrepreneurs to make the difference.

If this is to be realised we will have apply the principles outlined earlier to ever more territories: break down barriers, reduce bureaucracy, find ways of resourcing and overcoming the cycle of ignorance and the missing middle, and fund to the golden rule.

A recent study of 439 social enterprises – referred to as 'market-based solutions' – in Africa found that only 57 had achieved a significant size.[19] Often these organisations are facing an environment that is at best poorly set up to accommodate their activities, and at worst is outright hostile to their innovations, and in which organisations fall straight into the missing middle. If we follow the playbook outlined in this book, we have a chance of turning this around.

We know that some powerful advocates are on our side. Amina Mohammed, the UN Secretary-General's Special Adviser on Post-2015 Development Planning, was quite right when she argued that there would be a major role for entrepreneurs and innovators in the implementation of the SDGs. Bill Gates is another and his interventions swing us into another related plane of thought.

A financial transactions tax to support social entrepreneurship

At the G20 summit in Cannes in 2011, Gates came out in favour of *a financial transactions tax*, which would provide billions to tackle the world's biggest social problems.

The reasoning was clear: there is need, a need which conventional philanthropy (including his own foundation) cannot fulfil. And there is opportunity, an opportunity which social entrepreneurs and innovators are stepping up to meet. He spoke about new kinds of crops, new kinds of money transfer service, the entire gamut of social innovation that we have touched over the course of this book to service his argument.

Should we join his call? Certainly the idea is seductive, a form of redistribution that could provide a war-chest which social entrepreneurs can spin into massive social and economic gains. Perhaps now is the time to back them?

There are many forms of financial transaction tax, different kinds of trade and asset that may fall under its purview. The UK has had it in some form since the 'knavish and treasonous' stock jobbers of Sweetings Alley were forced to pay a stamp duty on their trades.

Some jurisdictions, such as France, have recently gone ahead. Others, such as Sweden, had one and then dropped it. The EU has attempted to drive continent-wide movement but meets resistance from entrenched interests, who fear unintended consequences, such as reduced liquidity or the costs being passed on.

It is beyond the scope of this book to outline the schematic of a global financial transactions tax that might work; to be credible this would involve a look at the entire spectrum of global arrangements including tax havens and national taxation policies.

Let us have this argument beyond these pages. These taxes exist in piecemeal; harmonising them would require immense co-operation but would yield an incredible legacy through which we can platform and drive the ingenuity and ambition of more of us.

Surely it is beholden on us, not to dismiss the idea out of fear or self-interest, but to properly engage with it, not just for a moment, but in sustained, evidence-driven debate?

5. A mass co-operative public sector

In 2011, I wrote in the *Guardian* newspaper about Katy Thorpe.[20] She was a teenager with a boyfriend who abused her. She fell pregnant and she went to live with her parents, overwhelmed at the prospect of becoming a young parent. It was her local family nurse, a member of a scheme run by the local hospital trust, who helped her, offered Katy simple advice about how to care for and eventually bond and play with her baby, as well as show him love and affection.

Family Nurse Partnerships all over the world can be an invaluable aid to young or overwhelmed new mothers. They are an example of that preventative or early intervening care: services that do not wait for social problems to materialise when relationships are not built, but rather that identify and work with vulnerable people to avoid problems before they occur.

Interventions like these build social capital but they also pertain to another piece of this puzzle. Katy's story emerged after she spoke at an event in which the local Family Nurse Partnership changed hands. Based in the UK, it 'span out' of Britain's National Health Service with a grant from the Department of Health and formed a social enterprise called RippleZ.[21] From April that year, nurses rather would run the service, as owners of their own independent organisation.

The benefits of a country's public sector 'going social enterprise' are many. Operating beyond the public sector with its various bureaucratic constraints gave RippleZ more freedom to raise its own funds and bring in its own advice so that it might grow, and help more people. I was there as RippleZ took its first steps in venture philanthropy with help from Impetus, having been set on its way as a new mutual – a community interest company – by UnLtd, as part of the foundation's initiative to change the systems around how we improve services for children.

It was a fraught couple of months. Building company infrastructure, making sure the back office is worthy of its product and getting some good mentors to give the company the benefit of their wisdom were the start. Its employment structure changed, and so did its system of pensions, which created further headaches. Working through problems like these systematically saw RippleZ double its turnover within those first two months – and in theory double the number of young parents its services could reach.

Within a small structure of public service workers, onerous targets and management structures often actively get in the way of good service. The argument is that creating co-operatives removes these structures. Remember the pioneer principles: the arrangement places the beneficiary rather than the bureaucracy or politics or capitalists at the centre of the organisation, places control and responsibility for those beneficiary's results in the hands of the workers, who decide democratically the direction of the social enterprise.

Empowered professionals who work with community members are more likely to be attuned to the work of other inventive social entrepreneurs working at ground level too; to link, learn, and leverage without the yoke of the bureaucrat holding them back. Indeed, that is a co-operative principle too. This is not so much a case of 'less state' as 'more social entrepreneurship'.

These are positive ideas that speak to the work of so-called 'systems thinkers' such as the USA's Russ Ackoff or the UK's John Seddon, who contend that often systems are designed that focus on 'internal requirements' (for example targets) rather than 'true objectives': meaningful improvement in people's lives. Such systems ultimately achieve the unenviable double of not doing what they are supposed to do and wasting money.

Systems thinkers argue that the role of managers should be first and foremost to study demand from the customers' point of view: to identify patterns, determine predictable and preventable demand, and facilitate frontline workers in tackling that demand. This will not only increase efficiency but improve user and citizen satisfaction. Co-operative structures give the flexibility to create such studies and adapt as required.

I flew a kite along these lines in another of my columns for the UK's *Guardian* newspaper in 2014. I questioned whether it might be possible to spin out job centres (or similar local state employment and entitlement agencies) from the main public system and help them reconstitute as independent social enterprises.[22]

Spinning out job centres could have significant virtues. Different areas could be offered different sets of services depending on the existing skillsets of its workers. A job centre might take on, say, online-based self-help services in an area with a younger population, while a more traditional face-to-face approach might work in other areas. Those are just two ideas.

Differing labour market conditions could be responded to with new initiatives rather than being hampered by a centralised bureaucracy that requires the same old papers and the same old assessments. These organisations would be more agile, more nimble, better able to thrive.

A co-operative driven service like this is not appropriate in every context and requires a good deal of support. Crucially, it must be led by the workers who will make up the mutual. Even today there are a few examples of spin outs – the semi-constructed West Mercia and Warwickshire mutual in the UK probation service was one, and its restructuring has been driven by skewed political and financial incentives and it ran into early difficulties as a result.

Do it well and the possibilities are considerable. The government agency British Waterways spun out into a charitable trust and a company limited by guarantee in 2012, after a funding crisis left it with a £30 million budget deficit. It is run by a board of trustees, responsible for making sure the organisation's charitable objectives are met, and who are advised and overseen by a council of elected and nominated members. The change has also helped the trust improve its operations, so that in 2013/14 it actually raised £5 million more income than it had targeted – which it was then able to spend on maintaining Britain's beautiful canals.

From nursing to job centres to waterways, mutualisation promises to return a real sense of community ownership to service-delivering organisations. Governments have every reason to push it, agitate for it and support it, as do we.

6. Free up and cherish our grass-roots community campaigners

The movements in this book flow from injustice, from anger, from wanting to solve a problem or right a wrong. They ripen into campaigns, and solutions, which ripen into movements, organisations and enterprises. Common to all of the above is that sense of justice, that need to stick to the mission; to debate and discern the values that we share and the solution that best tackles the challenge before us.

Central to all of this is advocacy. We live in an age of advocates who reach out and rally. Each link in the chain of social entrepreneurship depends upon this advocacy.

The future of social action is a future where advocacy becomes an increasing part of the work of socially minded organisations; where debate and interrogation accompanies the work they do.

Solidarity funds depend on community buy-in and awareness to generate their returns. There is a digital future of action beyond the echo chamber. There is the entire question of whether certain organisations are social enterprises with their beneficiaries' best interests at heart or 'corporations in drag' who use the badge cynically to get more work. The only way to nullify them is to expose them, publicly.

Feedback requires advocacy or else it is left on the shelf. Charities, social enterprises and the people who support them must campaign, be politically active, advocate for their beneficiaries, and lobby now more than ever before, for the future will not forgive them if they do not.

All of this places a greater duty on us than ever before to take part in public debate and for government to jealously protect the public square. For social enterprises and charities of all stripes, campaigning is no longer an 'optional extra'; in truth, it never was.

There are times even when social entrepreneurs will need to be protected from government itself. One painful example I remember is that of MyPolice, a social enterprise designed to foster engagement between communities and their local police forces. Its name was duplicated by the government for its own police engagement website, which was not terribly helpful to the cause of the business.

There is a happy ending to that story and it required the sort of public debate we talk about here. A 2010 flash online campaign supporting MyPolice utilised robust, punchy articles by me and advocacy from others including *Financial Times* journalist James Crabtree to arrow this issue up the agenda. Within a day, the government conceded that it had made an error.

A small victory then, and instructive. Power is inevitably arrogant; it resists challenge and change. Sometimes we must explain the error of its ways.

Small victories like are one thing; taking on legislative injustice directed at independent organisations is another. All over the world, repressive regimes crack down on independent action. Governments with atrocities to hide do not like it when groups of independent citizens come together, when leaders step forward and offer hope beyond the government teat.

One tranche of social enterprises registered by the South Korean government looks specifically at creating dialogue between citizens of the south and dissidents of the north. The regime in Pyongyang should be concerned. Social entrepreneurship is bad for dictators.

But these threats do not only come from these regimes. The Trump administration in the USA recently signed into law amendments that prevent independent organisations funded by USAID taking certain policy positions with regard to abortion. Regardless of your position in this debate, this is a remarkable attempt by a government to diminish the independent civic voice. And this is happening in the developed world.

Even the British government, for so long the vanguard of working with charities and social enterprises, has joined the authoritarian bandwagon. By passing the so-called 'Lobbying Act' in 2014 the government restricted the amount that social enterprises and other NGOs could raise their voices that election year and so gagged them at a crucial point in the democratic cycle. To deny vulnerable people a voice during an election was a bewilderingly undemocratic act; the principled argument against it continues.

Then in 2015, there came another authoritarian move. The government sought to ban advocacy groups from using grant funding from government to examine policy decisions and suggest improvements of any kind.

If the US measure was about gagging the independent voice as applied to abortion and the Lobbying Act was about gagging it at certain points in the calendar, this was something akin to a blanket ban on speaking up for those organisations with the temerity to think that working with government might be in the public interest.

The last story, at least, has a happy ending. I lobbied a group of charities and social enterprises to join me in contesting that decision – and together we sought to take the government to court.

Terse legal exchanges got us into a meeting with the legislator, who paused the implementation of the clause as they scratched their heads about what to do next. Then: Brexit. Britain voted to leave the European Union. The prime minister resigned. A new one came in who wanted to do it differently. And within a few weeks, the clause was gone.

The thought occurs: despite all of the patient diplomacy, principled debate and legal argument, it was the political change that got us the right result. That is campaigning for you. Sometimes it requires smart politics as well as shifts in law – and why social entrepreneurs and charities must brush up on their public affairs skills as well as their campaign savvy.

Our task here is constant. We are the vanguard that fights dismal authoritarianism. The elites; those with power: they will not give up that power without a fight. Independent organisations are in their crosshairs for independent organisations threaten everything. And as the old orders of politics, social segregation and inequality and economics are overturned, the agents of that change, the social entrepreneurs of this book, will be pressured.

Regimes of all stripes, bonded only by their malicious addiction to power, will react by attempting to strangle the independent voice; by outdoing each other's high-handedness and moral cowardice.

In so doing, they push societies and our democracies backwards and that is why our campaign must be to resist this at all costs.

Alongside the freedom of press, the freedom of speech of independent groups is one of the highest virtues we hold. Such groups perform an essential ameliorative function on the state and society, to the quality and humanity of our public conversation. In our time, their spirit and fire is the foundation on which some of the biggest social change movements of our era are founded. It begins and ends with democracy: an ideal worth fighting for.

CONCLUSION

Creating a new kind of capitalism

As I write these last paragraphs, the global economic system we have continues to do very well indeed for a minority of people. At the same time, the rate of extreme poverty worldwide remains high. The inroads into extreme poverty that we have made over these last few decades have been largely the result of the work of a few countries, notably China. There remain, in extreme poverty, a few hundred million in India, more across Africa. Others are spread around in parts of South America and elsewhere. We are talking here about people in our time living on around US$1.90 or less a day. The World Bank wants to get that figure to zero by 2030 but this is really very ambitious and every day this situation persists, people suffer and children are born into servitude.

Consider also, since the mid-1970s, both the USA and the UK have become less rather than more equal (per the gini coefficient, a widely used measure of equality). As of 2012, the bottom half of society in the USA owns just 3% of the wealth and 19% are below the poverty line. In the UK these figures stand at 5% and 9% respectively.

Those are but two examples of the negative consequences of our system. Persistent extreme poverty in the developing world sits alongside persistent inequality in the developed world.

As we live through global recessions and austere governments, thin gruel for savers and bone-dry public services, as market failures that mean that the poor pay poverty premiums for basic goods and lack access to the things we take for granted persist, the question is asked repeatedly and honestly: are we really happy that this must be our lot? Put more constructively: how do we improve on the system we have so that the fruits of the good life can be enjoyed by more of us?

Throughout this book we have adumbrated the idea of the moral marketplace being a rebuke to the system – the capitalism – we have. We asked whether, at the point where capitalism meets philanthropy, something new emerges that may be fairer and greater than the current dispensation.

Let's try to clarify that idea. We are not talking here about doing away with money, marketplaces or exchanges. Several of the technologies we have discussed in this book develop and evolve these things. But pretty much every society in human history has had some form of these things for they are useful.

Of more interest is the idea that we might repair and reform *capitalism*, the system founded on private ownership, free markets and profit, whose logical conclusion suggests that the owners of capital and the needs of capital are the determining factor of our collective future.

On one reading, the movements in this book accept the capitalist thesis. They are positive about private ownership and enterprise; about profit, in moderation. They work with the apparatus we have as a matter of pragmatism, surfing investment funds, trading floors and the like.

However, there are many points of discord and reform. In social entrepreneurship, profit maximisation is very rarely the name of the game: profit mediated by a public duty based on our shared values is the overwhelming majority of the movement.

Ownership is good, but only if ownership is diversified. For a truly free market we need a society of owners. This is what the co-operative-movement's Rochdale pioneers envisioned. Indeed, in the case of co-operatives, it is value-creating activity, not the mere ownership and accumulation of assets, that confers rights.

Where the moral marketplace is concerned, the behaviour of the market and the preferences of the owners of capital are to be joined by a third force in determining the future: the humanitarian needs of the planet. The greatest influence on the structure of the moral marketplace is the desire to end human misery and promote human progress.

This may be capitalism, but it is not as we know it.

This is not the time to develop a complex economic thesis. Consider this a gentle prod designed to open up the possibilities presented by the moral marketplace just that little bit further.

As our version of capitalism staggers from shock to collapse, as the world continues to bifurcate and splinter, as the systems of government that depend on this capitalism suffer from a failure of political vision, it is worth asking whether the movements we have discussed in this book offer an alternative. Could they, in sum, contribute not only to economic improvement at the grassroots, but to a genuine economic and political re-imagining; a democratisation of the economic space that serves to tilt the balance of power?

Think of it this way. At the heart of a more co-operative economy is the notion of collective ownership and community empowerment.

At the heart of a more mutualised state is the idea that workers and beneficiaries should determine how tax dollars are used, not bureaucrats.

At the heart of user-driven public services is the idea that communities can self-organise to arrange complex services and take charge of swathes of tax dollars and public patronage – if given tools and support.

The idea behind Chapter Seven's three-dimensional investment is that we live in a world where people can choose to operate with the best interests of society in mind or not and be judged in business terms on that basis.

The idea behind Chapter Three's shared value is that corporations will cease to exist without acknowledging their status as citizens of the society in which they operate: that corporations that thrive should not be those that cut corners but those that help society's corners flourish.

Rewiring business, investment, technology to the end of social good: these are strong foundations. A system where capital is allocated not on the instructions of those who possess it but on the needs of those who do not presents us with a radical vision with which I reckon we can work. The pieces fit together and something beautiful and momentous takes shape.

Discerning the good

But look: there is some way to go before we get to that point. By now you know that some of the elements of this movement are more solidly realised than others. In some areas, there are question marks and debates, questions of value and judgement. We have come such a long way, but there remain at least three futures for the movement and I leave you now with the view that only one of them is desirable.

Let's call the first future the *super-hyper-capitalist nightmare*. Here, the stellar growth of community movements results in a social enterprise sector that completely forgets its roots. This is a vision of a future social economy that is dominated by the economic elite.

With their size and scale and power, their reach into the hearts of governments, the cogs and wheels of big business subsume the social entrepreneur in her entirety. From the kinds of people that become social entrepreneurs, to the kinds of projects the movement indulges; from the metrics to the jargon to the objectives of the movement: the whole thing becomes about efficiency and money and passes the work of actual community activism back to the charity sector.

Such a vision would take this creature wrought of the ingenuity and labour of grassroots communities and ruin it. Thus repackaged beyond recognition it stops being the thing we knew it to be and we lose hope in it, in ourselves. The dream of a powerful alternative powered by us, created by us, will crumble to the sound of the eternal clunking mantra: 'there is no alternative'.

The nightmare scenario is of capitalism swallowing this insurgency, like some massive yellow amoeba playing online multiplayer agar.io, swallowing all dots in its path.

Remember the anti-neoliberals, academics like Robert Skidelsky and William Davies, who *insist* that our capitalism has created a culture of unbridled envy, competition, desolation and dismay and these become the only emotions we are capable of truly feeling. Social entrepreneurship suggests another way but a world in which the ear to the ground is closed off will only add grist to the anti-capitalist mill. In these horror-shows, profit-motivated juggernauts come to occupy our every waking moment, our dreams and our nightmares. Brands litter our streets, the cyberpunk authors write of future planet sponsored by burger chains while here on earth billionaires reclaim land in oceans and envision great offshore working spaces that circumvent employment laws. Social entrepreneurship is little better than that.

Okay, so there was a bit of poetic licence there. We don't need to go quite that far to think that a balanced economic equation, with the needs of the many, rather than the few at its heart could be a good thing.

Or that bringing the virtuous impulses of generosity, equality, collaboration, belief and hope and its centre sitting alongside the purifying principles of competition and self-interest might represent a better balance on which to structure the bigger part of our world.

You do not have to be blessed with great foresight to see in the rise of social entrepreneurship, a healthy balance between charity and change; business and progress.

And if you go that far, if these things are important, a future in which the moral marketplace moves from the edges of our consciousness into the mainstream; from a tool of development to a tool of mass empowerment wrought of the economic and political centre becomes that much more critical.

Which brings us to the second future. Let's call it, for the sake of novelty, *the age of the moral marketplace.*

The moral marketplace is on the move. We have witnessed its logic; have seen how social entrepreneurship transitions seamlessly from leadership style to development technique to industry maker, to capitalist powerhouse, to economic fundamental.

The scope of what was once a series of passionate but local community movements has ballooned beyond the wildest imaginations of its pioneers. And when this has been done really well, it has retained a laser-focus on the people that matter, has been driven, run and owned by people on the ground.

The solidarity economy, the gift economy, the social economy: call it what you will. This is what we are trying to protect and grow: that which burnishes hope and transmits its light.

There is no single way of inaugurating this future, or mitigating the risks of the first. The only possible approach is vigilance and dialogue; understanding and nurturing these movements. In this, I think, we all have a role to play. So here are my final set of pleas to you that might help us avoid the dismal and embrace the glorious.

Support your social entrepreneurs

That's right. Buy more from them; buy social as often as you can. People like me will try to help by providing advice and insight. There are apps, and there will be better ones that make this stuff more convenient. Share them.

Look to support them in your investments and savings; in your pension pot choices and your current accounts. Badger your advisers to give you these options.

If you come into some money or want to leave something behind, don't set up family foundations, think about setting up family impact investment funds, like Charly Kleissner, a trailblazer in the space who decided to turn his family foundations to such investments, sacked his accountants and went for it alone.

And if you are setting up a social venture of your own: be entrepreneurial. Choose flexibility over tax breaks, aspiration over regulation, social impact and the social economy over endless fundraising drives and the donations dilemma. If you don't back yourself to create something sustainable, no one will.

Agitate for political change

The age of the moral marketplace requires a political humanitarianism to go with its economic humanitarianism.

That means we need to know from our politicians the extent to which they are prepared to come clean, seek help beyond the comfortable and known, their own bureaucracies or the private sector super-providers who live and breathe profit – and reach out to social entrepreneurs.

Will they place social entrepreneurs at the front and centre of our politics? Six sets of major ideas, some 30 major policy recommendations are contained in this book. Let's get them on the table.

By now, we know: governments that do anything but send for the social entrepreneurs are not being serious. Corporate culture is arid and self-interested. Government is atrophied, sclerotic and out of ideas. Charity is good but not good enough.

People ask for greater taxation and for corporations to pay what they owe and that is important. It is the base on which good rests. That good is articulated and delivered by communities, working with social entrepreneurs.

An economics rooted in communities could be augmented by a genuine communitarian politics. Let us see who can best approximate this vision; let us back it.

Own the conversation

You are initiated; you are now in the box seat to decide the future. The conversation is yours to take on.

You should not be alone. This movement is huge, remember. It is the product of a quiet revolution that grew unknown to most. Now we can state with confidence what is and isn't a social enterprise, whether such and such meets the 'smell' test for being social enough; we can put forth our views enough to disagree with each other and that is enough.

Talk about the changes that you want to see and which organisations you trust to deliver it.

Just as we have caught up with all of this, a key ally – the media – has to go through the same journey.

Let's help them. We need the media on our side. A number of social entrepreneur movements have been set up to attempt to shift this needle. They call it constructive journalism. There are centres across the world; key nodes include David Bornstein, an author whose work influenced this book and who writes the excellent 'Fixes' blog.

Despite what some might have you believe, it is not that the media does not report on constructive stories. Quite the reverse. But if a story is to carry, it needs to be framed properly and its newsworthiness understood and communicated. That is a job in itself.

It need not take a huge amount of dumbing down – it is not only stories about animals and celebrities and randy politicians that sell. Stories about communities turning around their situations, high streets transforming from broken to pristine: the things that social entrepreneurs do as a matter of course. Framed correctly, they could become a recurrent part of the stories we see every day, alongside all of the miserable stuff.

If old media seems too restrictive, what about the internet? Here, people power can and must push the difference.

Releasing a story in the new media that gains attention forces the rest to take a look.

That's the ambition of a whole new type of online social enterprise. UpWorthy.com is one such site, which allows people to share and vote on great social stories.

Targeting new and old media with great social entrepreneur stories should be our collective aim. It will help.

Join forums, use your knowledge to inform the debate the debate, help others make good choices and share good news. It really is easier than ever before to do play your part and do a whole lot of good.

Take responsibility, no matter how small

We use words like democratise, people power, radical, revolutionary and it can sound grandiose. But, really, there is a simple concept is at the heart of all this.

The best social entrepreneurs act as lenses that enable us to see it that much more clearly. They encourage each of us taking responsibility for the things that matter and facilitate that which is beautiful within us.

I said there were three futures, didn't I? Well, the third future is no future at all.

It consists of us choosing to remain where we are. Call it *do-nothing-and-pray*.

We remain precariously balanced between these two eventualities, tip-toed on the edge of a knife. Following that metaphor through to extremes: you tilt, you slip, you fall on the sword.

If we do nothing, we are surely offering everything we have achieved together on a plate to those who only know how to take and we will receive so little in return. We will thus acknowledge that the purpose of this work is to perpetuate the status quo, to offer that release valve for the system we have.

We eschew the possibility of something better because we do not truly believe that better is possible. I just don't believe that anyone who has read this far really believes that.

I think for us, there is no going back now. The risk to remain is greater than the risk to flower. Our work is to support the biggest community movement in human history; which with your support we can make even bigger.

This is not just about agitating for the big ideas in this book – though that would be a start.

This is about you. You can connect to it in so many different ways. If you are minded to give to charity, to write a cheque, to drop a few coins in a bucket, that is good. But why stop there? There is a wealth of opportunity to make an even bigger difference.

This is a movement that needs your ideas and input; that wants to combine your skills and abilities with your spirit of generosity and create not just instances but legacies of change.

Consider the alternatives it provides when you are going to the supermarket, considering a project at work, chilling at home wondering what to do, taking out or recycling your garbage or messing around on the internet.

Each of us has the tools at our disposal to empathise with others, find common connection, influence and improve lives. A smile is good; a piece of computing power, a P2P loan or your skills put to the service of mentoring a child who has no one else are often even better.

Really, the possibilities are endless.

As endeavours go, as things to do, projects to while away a few minutes, hours, months, or whole lives: it doesn't get much better than this. Reform capitalism; create the world's first ever multi-trillion dollar platform for social good; inaugurate the age of the moral marketplace: what's stopping us?

Notes and references

Introduction

[1] Cabinet Office/Office of the Third Sector (2008) 'Is Social Enterprise at a Crossroads?', p 21. Accessed 27 April 2010 at: http://www.cabinetoffice. gov. uk/media/cabinetoffice/third_sector/assets/COI%20SE%20 presentation%20FINAL.pdf

[2] World Bank estimates. See also http://www.worldbank.org/en/news/ feature/2015/03/30/does-microfinance-still-hold-promise-for-reaching-the-poor

[3] Figure for total global wealth of $241 trillion retrieved 29 June 2017 from: https://publications.credit-suisse.com/tasks/render/ file/?fileID=BCDB1364-A105-0560-1332EC9100FF5C83

[4] Coley, R. and Baker, B. (2013) *Poverty and Education: Finding the Way Forward.* Retrieved 29 June 2017 from: https://www.ets.org/s/research/ pdf/poverty_and_education_report.pdf.

[5] Charities Aid Foundation (2015) *UK Giving 2014.* Retrieved 29 June 2017 from: https://www.cafonline.org/about-us/publications/2015-publications/uk-giving-2014

Chapter One

[1] Some of this case study emerges from material that I was directed to by Keggfarms CEO Vipin Malhotra, and for which I was very grateful, given that Vinod Kapur, at the time of writing, had some difficulty with hearing loss. Some of the details of Kapur's and Keggfarm's rise are taken from Isenberg, D. (2007) *Keggfarms (India)—Which Came First, the Kuroiler™ or the KEGG™?,* Harvard Business School, 9-807-089.

2   Studies were conducted by Professor Jagdev Sharma (2011) at the Biodesign Institute of the University of Arizona; see, for example, Sharma, J., Xie, J., Boggess, M., Galukande, E., Semambo, D. and Sharma, S. (2015) 'Higher weight gain by Kuroiler chickens than indigenous chickens raised under scavenging conditions by rural households in Uganda', *Livestock Research for Rural Development*, volume 27, article #178. Retrieved 26 June 2017 from: http://www.lrrd.org/lrrd27/9/shar27178.html

3   Retrieved 29 June 2017 from: www.groupe-sos.org

4   Retrieved 29 June 2017 from: http://www.nielsen.com/ug/en/press-room/2015/consumer-goods-brands-that-demonstrate-commitment-to-sustainability-outperform.html

5   OECD (2013) *Policy Brief on Social Entrepreneurship: Entrepreneurial Activities in Europe*. Retrieved 29 June 2017 from: www.oecd.org/cfe/leed/Social%20entrepreneurship%20policy%20brief%20EN_FINAL.pdf

6   British Council (2015) *Social Enterprise: An Overview of the Policy Framework in India*. Retrieved 29 June 2017 from: www.britishcouncil.org/sites/default/files/social_enterprise_policy_landscape_in_india_british_council.pdf

7   Alter, K. (2007) *Social Enterprise Typology*, Washington: Virtue Ventures.

8   Schumpeter, J.A. (1934, 2008) *The Theory of Economic Development: An Inquiry into Profits, Capital, Credit, Interest and the Business Cycle*, translated from the German by Redvers Opie, New Brunswick and London: Transaction Publishers.

9   Von Mises, L. (ed) (1998) *Human Action*, Auburn, Alabama: Ludwig von Mises Institute, p 255.

10 Schumpeter, J.A. (1942) *Capitalism, Socialism, and Democracy*, Harper & Bros, p 83.

11 Bornstein, D. (2004) *How to Change the World*, Oxford: Oxford University Press.

12 Alter, K. (2007) *Social Enterprise Typology*, Washington: Virtue Ventures.

13 Ibid. Several efforts were made by the publisher and author to contact the academic in question, alas without success.

14 Yunus, M. (2007) *Creating a World without Poverty*, Yunus Foundation.

15 Mirsa, U. (2015) 'Explained: Meaning of a Section 25 Company', *Indian Express*, http://indianexpress.com/article/explained/explained-meaning-of-a-section-25-company/

16 Retrieved 29 June 2017 from: www.tatasechallenge.org

17 Prahalad, C.K. (2004) *The Fortune at the Bottom of the Pyramid*, University of Pennsylvania, Wharton School Publishing.

[18] Young, D.R. and Grinsfelder, M.C. (2011) 'Social Entrepreneurship and the Financing of Third Sector Organisations', *Journal of Public Affairs Education* vol 17, no 4, pp 543–67.

[19] Retrieved 29 June 2017 from: www.thegiin.org

[20] The story of Mirakle is told in Yunus, M. (2011) *Building Social Business: The New Kind of Capitalism that Serves Humanity's Most Pressing Needs.* New York: Public Affairs.

[21] Retrieved 29 June 2017 from: www.socialenterprisecensus.org

[22] *Beyond Profit Indian Social Enterprise Landscape Survey* (2010, as reported by the Sankalp Forum, see: http://www.sankalpforum.com/wp-content/uploads/2013/05/india-social-enterprise-landscape-report.pdf

Chapter Two

[1] Details of Betty Makoni's life are taken from an interview she conducted with New Zimbabwe: www.newzimbabwe.com/news-1148-The+Truth+About+Betty+Makoni/news.aspx

[2] Retrieved 29 June 2017 from: http://www.girlchildnetworkworldwide.blogspot.co.uk

[3] Ibid.

[4] Makoni, B., 'The Girl Child Empowerment Strategy', GCN, retrieved 29 June 2017 from: http://projects.essex.ac.uk/ehrr/V7N1/Makoni.pdf

[5] van der Paauw, C. (2016) *The Critical Success Factors and Barriers of Social Enterprises in the Health and Social Care Sector,* Vrije Universiteit of Amsterdam, http://nieuw.multivation.nl/wp-content/uploads/2016/09/Succes-factors-of-social-enterprises-in-health-and-social-care.pdf

[6] Mustapha, E.B. (2008) 'Social Entrepreneurship in Indonesia and Chine: From Micro Credit to Community Development', National University of Malaysia, www.ufhrd.co.uk/wordpress/wp-content/uploads/2008/06/must-186-wp.pdf

[7] Singh, A. (2010) *The Venture Society*, ResPublica, available at: www.respublica.org.uk/wp-content/uploads/2015/01/Venture-Society.pdf

[8] www.shaftesburypartnership.org/

[9] As quoted in Singh, A. (2010) *The Venture Society*, ResPublica, www.respublica.org.uk/wp-content/uploads/2015/01/Venture-Society.pdf

[10] Ibid.

[11] Retrieved 29 June 2017 from: http://csip.vn/en

[12] Retrieved 29 June 2017 from: altcity.me

[13] UnLtd (2014) *Impact Report 2014*, available at: https://unltd.org.uk/2015/04/09/unltd-impact-report-2014/

[14] Ibid.

[15] Retrieved 29 June 2017 from: www.tides.org

16 Global Social Entrepreneurship Network (GSEN) (2016) 'Meet our Members', www.gsen.global/members

17 Updated data can be found at socialcapitalmarkets.net

18 Retrieved 29 June 2017 from: https://www.theguardian.com/social-enterprise-network/2014/apr/08/social-enterprise-women-leaders

19 As quoted in Singh, A. (2010) *The Venture Society*, ResPublica.

Chapter Three

1   Retrieved 29 June 2017 from: www.aidtoartisans.org

2   Quoted in Judah, H. (2009) *Crafted with Care*, London: Financial Times.

3   Retrieved 29 June 2017 from: www.nytimes.com/2005/09/18/style/tmagazine/puff-dada.html?_r=0

4   Judah, H. (2009) *Crafted with Care*, London: Financial Times.

5   Retrieved 6 June 2017 from: http://ica.coop/en/history-co-op-movement/rochdale-pioneers

6   Retrieved 6 June 2017 from: https://ica.coop/en/what-co-operative

7   For more information on the structure and history of Amul, see their website at: http://www.amul.com/m/organisation

8   International Cooperative Alliance, (2013) 'Blueprint for a Co-operative Decade', Oxford, available at http://ica.coop/sites/default/files/publication-files/blueprint-for-a-co-operative-decade-english-1707281677.blueprint-for-a-co-operative-decade-english (accessed 29 June 2017)

9   Retrieved 29 June 2017 from: https://coopseurope.coop/2012-coops-year/un-secretary-general-ban-ki-moon-says-co-operatives-build-better-world

10 Retrieved 9 October 2016 from: https://www.foodcoop.com/home

11 Retrieved 29 June 2017 from: https://www.ipsos.com/ipsos-mori/en-uk/ipsos-mori-global-trends-2017-biggest-survey-its-kind

12 Retrieved 29 June 2017 from: http://news.gallup.com/poll/1597/confidence-institutions.aspx

13 Weinstein, A. (2014) 'Andrew talks B Corp and shared value', B the change: The Blog, retrieved 29 June 2017 from: http://www.bcorporation.net/blog/andrew-talks-b-corps-and-shared-value

14 Hilton, S. and Gibbon, G. (2002), *Good Business: Your World Needs You*, Texere Publishing, pp 62–3.

15 See eg Schwartz, M.S. and Saiia, D. (2012) 'Should Firms Go "Beyond Profits"? Milton Friedman versus Broad CSR'. *Business and Society Review*, 117: 1–31.

16 Porter, M. and Kramer, M. (2011) 'Creating Shared Value', *Harvard Business Review*, nos 1-2 (January–February): 62–77.

17 See hwww.goodmustgrow.com/ccsindex/downloads/GmG_Infographic. pdf (accessed 29 June 2017).

18 See www.fairphone.com (accessed 29 June 2017).

19 See www.solerebels.com (accessed 29 June 2017).

20 See https://www.forbes.com/forbes/welcome/?toURL=https://www. forbes.com/sites/mfonobongnsehe/2012/01/05/africas-most-successful-women-bethlehem-tilahun-alemu/

Chapter Four

1   See, for example, Myers-Lipton, S. (2006) *Social Solutions to Poverty: America's Struggle to Build a Just Society*, Boulder, CO: Paradigm Publishers.

2   Croke, K. (2014) *The Long Run Effects of Early Childhood Deworming on Literacy and Numeracy: Evidence from Uganda*, available at: http://scholar. harvard.edu/files/kcroke/files/ug_lr_deworming_071714.pdf

3   Duflo, E. and Banerjee, A. (2011) *Poor Economics*, New York, NY: Public Affairs.

4   Retrieved 6 June 2017 from: www.charitystar.org

5   Retrieved 29 June 2017 from: http://www.thinknpc.org/blog/sroi-not-enough/

6   Quoted in Singh, A. (2010) *The Venture Society*, ResPublica.

7   Ipsos MORI (2014) *Public Trust and Confidence in Charities*, available at: https://www.ipsos.com/ipsos-mori/en-uk/public-trust-and-confidence-charities-2014?language_content_entity=en-uk

8   In keeping with its focus on impact, GiveWell publishes its own impact statistics on its website: www.givewell.org

9   This data is taken from the National Center for Charitable Statistics, which publishes an array of data on the state of charities in the USA; see www. nccs.urban.org

10 This information, as well as a variety of other facts and figures on the Gates Foundation, can be found on the Foundation's website: www. gatesfoundation.org

11 As reported in *The Guardian*, see: https://www.theguardian.com/global-development/poverty-matters/2011/nov/04/bill-gates-speech-g20-capital-flight (accessed 29 June 2017).

12 Retrieved 6 June 2017 from: nccs.urban.org

13 Singer, P. (2010) *The Life You Can Save: How to Play your Part in Ending World Poverty*, London: Random House; Singer, P. (2016) *The Most Good You Can Do: How Effective Altruism is Changing Ideas About Living Ethically*. New Haven: Yale University Press.

14 Giving What We Can is a charity evaluator and movement to get people
    to give more of their income: see www.givingwhatwecan.org (accessed
    29 June 2017)

15 MacAskill, W. (2015) *Doing Good Better*, London: Guardian, Faber.

16 Singer, P. (1972) 'Famine, Affluence, and Morality', *Philosophy and Public
    Affairs*, 1(1): 229–43.

17 IFC (2010) *M-Money Channel Distribution Case – Afghanistan: Roshan M-Paisa*.
    www.ifc.org/wps/wcm/connect/cad6888049585efe9e8abf19583b6d16/
    Tool%2B6.9.%2BCase%2BStudy%2B-%2BM-Paisa%2BAfghanistan.
    pdf?MOD=AJPERES

18 Heinrick, E. (2013) 'How Afghanistan is on the Leading Edge of a Tech
    Revolution', *TIME*, 2 March, http://world.time.com/2013/03/02/how-
    afghanistan-is-on-the-leading-edge-of-a-tech-revolution/

19 Ibid.

20 Bryce, R. (2014) 'How Digital Currency Could End Corruption in
    Afghanistan', *WIRED*, 30 May, www.wired.com/2014/05/how-digital-
    currency-could-end-corruption-in-afghanistan/

Chapter Five

1   Retrieved 6 June 2017 from: www.robinhood.org

2   Feldman, A. (2010) 'Helping Nonprofits Raise Money like Goldman
    Does', retrieved 6 June 2017 from: https://www.bloomberg.com/news/
    articles/2010-02-11/helping-nonprofits-raise-money-like-goldman-does

3   Retrieved 6 June 2017 from: https://data.ncvo.org.uk/category/almanac/
    voluntary-sector/?publication=almanac12

4   Age UK (2015) *Report of Trustees and Annual Accounts 2014/15*, available
    at: http://www.ageuk.org.uk/about-us/what-we-do/previous-reports/

5   Alter, K. (2007) *Social Enterprise Typology*, Washington: Virtue Ventures.

6   Acevo (2017) *Charity Today*, retrieved 19/11/2017 from: https://www.
    acevo.org.uk/news/charity-today-2017

7   CGAP (2011) *How Generous is the UK? Charitable Giving in the Context of
    Household Spending*, retrieved 6 June 2017 from: http://www.cgap.org.uk/
    uploads/Briefing%20Papers/CGAP%20BN7%20How%20generous%20
    is%20the%20UK.pdf

8   NCVO (2015) *NCVO Almanac 2015*, retrieved 6 June 2017 from: https://
    data.ncvo.org.uk/

9   Coley, R. and Baker, B. (2013) *Poverty and Education: Finding the Way
    Forward*, retrieved 29 June 2017 from: https://www.ets.org/s/research/
    pdf/poverty_and_education_report.pdf.

[10] Hirsch, D. (2013) *An estimate of the cost of child poverty in 2013*, retrieved 29 June 2017 from: /www.cpag.org.uk/sites/default/files/Cost%20of%20 child%20poverty%20research%20update%20%282013%29.pdf

[11] Charities Aid Foundation (2015) *UK Giving 2014*, retrieved 29 June 2017 from: https://www.cafonline.org/about-us/publications/2015-publications/uk-giving-2014

[12] US figures from Giving USA Survey; UK figures from NCVO Almanac. Both publications are updated annually and are available online, providing a useful source of information on charity funding.

[13] Berger, K. and Penna, R.M. (2013) 'The Elitist Philanthropy of So-Called Effective Altruism', *Stanford Social Innovation Review*, 25 November, https:// ssir.org/articles/entry/the_elitist_philanthropy_of_so_called_effective_ altruism

[14] Harford, T. (2012) 'Charity begins… in the back office', *Financial Times*, 17 March.

[15] Drayton, B. (2004) 'Needed: A Social Financial Services Industry', *Alliance*, 9(1).

[16] See for example his book: Pallotta, D. (2012) *Charity Case: How the Non-Profit Community Can Stand up for Itself and Really Change the World*, San Francisco, CA: Jossey-Bass.

[17] Lesley-Anne Alexander's speech given to Acevo annual conference, November 2014.

Chapter Six

[1] Jacobs, J. (1961) *The Death and Life of Great American Cities*, New York, NY: Random House.

[2] See www.muhammadyunus.org/index.php/yunus-centre/yunus-centre-highlights/850-fukuoka-declared-social-business-city-by-mayor-as-asian-forum-for-social-business-closes (accessed 30 August 2016).

[3] More on the SI Park can be found here (in Spanish): http://denokinn. eu/?page_id=14&lang=en (accessed 10 October 2016).

[4] Retrieved 29 June 2017 from: www.reserveinc.org

[5] See www.thenewbarnraising.com (accessed 29 June 2017).

[6] Young, D.R. and Grinsfelder, M.C. (2011) 'Social Entrepreneurship and the Financing of Third Sector Organisations', *Journal of Public Affairs Education* vol 17, no 4, pp 543–67.

[7] Bennion, J. (2005) *South Africa: The Play Pump*, Frontline World, PBS, www. pbs.org/frontlineworld/rough/2005/10/south_africa_th.html

[8] Prahalad, C.K. (2004) *The Fortune at the Bottom of the Pyramid*, University of Pennsylvania, Wharton School Publishing.

9   Sherradan, M. (1991) *Assets and the Poor: A New American Welfare Policy.* Armonk, NY: Routledge.

10 World Bank (2015) 'Mobile payments go viral: M-Pesa in Kenya', http:// web.worldbank.org/WBSITE/EXTERNAL/COUNTRIES/AFRICA EXT/0,,contentMDK:22551641~pagePK:146736~piPK:146830~theSit ePK:258644,00.html (accessed 7 August 2016).

11 Smith, D. (2014) 'Internet use on mobile phones in Africa predicted to increase 20-fold', *Guardian*, 5 June.

12 World Economic Forum (2014) *The Global Information Technology Report 2014*, http://www3.weforum.org/docs/WEF_GlobalInformationTechnology_Report_2014.pdf

13 Smith, D. (2014) 'Internet use on mobile phones in Africa predicted to increase 20-fold', *Guardian*, 5 June.

14 See, for example, http://nextbillion.net/a-closer-look-at-conversion-franchising/ (accessed 10 October 2016).

15 Retrieved 10 October 2016 from: www.drishtee.org

16 See www.826national.org (accessed 29 June 2017).

Chapter Seven

1   Defoe, D. (1719, 2010) *The anatomy of Exchange-Alley: or, a system of stock-jobbing. Proving that scandalous trade, as it is now carry'd on, to be knavish in its private ... By a jobber. The second edition corrected.* Gale ECCO Print Editions (online).

2   Retrieved 29 June 2017 from: https://www.fastcompany.com/42111/perfect-vision-dr-v

3   His website www.muhammadyunus.org is a good all-purpose starter resource and a key to a quite remarkable vocation.

4   See, for example, Polgreen, L. and Bajaj, V. (2010) 'India Microcredit Faces Collapse from Defaults', *New York Times*, 17 November.

5   Useful statistics available at: https://www.credit-suisse.com/uk/en/about-us/responsibility/economy-society/focus-themes/microfinance.html

6   The story is told in: Gonzalez, A. (2010) 'Analyzing Microcredit Interest Rates', MIX Briefing note. It is updated in Gonzalez, A. (2011) 'Sacrificing Microcredit for Unrealistic Goals', www.themix.org/publications/microbanking-bulletin/2011/01/sacrificing-microcredit-unrealistic-goals

7   Bateman, M. and Chang, H.-J. (2009) 'The Microfinance Illusion', 25 May. Available at SSRN: https://ssrn.com/abstract=2385174 or http://dx.doi.org/10.2139/ssrn.2385174 (accessed 25 September 2017).

8   Dahl, R. (1953, 2011) *Someone Like You*, London: Penguin.

9   Defoe, D. (1719, 2010) *The anatomy of Exchange-Alley: or, a system of stock-jobbing. Proving that scandalous trade, as it is now carry'd on, to be knavish in its private … By a jobber. The second edition corrected.* Gale ECCO Print Editions (online).

10   Retrieved 29 June 2017 from: www.friendslife.co.uk

11   Under an amendment to the UK 1995 Pensions Act which came into effect in 2001, pension funds have been required to state in a Statement of Investment Principles 'the extent (if at all) to which social, environmental or ethical considerations are taken into account in the selection, retention and realisation of investments'.

12   Governments had long ago began to sense that this movement might be worth something to them and their own social objectives. In the UK for example pension funds must invest in ethical stocks (though an amendment to the UK's 1995 Pensions Act allowed funds to include, for example, the shares of supermarkets that sell tobacco and alcohol only as a small proportion of their revenue).

13   Further details can be found in The Association of Chief Executives of Voluntary Organisations (2014) *Good with Money,* https://www.acevo.org.uk/news/goodwithmoney (accessed 29 June 2017).

14   Retrieved 29 June 2017 from: www.eiris.org/media/statistics/

15   Solomon, A. (2003) *Is a Virtuous Circle for Corporate Social Responsibility arising from the New Socially Responsible Investment Disclosure Requirement for Pension Fund Trustees?,* https://pdfs.semanticscholar.org/e4d8/b63c6f9cfd1b3a0a2f7168abdb0433729a4d.pdf (accessed 29 June 2017).

16   Retrieved 29 June 2017 from: www.unpri.org

17   O'Donohoe, N., Leijonhufvud, C., Saltuk, Y., Bugg-Levine, A. and Brandenburg, M. (2010) *Impact Investments: An Emerging Asset Class*, JP Morgan/Rockefeller Foundation/GIIN, https://www.jpmorganchase.com/corporate/socialfinance/document/impact_investments_nov2010.pdf (accessed 29 June 2017).

18   *Economist* (2011) 'Happy returns: the birth of a virtuous new asset class', 10 September.

19   See www.aravind.org/ (accessed 29 June 2017).

20   More on David Green and his journey through social entrepreneurship with Auroblab can be found at www.schwabfound.org/content/david-green

21   The interview was with FastCompany and is available at www.fastcompany.com/42111/perfect-vision-dr-v (accessed 29 June 2017).

22   All reports can be accessed at http://www.ronaldcohen.org/initiatives/social-investment-task-force

23   Retrieved 29 June 2017 from www.triodos.co.uk

24   See www.bridgesventures.com (accessed 29 June 2017).

[25] See www.bigsocietycapital.com (accessed 29 June 2017).

[26] O'Donohoe, N., Leijonhufvud, C., Saltuk, Y., Bugg-Levine, A. and Brandenburg, M. (2010) *Impact Investments: An Emerging Asset Class*, JP Morgan/Rockefeller Foundation/GIIN, https://www.jpmorganchase.com/corporate/socialfinance/document/impact_investments_nov2010.pdf (accessed 29 June 2017).

[27] Prahalad, C.K. (2004) *The Fortune at the Bottom of the Pyramid*, University of Pennsylvania, Wharton School Publishing.

[28] Sullivan, P. (2010) *With Impact Investing, a Focus on More Returns*, http://www.nytimes.com/2010/04/24/your-money/24wealth.html?dbk (accessed 29 June 2017).

[29] See www.toniic.com (accessed 29 June 2017).

[30] See www.impactassets.org (accessed 29 June 2017).

[31] See www.socialstockexchange.com (accessed 29 June 2017).

[32] UNDP (2006) *Human Development Report 2006*, http://hdr.undp.org/en/content/human-development-report-2006

[33] Retrieved 29 June 2017 from: www.gavi.org

[34] Light, D.W. (2010) 'GAVI's Advance Market Commitment', *The Lancet*, vol 375, no 9715, p 638.

[35] Duflo, E. and Banerjee, A. (2011) *Poor Economics*, New York, NY: Public Affairs.

[36] See www.iffim.org (accessed 29 June 2017).

[37] Bateman, M. and Chang, H.J. (2012) 'Microfinance and the Illusion of Development: From Hubris to Nemesis in Thirty Years', *World Economic Review*, 1: 13–36.

[38] Rowell, S. (2015) *Good Pensions*, London: Social Market Foundation.

[39] De Soto, H. (2001) *The Mystery of Capital*, London: Black Swan.

[40] See www.Clearlyso.com (accessed 29 June 2017).

Chapter Eight

[1] See www.hole-in-the-wall.com/Beginnings.html.

[2] A number of interesting papers by Professor Heeks on this subject can be found at www.manchester.ac.uk/research/richard.heeks/publications (accessed 29 June 2017).

[3] See www.goodgym.org (accessed 29 June 2017).

[4] See www.mysociety.org (accessed 29 June 2017).

[5] See www.paulocoelhoblog.com (accessed 29 June 2017).

[6] Oren Yakobovitch is another Ashoka Fellow: www.ashoka.org/fellow/oren-yakobovich (accessed 29 June 2017).

[7] www.videreonline.org (accessed 29 June 2017).

8   See https://hbr.org/2009/02/breakthrough-ideas-for-2009 (accessed 25 September 2017).

9   Retrieved 29 June 2017 from: http://blog.zopa.com/2007/09/25/opaque-banking-practices/

Chapter Nine

1   *Correspondance diplomatique, vol 2*. Paris: Michel Lévy frères libraires éditeurs, 1860, p 196.

2   See www.nationalservice.gov/programs/social-innovation-fund (accessed 29 June 2017).

3   See www.nokidhungry.org (accessed 29 June 2017).

4   FOMIN (2016) 'Ecosystem for Supporting Social Business in South Korea', 10 May, www.fomin.org/Home/FOMINblog/Blogs/DetailsBlog/ArtMID/13858/ArticleID/7098/Ecosystem-for-supporting-social-business-in-South-Korea.aspx

5   Ibid.

6   Leadbeater, C. and Cottam, H. (2007) *The User Generated State*, http://charlesleadbeater.net/wp-content/uploads/2007/03/PSRG3.pdf

7   See www.in-control.org.uk (accessed 29 June 2017).

8   See www.m2m.org (accessed 29 June 2017).

9   Small, M. (2010) *Unanticipated Gains: Origins of Network Inequality in Everyday Life*, Oxford: Oxford University Press.

10 Acevo (2016) *Coming in from the Cold*, https://www.acevo.org.uk/sites/default/files/Coming%20in%20from%20the%20Cold%20Full%20Report.pdf (accessed 29 June 2017).

11 Cawley, J. and Meyerhoefer, C. (2012) *The Medical Care Costs of Obesity: An Instrumental Variables Approach*, available at: http://www.nber.org/papers/w16467.pdf (accessed 29 June 2017).

12 Szabo, L. (2014) *Cost of not caring: Nowhere to go*, see, eg https://www.usatoday.com/story/news/nation/2014/05/12/mental-health-system-crisis/7746535/ (accessed 29 June 2017).

13 NHS England (2013) *A Call to Action*, available at: https://www.england.nhs.uk/2013/07/call-to-action/ (accessed 29 June 2017).

14 Action for Children (2010) *The Red Book*, available at: https://www.actionforchildren.org.uk/resources-and-publications/reports/the-red-book-review/ (accessed 29 June 2017).

15 Hutton, W., Owen, R. and Singh, A. (2015) *Remaking the State*, available at: https://www.acevo.org.uk/sites/default/files/REMAKING%20THE%20STATE%20RESEARCH%20REPORT%20FINAL_1.pdf (accessed 29 June 2017).

16 Ravallion, M. and Chen, S. (2004) *China's (Uneven) Progress Against Poverty,* September, World Bank Policy Research Working Paper No 3408. Available at SSRN: https://ssrn.com/abstract=625285 (accessed 29 June 2017).

17 Pritchett, L. (2015) 'The New Global Goals Spell the End of Kinky Development', Center for Global Development, 20 October, www.cgdev.org/blog/new-global-goals-spell-end-kinky-development (accessed 29 June 2017).

18 Retrieved 9 October 2017 from https://www2.deloitte.com/global/en/pages/about-deloitte/articles/social-progress-index.html

19 Kubaznasky, M., Cooper, A. and Barbary, V. (2011) *Promise and Progress: Market-based Solutions to Poverty in Africa,* available at: http://web.mit.edu/idi/idi/Africa-%20PromiseAndProgress-MIM.pdf (accessed 29 June 2017).

20 Singh, A. (2011) 'Support is Key to Success in Early Years Intervention', *Guardian,* 11 July.

21 See www.ripplez.co.uk (accessed 29 June 2017).

22 See www.theguardian.com/public-leaders-network/2014/aug/11/jobcentre-plus-dwp-long-term-work-social-enterprise (accessed 29 June 2017).

Index